Praise for

Global Diversity

"***Global Diversity*** focuses adeptly on the culture within cultures. A must-read for anyone who wants to navigate successfully in the world market and is not satisfied with cursory descriptions."

—Malini Janakiraman, Director, Corporate Learning, Honeywell

"This book offers a unique approach to global diversity, one that goes beyond country-to-country communication, emphasizing the need—and tools—to understand the diversity within each country. Framing chapters expertly inform readers why this approach is effective and offer tips on how to use it, while the interior chapters present necessary information on the diversity within specific countries. It's quite an addition to the literature!"

—William Sonnenschein, Senior Lecturer, Haas School of Business, University of California, Berkeley and Author of *The Diversity Toolkit*

"***Global Diversity: Winning Customers and Engaging Employees within World Markets*** charts a course for approaching diversity and inclusion within an organizational context. The framework is pragmatic and provocative, helping evoke healthy discussion among senior leaders, colleagues and change facilitators. It is refreshing to have the authors work with diversity and inclusion as a change process and not simplify the complex topic. The thinking reflected in this book will help me, my global colleagues and others broaden our perspectives of what is possible—and will help make the world smaller."

—Tracy Ann Curtis, Senior Manager, Asia Pacific Diversity & Inclusion, Cisco Systems Inc.

"This lucid and practical book is an essential introduction to the intercultural world of the global manager. The authoritative and thoughtful contributors have produced sophisticated analyses as well as pragmatic recommendations that will be valued by both experienced and novice professionals."

—Janet Bennett, Executive Director, The Intercultural Communication Institute

"This book takes the reader beyond the broad brush strokes and cultural 'tip' sheets that may be interesting but largely ineffectual in building meaningful cultural understanding and competency. ***Global Diversity*** offers a nice balance between in-depth and practical information on each country profiled. The invitation to critically think about and discuss the diversity *within* cultures is implicit in the content, and that approach is a refreshing one given the increased need for cross-cultural collaboration in a globally integrated world."

—Nadia Younes, Director, Diversity & Work-Life, Amgen, Inc.

global diversity

global diversity

Winning Customers and Engaging Employees within World Markets

ERNEST GUNDLING and
ANITA ZANCHETTIN, Editors
with Aperian Global

NICHOLAS BREALEY
INTERNATIONAL

BOSTON • LONDON

Paperback edition first published by Nicholas Brealey Publishing in 2010.
Original hardcover edition first published in 2007.

Nicholas Brealey Publishing
20 Park Plaza, Suite 115A
Boston, MA 02116
Tel: + 617-523-3801
Fax: + 617-523-3708
www.nicholasbrealey.com

Nicholas Brealey Publishing
3-5 Spafield Street, Clerkenwell
London, EC1R 4QB, UK
Tel: +44-(0)-207-239-0360
Fax: +44-(0)-207-239-0370
www.nicholasbrealey.com

Printed in the United States of America

14 13 12 11 10 1 2 3 4 5

ISBN: 978-1-904838-26-5

The Library of Congress has previously cataloged this edition as follows:

Gundling, Ernest.
Global diversity : winning customers and engaging employees within world markets / Ernest Gundling and Anita Zanchettin with Aperian Global.

p. cm.

Includes bibliographical references and index.

ISBN: 978-1-904838-26-5

1. International trade—Cross-cultural studies. 2. International business enterprises—Cross-cultural studies. 3. International economic relations—Cross-cultural studies. 4. Cross-cultural studies. I. Zanchettin, Anita. II. Aperian Global (Firm) III. Title.
HF1379.G778 2007
658'.049—dc22

2006027128

To my parents, who started me on the global diversity journey with our family adventure to Iran; your curiosity and openness showed me how to approach new cultures and situations. And for my family—Richard, Michael, and Jonathan—for living "cultures within cultures" with me every day.

AZ

To Chris and to Katherine—this is about the global working world that lies ahead; I hope that you will each find your own way to build bridges beyond prejudice.

EG

Contents

Acknowledgments

We are grateful to our clients who are working to make a difference on the job and around the world. They have been generous in sharing their challenges, successes, and lessons learned on the global diversity journey as well as reviewing and providing input on the book. We would like to extend our thanks and appreciation to Wes Bean, Lynn Castrataro, Shari Chapman, Tracy Ann Curtis, Sam Dolinsky, Anne Drewry, Tracy Kellum, Ron Mortensen, Malini Janakiraman, Jim O'Hern, Eddie Pate, Lakiba Pittman, Victoria Posternak, Fernando Serpa, Nicole Siddall, Alma Vigo-Morales, Janet Winters-Smith, and Nadia Younes, along with many others. These clients have been valued partners who have given us both great opportunities and lots of good ideas; if there are any less useful ideas in the book those undoubtedly come from the authors instead.

It has been our privilege to work with our fellow Aperian Global team members and primary writers of the country chapters. This book is a result of their dedication and commitment to providing insights and fresh perspectives on "cultures within cultures." We are grateful to:

- Charles Bergman, China
- Bidhan Chandra, India
- Graziella Figi, Egypt
- Pamela Leri, United States

- Rossana Miranda-Johnston, Mexico
- Nigel Richards, United Kingdom
- Paul and Maria Wayne, Russia.

You are all pros and have been very patient with us!

Many friends and colleagues shared with us their expertise on the eight countries included in this book. They reviewed content, re-read chapters and provided new insights. We would like to express our appreciation in particular to Carmen DeNeve, Lupita Rodriguez Bulnes, Liliana Cantú, Carmen Dávila, Marion "JR" Johnson, Nina Kostromina, Vitaly Kostomarov, Ed Charrier, John Proverbs, Alex Freedland, Mikhail Ivanov, David Shusterman, Dr. Adel Omar Sherif, Dr. Elie K. Mangoubi, Sonya Kaleel, Osama El Enany, Anju Bhargava, Dinesh Chandra, Rajesh Parwatkar, Ashutosh Phadke, Abhijit Bhattacharjee, Hari Krishna Lal, Tony Pan, Kay Jones, Ming Yang, Liisamaria Keates, and Yukiko Kuroda. Dr. David Matsumoto of San Francisco State University generously provided both statistical data and critical insights for the Japan chapter, and his book *The New Japan* was a stimulating resource. We are thankful also to a number of others who read earlier drafts and are not named here.

More than a decade of graduate students in classes on "Global Management Skills" at the University of California Berkeley's Haas School of Business have contributed in significant ways to the book's contents. The process of lively class discussion and debate in response to persistent questions about cultural variation within countries gave shape to some of the central ideas in the book. The atmosphere of academic freedom and exploration at Berkeley as well as the presence of students from a wonderfully diverse array of countries has offered fertile ground for generating new perspectives.

We would like to extend special appreciation as well to a group of students from the Monterey Institute of International Studies who participated in a class on the subject of "Global Diversity" taught by one of the authors. These students included Lorena Davalos, Jacqueline Fong, Luis Gonzales, Yuka Mori, Umoloyouvwe Onomake (Ejiro!), Heather Schultes, William Sells, Hiroko Shimota, and Monika Szewczyk. They provided valuable critiques of early chapter drafts, obtained input from country experts, researched and verified facts and supporting information, and offered good suggestions for modifications and additions based upon their own international experience. Several students continued to help after the conclusion of the class. Luis Gonzales gave particularly welcome assistance with some of the nitty-gritty tasks such as footnotes and permissions. Thanks to Tsuneo Akaha and to Dean Amy Sands at the Graduate School of International Policy Studies for making the Monterey Institute class possible.

We are grateful to Gary Alveranga, Doug Harris, and Gloria Woods of the Kaleidoscope Group for sharing their experiences and insights into the current issues of diversity in the United States. Many colleagues on the diversity journey have been wonderful teachers and friends, including Bill Harris, Enidio Magel, Pam Ex, Jonamay Lambert, Gloria Cotton, Scott Hoesman, and Troy Cicero. Anita is especially grateful to two wonderful mentors and friends: Rita Bennett provided an eager yet inexperienced new hire with extraordinary opportunities for professional growth; Bea Young demonstrated that diversity and inclusion are more than a business imperative, they are a way of life.

Other Aperian Global employees who helped in various phases of content creation, editing, and book production include Brent Ackerman, Rita Bennett, Christopher Bernard, Karen Cvitkovich, David Dickey, Heather Hinrichs, Laurie Mack, Jeneva Patterson, Keiko Sakurai, and Jennifer Marquez. Keiko Sakurai provided both editorial assistance and input on the Japan chapter from a bicultural perspective.

About the Editors and Contributors

Charles K. Bergman—China

Charles Bergman has been involved with China for over 20 years, having initially visited Taiwan in 1980. He is fluent in Mandarin and has a first-hand understanding of China, its history, and business practices. Mr. Bergman's work has focused on leadership and organization development for multinational firms and improving the performance of teams within the broader organizational context. He provides consultation to management teams, and training and coaching for executives who seek to expand their range of leadership and management skills. Mr. Bergman worked for ten years with IBM in marketing, management, and business development both in the United States and in Asia, and was a member of the start-up team for IBM's China subsidiary in Beijing. Mr. Bergman has a B.A. in mathematics from Amherst College, an M.S. in mathematics from the University of California at Berkeley, and an M.A. in East Asian Studies from Stanford University. He currently teaches world history, Chinese studies, and philosophy at Albuquerque Academy in Albuquerque, New Mexico.

Graziella Figi—Egypt

Graziella Figi specializes in African, Arab, Islamic, and Asian subjects and countries for multinational corporations and international institutions. Ms. Figi has served as a political risk expert at emerging market conferences in Egypt, Hong Kong, Morocco, New York, and Tunisia. She was sponsored for a Middle East business course at the John F. Kennedy School of Government at Harvard University. In 1995 she was a member of the U.S. Delegation to the Middle East/North Africa (MENA) Economic Summit conference in Amman, Jordan. Ms. Figi is a Eurasian-American Muslim born in Chicago. She completed undergraduate work at De Paul University, and a Certificate Program on International Leadership at the Institute of Leadership & Public Affairs at the University of Bahcesehir in Istanbul, Turkey. Ms. Figi speaks French, Arabic, and Bahasa.

Bidhan Chandra—India

Dr. Bidhan Chandra provides consultation, coaching, and training in the areas of intercultural management, international business, global cultural diversity, multicultural team building, and e-learning. He has designed and delivered a diverse range of training programs for both U.S. and Indian professionals involved in offshore outsourcing or captive development work related to IT, R&D, business processes, and manufacturing. Born and raised in India, Dr. Chandra earned a B.S. degree in mechanical engineering from Ranchi University (India), an M.B.A. in Finance, an M.A. in International Trade, and a Ph.D. in International Business from the State University of New York at Buffalo. He has taught on the faculties of Empire State College, Saint Bonaventure University, and University at Buffalo School of Management's EMBA programs in Beijing. He is currently an Associate Professor in management and international business in the Center for Distance Learning, Empire State College, Saratoga Springs.

Ernest Gundling—Japan

Ernest Gundling is a senior Asia specialist and co-President of Aperian Global. He assists clients in developing strategic global approaches to leadership, organization development, and executive level relationships with key business partners. Dr. Gundling has been involved with Japanese language, culture, and business for over 25 years, including more than six years' residence in Japan. He holds a Ph.D. from the University of Chicago and wrote his dissertation on Japanese management training programs; his field research was funded initially by a U.S. Department of Education Fulbright Fellowship. He also received a Master's degree from the University of Chicago, and a B.A. from Stanford University. Dr. Gundling is also currently a Lecturer at the Haas School of Business at the University of California, Berkeley, where he teaches a course called Global Management Skills.

Rossana Miranda-Johnston—Mexico

Rossana Miranda-Johnston is an experienced intercultural trainer who delivers client-tailored training to improve intercultural business interactions, international relocation, teambuilding, customer service, and cultural diversity. She has delivered training on doing business in Mexico, the United States, Argentina, Chile, Puerto Rico, Venezuela, Spain, England, and Italy. Born and raised in Mexico, Ms. Miranda-Johnston received an M.A. in Intercultural Management from the School for International Training in Brattleboro, Vermont, and has completed many training courses from the National Multi-Cultural Institute in Washington, D.C. She has lived and worked in Mexico, the United States, Portugal, Israel, England, and Italy. Ms. Miranda-Johnston is a member of the Society for Intercultural Education, Training and Research, SIETAR USA, and founding member of the SIETAR Rocky Mountain Chapter.

Maria Kostromina-Wayne—Russia

Maria Kostromina-Wayne specializes in global teams, productivity, and leadership development. As Governance Manager for a major Silicon Valley corporation, she managed the start-up and operations of an offshore Technology Development Center in Moscow. Currently, Dr. Wayne holds the position of Director of Global Leadership Development for Seagate Technology. Since 1993, she has been part of a team providing support and cultural training for the United States Astronauts who fly on the Mir Space Station, as well as for Astronaut families. In 1993, she worked in Siberia in a joint venture between Occidental Petroleum and Chernogorneft. Born and raised in Moscow, Dr. Wayne completed her undergraduate studies at Moscow State University. She received her Ph.D. in Russian Linguistics from the Russian Academy of Sciences. Dr. Wayne is the co-author of "Moscow at Your Door."

J. Paul Wayne—Russia

Mr. J. Paul Wayne has lived and worked in Russia for more 16 years, supporting and leading international projects with American, British, French, German, Italian, and Russian organizations. Mr. Wayne's professional skills in the areas of organization development, strategic planning, management development consulting and privatization/restructuring are complemented by his in-depth knowledge of Russian business culture and fluent language skills. He has a successful track record of project management in Russia and long-term consulting relationships with prominent public and private projects. Mr. Wayne holds a Master's degree in Organization Development from Pepperdine University.

Nigel Richards—United Kingdom

Nigel Richards has been involved in management training and corporate development for over 15 years. A highly experienced trainer, coach, and facilitator, he has conducted cross-cultural training, team building, negotiation skills workshops, and expatriate coaching. He focuses primarily on helping businesspeople and professionals to successfully manage, communicate, and adapt when operating across diverse cultures or going on international assignments. Born in the United Kingdom, Mr. Richards graduated in law and received an LLB with Honors, and has an M.A. in Education. He originally worked as a business lawyer and coach in the corporate sector before moving into global training and development. Over the last 20 years Mr. Richards has himself been a permanent expatriate, living and working in England, Italy, Japan, and Thailand; he is now based in San Francisco.

Pamela Leri—United States

Pamela Leri provides consulting, training, and coaching on global business issues including outsourcing, global teams, and collaboration. Previously, Ms. Leri was senior vice president of Human Resources and Manager of Diversity and Intercultural Strategy for Mellon Financial Corporation. She originally joined Mellon as part of its acquisition of PricewaterhouseCoopers' Human Resources consulting practice (Unifi). Before joining PricewaterhouseCoopers, Ms. Leri gained valuable experience as the director of Global Business Development at the Kaleidoscope Group, a diversity consulting firm, where she conducted diversity training for Fortune 500 companies and governmental agencies. Ms. Leri received her Master of Fine Arts degree in Creative Writing, Fiction, from The University of Iowa Writers' Workshop, where she received the prestigious Iowa Arts Fellowship; and her bachelor's degree in Literature, Creative Writing with honors from the University of California, Santa Cruz.

Anita Zanchettin—United States

Anita Zanchettin has more than 18 years' experience providing training and consulting for global corporations on the impact of culture on job effectiveness, teamwork, leadership, project management, marketing, joint ventures, technology transfer, and other business systems and processes. She has designed and delivered culturally appropriate global diversity training for the United States, UK, Belgium, Brazil, Japan, the Philippines, Italy, and Mexico. Ms. Zanchettin has worked extensively with CEOs and senior leadership teams, human resources, and diversity councils to improve the organizational environments, systems, and processes. Prior to joining Aperian Global, Ms. Zanchettin worked at the Kaleidoscope Group, where she conducted diversity training for Fortune 500 companies and government agencies. Ms. Zanchettin holds a Master's degree in Intercultural Management from the School for International Training in Brattleboro, Vermont, and a B.A. degree in French and Spanish from Dominican University in River Forest, Illinois. She has lived in Spain, Iran, Saudi Arabia, and Kuwait.

CHAPTER 1

Introduction

Mastering global diversity means understanding the differences that exist within countries as well as between them. The most successful business strategies utilize not only global scope but also a depth of knowledge about the various circumstances faced by local customers, employees, and suppliers. Such knowledge is vital for individual managers who are selling their company's products and services in foreign markets, expatriates who work both with headquarters and with subsidiary operations, organizational leaders who want to upgrade and/or better leverage the capabilities of their workforce in key growth markets, and diversity professionals with limited global experience whose job is to extend corporate diversity initiatives abroad.

Global Diversity and Local Knowledge

What kind of local knowledge is necessary? Financial progress reports portray current results but provide limited insight. Business publications feature the most current stories yet sometimes lack historical and cultural perspective. It is insufficient for the virtual team member or business traveler—not to mention expatriates or corporate executives—to learn just a few dos and don'ts or key phrases pertaining to a given country. The convenient argument that the world is converging toward a single set of global commercial practices and standards with English as a common language looks increasingly dubious as many countries explicitly reject Western and particularly U.S.-based standards.

Global Diversity: Winning Customers and Engaging Employees within World Markets addresses the complexities of various countries on their own terms and describes differences among people in each location through the eyes of people who actually live there. It does more than provide facts and figures or stress the usual contrasts between the cultural values of one country versus another. Too many graduates of training programs about countries such as China, India, Germany, or the United States have discovered that although basic facts and generalizations about country norms may have some usefulness, they only go so far when one is confronted with the blooming, buzzing diversity of a major national player in the world economy.[1] India, for example, has a plethora of different languages, regional cultures, religious beliefs, socioeconomic strata, and levels of education—with change occurring at various rates in each area. Savvy firms and their employees are looking for new ways to both fully grasp and leverage the tremendous internal diversity that each country holds.

How Much Is Local Knowledge Worth?

Successful diversity efforts are usually based on a strong business case. The value of extensive local knowledge about key markets around the world is underlined by the following thought exercise.

> You are a potential buyer of a product or service. You have the choice of two offerings. One is provided by a firm that speaks your language, has a facility located in your part of the country, and has incorporated features that appeal to people of your particular age, gender, and socioeconomic background. The other product, although technically superior, is being sold by a foreign company that does not have those other advantages. Which product will you choose to buy?

Customers around the world make such choices countless times each day. The consistent winners in the marketplace are firms offering products adapted to fit local variations in needs and tastes that are presented by people who know how to use the buyer's own language, both literally and figuratively. The end result is that the potential customer feels a level of comfort that leads to a purchase: "They understand me and I can trust them."

Domestic enterprises have no monopoly on the advantages of local knowledge. Customers may mistakenly assume that foreign firms are local enterprises if they are sufficiently well adapted; foreign origin is even seen as a plus in some countries when it is accompanied by quality, price, and features that fit local circumstances. It is not always necessary to get everything right the first time. Japanese automakers were laughed at when they first started to export boxy, cheap-looking, low-priced vehicles abroad. Today in Europe they offer a range of sporty subcompacts with diesel engine options and attractive styling, while buyers in North America can select from a full menu of sedans, SUVs, and high-powered pickups with rugged-sounding names like "Titan" or "Tundra."

The experience of Microsoft in India offers a sense of the spectrum of potential economic consequences that stem from local knowledge—or the lack of it. It might seem that such a sophisticated competitor, with an enviable number of advanced academic degrees among its employees, would be immune to cultural errors of the "Pepsi Brings Your Ancestors Back from the Dead" variety that became urban legends in previous eras.[2] However, in a recent talk, Tom Edwards, a Microsoft executive, confessed to a mistaken coloration of pixels on a map of India that depicted disputed Kashmiri territory in the north of the country as non-Indian. Because this touched a sensitive nerve related to decades of conflict and territorial dispute between Pakistan and India as well as internal conflicts with Muslim separatists in the region, the Microsoft product that contained it was immediately banned in India, and the company had to recall 200,000 copies at a cost of millions of dollars. Edwards' comment was, "Some of our employees, however bright they may be, have only a hazy idea about the rest of the world."[3] This lack of knowledge led to neglect of a volatile subject related to India's own internal religious diversity and political history that almost any Indian would recognize.

Yet Microsoft has also made some very smart moves in India that reflect sensitivity to its internal diversity. The larger issue for Microsoft in India is whether the country's institutions and burgeoning software industry will ultimately favor Microsoft's operating system or competing open-source software from Linux—in this case, there are not just millions of dollars at stake but billions. Microsoft has recognized that Indian attitudes toward its products in both the government and private sectors will be shaped by the contribution the company makes to address the issues crucial to contemporary India, such as economic development, education, and health care. Microsoft needs to defend and expand its market presence through its local knowledge of the huge disparities that exist among Indians themselves.

This challenge has received top-level attention at Microsoft, which is pushing forward on all fronts. During a trip to India several years ago, Bill Gates discussed substantial new investments in Microsoft's software development center in Hyderabad, a burgeoning city in the south of India; he also made public a $20 million contribution to an online training program targeted at training tens of thousands of teachers and several million students over several years. On the initial day of the same trip, during the course of a full day devoted to philanthropic activity described as being unrelated to the commercial purposes of the visit, Gates announced a $100 million grant from the Gates Foundation to help address the growing issue of AIDS. At the time, this was the single largest donation given by the foundation to any country.[4]

Meanwhile, Microsoft is busy addressing a uniquely Indian business opportunity—calling upon its Hyderabad software engineers to provide translations of standard Microsoft products into local languages such as Hindi, Bengali, and Malayalam. India has one of the world's most diverse collections of languages[5] as well as a huge and growing consumer base. Companies like Microsoft that are alert to this situation can position themselves to profit from the localization of established software products for decades to come.

Defining Diversity: Key Variables

The dictionary definition of the term *diversity* refers to distinct elements or qualities—points of difference. It also means a condition of being different. The Latin root, *diversus,* suggests that historically this notion had a neutral, or even negative, connotation. Synonyms are different, unlike, opposed, or hostile.[6]

While of course differences exist across national boundaries, it is also important to recognize the contrasting ways that various countries signal and describe differences among their own people. This book explores cultures within cultures in China, India, the United Kingdom, Mexico, the United States, Russia, Japan, and Egypt refers to the diversity that exists within each of these countries. Such internal differences are handled in various ways—from tremendous creative ferment and friendly rivalries to armed combat—depending upon the country. In the United States, diversity in the cultural sense has been interpreted primarily with reference to racial, ethnic, or gender differences in the context of providing more equal opportunities. Contemporary usage has paired diversity with positive words such as valuing, leveraging, or even celebrating. Other countries around the world each have their own experience with and approach to ideas about how people differ, depending upon their historical and linguistic heritages.

The term *diversity* is used here to denote cultural differences in a broad sense that includes, but is not limited to, racial or ethnic differences. The following list of variables can serve as a descriptive template—a way of organizing and depicting the types of differences that appear to exist. It is also intended to be a tool for constructive inquiry or a means of discovering more, both about the possible factors that are listed and those that are not listed. The "Other" category included in this list is a conscious acknowledgement that there are bound to be additional variables important to particular countries, and that the list should remain open-ended.

Cultural Diversity: Key Variables

- Race and Ethnicity
- Gender
- Regional Origin
- Educational Background
- Age
- Religion
- Family Background
- Socioeconomic Status
- Language
- Organizational Affiliation
- Sexual Orientation
- Job Function
- Physical Disability
- Other

Differences that stem from these variables are not necessarily a matter for either celebration or consternation—what is most important for our purposes here is that they do have practical consequences in the workplace. The evidence available for culturally diverse groups suggests that in spite of some of the more cheerful rhetoric about cultural diversity, differences between people can have a positive, negative, or neutral impact on workplace performance. In a team context, for example, it is important to recognize and deal effectively with potential negatives associated with a diverse membership: trouble in reaching agreements, miscommunication, higher stress and levels of distrust, mutual stereotyping, and less overall cohesion. At the same time, cultural diversity can produce more options and better solutions when a team is managed properly, while avoiding the "groupthink" to which homogeneous groups more easily succumb.[7] Such positives and negatives are likely to be present whether cultural diversity takes the form of people from different countries or different cultural subgroups within the same country.

Generalizations versus Stereotypes

To say that Chinese are this way or French are that way may actually get in the way of learning about particular individuals if we deal primarily in stereotypes. It is important to probe beneath overly broad characterizations of the people of a given country in search of real internal diversity. However, this does not mean simply providing a more refined level of stereotypes that affirm local prejudices or the social status quo. Whether we are trying to describe common behaviors of people from an entire country or a subgroup within that country, it is best to share perceptions and offer generalizations in as objective a manner as possible rather than to reinforce stereotypes. Stereotypes are held in a way that is typically impervious to new information, while generalizations are more flexible constructs, permeable to new information or a fresh set of facts, as suggested by Figure 1-1.

What is needed is a new template for understanding global diversity that provides a common framework from one country to another while also approaching each country on its own terms. First and foremost, this

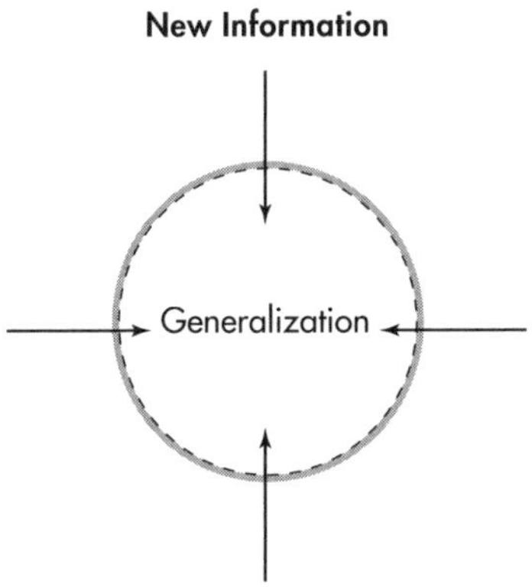

FIGURE 1-1. Formulation of Generalizations

template must serve as a tool for constructive dialogue with customers and employees about what aspects of local diversity are most significant to them. This does not mean viewing a country other than one's own through the lenses of our own historical experience or ideological perspective. Instead, it requires us to clear our vision as much as possible and engage in a fresh round of inquiry. What are the contrasts that exist in a given environment based upon its own historical, economic, and cultural context? What are the differences that make a difference to the members of a country's present workforce?

The Intercultural Field and Global Diversity

There are several streams of thought and practice that have contributed to current views about global diversity. These include the intercultural field as well as approaches to domestic diversity in the United States, Europe, and elsewhere. It is not only the strengths of these approaches, however, but also their limitations that have made the need for a fresh approach to global diversity more urgent.

Managing across Borders

The intercultural field has been particularly influenced by ideas about how to compare the cultural values of different countries. There have been many contributors to this area. Perhaps the best known is Geert Hofstede, whose book *Culture's Consequences: International Differences in Work-Related Values* is still regarded as a classic 25 years after its publication. Hofstede's research, based initially on surveys of IBM employees in 40 countries, identified four cultural dimensions: Power Distance, Individualism vs. Collectivism, Masculinity vs. Femininity, and Uncertainty Avoidance that highlighted contrasts in values between respondents from these countries.[8] Hofstede also incorporated a dimension related to time, Long-Term Orientation vs. Short-Term Orientation, based on research by Chinese scholars.[9]

Subsequent models have extended ideas about national dimensions of culture and have drawn out their applications to doing business across borders. Kluckhohn and Strodtbeck, Hampden-Turner, Trompenaars, Walker, Peterson, Schwartz, McCrae, Inglehart, and Matsumoto have all made useful contributions.[10] Thanks to the efforts of these people, as well as others, concepts that were once seen as marginal from a corporate perspective have now been integrated into standard programs for orienting expatriates, training global managers, facilitating the work of global teams, and developing corporate leaders.

Figure 1-2 shows a sample comparison of several countries covered in later chapters of this book across six dimensions; it incorporates data from

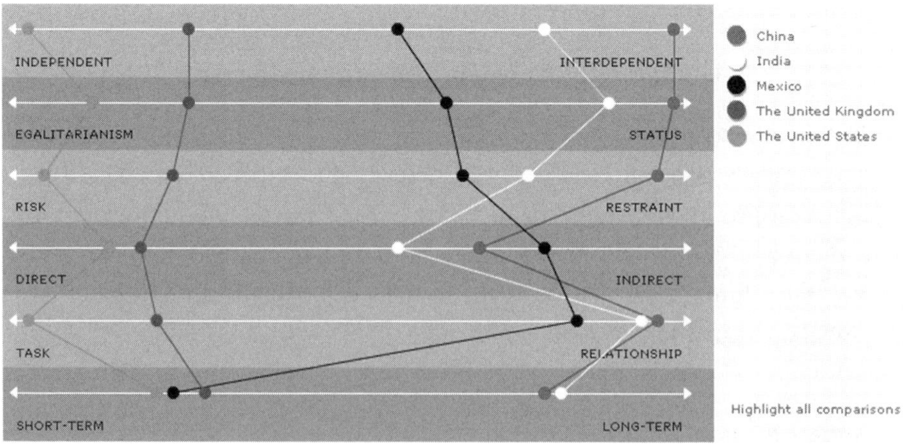

FIGURE 1-2. Comparison of Cultural Dimensions Among Countries
Source: Aperian Global; based upon the Matsumoto Self-Assessment Tool, Copyright 2004 Dr. David Matsumoto.

Hofstede as well as from other more contemporary sources. Participants in intercultural programs are commonly asked to consider the areas of overlap as well as gaps between their own personal profiles and the average scores for other countries they do business with. Implications for topics such as how to sell to customers, manage subordinates, or negotiate with suppliers in a cross-border setting are then considered. For example, a large gap between two countries on the first dimension could mean that a salesperson from the country with strong "independent" values takes an individualistic approach to a customer relationship, whereas the purchasing manager in the interdependent host country would respond more favorably to an approach that addresses a group-oriented decision-making process. This contrast suggests that a modified sales approach better suited to the host country customer's norms would be more effective.

Dimension Dogma?

Although the notion of cultural dimensions has been a powerful and useful tool for decades, its very strength can become an obstacle if it leads us to neglect equally important areas. Knowledge of national cultural differences and the dimensions used to characterize them is necessary, but it is not sufficient by itself. There is diversity not only between cultures but also within them. Those who complete training programs or read publications focused on these cultural dimensions sometimes react with comments such as, "I know that Chinese are less risk-oriented overall, but isn't there a lot of variety among them?" or, "India seems like such a big and complex country; I understand that they are more hierarchical, but isn't there a lot of variation between different industries such as software or manufacturing?" Unfortunately, all too often what they learn beyond the general dimensions is at best a smattering of disconnected facts and historical events.

The dimensions, even when they are taught well, provide only a partial framework for understanding cultural differences and some clues for how to modify behavior and/or seek a hybrid solution. A bell curve formula is used to define cultural norms, but these dimensions were never intended to be a complete solution for identifying cultural subgroups or for determining how to work effectively with them. Likewise, such dimensions can help us to understand other individuals from different environments, yet are by no means a complete guide to the tremendous individual variation that exists within every culture. As with most good maps they have edges, and there are important things that are off of the map.

One area that deserves more systematic investigation by the intercultural field is the implications of country-level comparisons for practical workplace skills. Such efforts are already underway.[11] A further step, which is the focus here, is to develop a more methodical approach to analyzing and conveying the tremendous diversity that exists within cultures around the world—that is, cultures within cultures. For this purpose, the dimensions that have served so well to identify broad differences between cultures must be supplemented by other variables. Interculturalists are increasingly being invited to design and deliver programs that have a global diversity label, or that are requested by people in a global diversity function. It is vital that their response does not impose the same familiar dimensions on what could be a fresh and intriguing question: What does global diversity really mean?

The Diversity Field in the United States

Diversity is well established in the United States as a subject that warrants attention by corporations. IBM, for example, claims that its diversity and inclusion efforts began as early as 1953 with a letter advocating equal opportunity. This letter was written by Thomas Watson, Jr., IBM's CEO at the time. Today, the majority of Fortune 500 companies have an individual or a team whose responsibilities focus on enhancing the diversity of an organization and developing strategies and initiatives to address diversity issues. At the most sophisticated level, diversity leaders are tasked with culture change. Their job is to ensure that the workplace environment is inclusive of all employees, whatever forms of diversity they represent, and that each employee has access to opportunities for development and promotion. On a more basic level, diversity leaders are tasked with the maintaining internal demographic data, compiling Affirmative Action (AA) and Equal Employment Opportunity (EEO) reports, and resolving employee issues related to discrimination on an individual or group basis.

The sophistication and scope of corporate diversity efforts are frequently related to the length of time that diversity has been acknowledged as a business and moral imperative for a particular corporation. Diversity consultants and theorists frequently use a continuum to characterize the three key areas of focus related to diversity and inclusion—opening doors, opening minds, and changing organizational cultures. Historically, these three phases came into being in and are associated with different eras—opening doors in the 1960s and 1970s, opening minds in the 1980s and early 1990s, and changing organizational cultures from the mid- to late 1990s to the present. The overall thrust in recent years has been to go beyond legal compliance to focus on potential sources of bottom-line competitive advantage.

Some U.S. companies have worked through all three phases in their historical sequence and have made considerable progress in enhancing representation and creating a work environment inclusive of all employees over the past 30 years. Recently, many of these companies have begun to make connections between dealing with the competitive challenges of globalization and involving their global employee population in workforce initiatives that have brought about positive results in their home country organizations.

Other companies are latecomers to diversity efforts and find themselves catapulted into a crash course in diversity after becoming a government contractor or the target of a high-profile lawsuit. Well-known cases of the latter include Mitsubishi Motors and the Denny's restaurant chain, which were both hit with costly lawsuits related to workplace discrimination. Diversity efforts in most companies have ebbed and flowed in visibility and intensity based on factors such as market realities, business growth and profit, mergers and acquisitions, global expansion, availability of critical labor, and public relations problems.

Another, more personal, factor has been the commitment to diversity by an individual CEO or business unit leader. Stories abound in the diversity field of corporate executives whose stance toward diversity resulted from having a family member who faced limited opportunities due to being disabled, gay, or female; some have also experienced their own challenges as a female or a person of color. These epiphanies by leadership, while they have an impact on the corporate culture for a time, may be as transient as the leaders themselves.

Diversity Fatigue and Global Diversity

It is, in fact, this inconsistent attention by corporations to diversity—whatever causes are behind it—that leads to the skepticism of employees when they are invited to a diversity seminar or hear about a new diversity-related program. Diversity leaders, especially in those corporations with a long-term focus on diversity, acknowledge a state of diversity fatigue, a kind of "been there, done that" feeling about programs that once again spotlight the intransigence of deep-seated issues related to race, ethnicity, gender, age, disability, and sexual orientation as well as the limited progress that has been made on such issues within the organization over time. The need to reinforce constantly the awareness that diversity issues exist in the workplace may even divert attention away from related and equally crucial tasks such as developing the interpersonal and team skills that will foster a truly inclusive work environment.

In the late 1990s and early years of the new millennium, the sense of diversity fatigue in many of the more diversity-savvy companies converged with the need and desire to extend outside of the United States the good work that was being done in the name of diversity. The term *global diversity* has increasingly been used in reference to these efforts. As other human capital initiatives are being rolled out to non-U.S.–based employees—learning and development, performance management, corporate values, and competencies—it is both sensible and cost effective to include diversity as part of this global organizational change package. This movement has been part of the third area of focus in the diversity continuum: changing organizational cultures. It advocates the involvement of all employees in diversity efforts and has multicultural, organizational development, and change management components; most important, it also focuses on return on investment (ROI) and competitive advantage. These trends are in contrast to the previous two phases—opening doors and opening minds—that were primarily domestic in focus.

Three Phases of U.S. Diversity

Global diversity is now being highlighted by many companies as a new and more comprehensive challenge than the domestic issues that have been of primary concern to date. It is seen as a natural extension of domestic diversity programs and as possibly offering wider promise from a business standpoint. Some firms prefer to have one department that handles both domestic and international diversity concerns. They also want this department to operate in a way that is parallel to the global business unit structure which requires each major unit or division of a company to run its own business worldwide, as opposed to having a separate international division or semiautonomous countries or regions. For anyone working in this type of structure who is interested in career advancement and a healthy budget, there is a great deal of pressure to say, "Sure, we can do global too."

Yet diversity professionals in the United States today face difficulties on a number of fronts. Some find that their backgrounds and work experience do not prepare them for being internal or external consultants on the complex issues of organizational development and change management that they now find themselves charged with. Others, while widely experienced in the issues of U.S. diversity, have spent little or no time outside the country, are unfamiliar with intercultural communication theory, and lack knowledge of the learning styles of people who have not been educated in the United States. This can lead to misdirected efforts and diversity training *faux pas.*

These professionals may suddenly find themselves leading a global diversity effort merely because they are situated at corporate headquarters. Without global experience, they sometimes lack the necessary credibility when trying to spread the diversity or inclusion message outside the United States. They can be stymied by budget and travel limitations outside of their control that force them to attempt to implement change through virtual methodologies such as video and teleconferences and online learning. They encounter resistance, passive or active, and receive bemused or confused looks when they attempt to explain their mission to local nationals. They might, with the best of intentions, impose the corporate U.S. stance on diversity without coming to a true understanding of local needs.

Global diversity of this kind is often met with resistance by non-U.S. employees who are on the receiving end of such well-meaning initiatives. Diversity is seen by some as a uniquely U.S. phenomenon based on its history and cultural institutions, with an emphasis on particular issues such as race relations or gender roles. When diversity is regarded as a U.S. problem, employees outside the United States may resist investing energy and allocating precious budget resources to address a problem they do not see as their own. In many cultures, diversity is also equated with focusing on differences, which may seem both countercultural and undesirable. The Balkans, for example, is a region where even in all-too-recent times cultural differences have been the cause of lethal conflict and grief rather than of celebration.

The resistance to U.S.-style diversity in other countries can be further exacerbated by well-intended training programs that are exported without adapting instructional techniques and content to fit local circumstances. As with other programs exported from headquarters, the learning and participation styles of overseas employees may run contrary to the expectations of facilitators accustomed to interacting with domestic audiences. A facilitator who equates heated debate and questioning with resistance would most likely be seen as hostile and defensive in Europe and Israel. More passive participants, who are accustomed to a lecture style of presentation, could be labeled resistant or disinterested by a U.S. facilitator, when instead what is required is adaptation of training styles to focus on small-group interactions and to accommodate limited English-language capabilities.

When introduced to a scenario depicting race relations in the United States, an Asian or Latin American audience may encounter names and faces that resemble their own, but feel no connection to the situations portrayed. French and Germans are understandably puzzled by and question the relevance of programs using videos that portray gender communication styles based on U.S. norms. Latin American men and women may question the imposition of U.S. rules around gender interactions in their own relationships with colleagues and customers. This is not to say that any of these audiences do not have their own diversity or inclusion issues, but often U.S.-based corporations neglect to ask or take the time to understand what kinds of diversity challenges exist for their employees outside the United States.

Other Approaches to Domestic Diversity

The primary focus of this book is both a critique and a response to global diversity models that have originated in the United States. With this in mind, however, it is valuable to consider approaches to diversity in other countries, as well as the regulatory framework that shapes their corporate policies and practices. Nations such as Canada, South Africa, and Sweden provide distinctive examples of homegrown diversity approaches that are different from U.S. paradigms (See Appendix A). Some of these directions, particularly the ones taken by multinational corporations based in Europe, are increasingly shaping global diversity policies that diverge from those of U.S. companies.

Global Diversity: Going from Questions to Answers

The topic of global diversity is thus a moving target. As indicated in this introduction, it refers to (1) differences that exist within national cultures as well as between them, and (2) a corporate movement with roots in the United States and in other countries that promotes equal opportunity and employee involvement with the aim of creating competitive advantage. This book will take a twofold approach that explores diversity within a number of national cultures while offering to organizations a model of inclusion that can be readily adapted to various national contexts.

Each of the chapters that follow focuses on a particular country and explores the differences that exist within it, applying the most relevant variables among the 14 outlined above to describe internal differences that are relevant to workplace interactions. The chapter authors are either natives of the country being discussed or have lived there for many years, and are all employees or associates belonging to the Aperian Global team.[12]

Countries have been selected for examination here based on several criteria, including population, economic significance, and geographical balance. They are

- China
- Egypt
- India
- Japan
- Mexico
- Russia
- United Kingdom
- United States

The final chapter will revisit the subject of global diversity as a corporate strategy for discovering new business opportunities through careful inquiry and equitable inclusion and involvement of employees around the world. It will propose a multifaceted approach to this subject that companies can use to shape their own initiatives. Domestic diversity principles and practices that travel well in a global context will be highlighted. The goal is to outline an approach to diversity that takes into account the true variety that exists within each country while also enabling every employee in a global enterprise to become an engaged and accountable contributor.

CHAPTER 2

Diversity in China

Charles K. Bergman

Why China?

- With a population of approximately 1.3 billion, China has more people than any other nation on the planet, accounting for almost one-fifth of humanity.
- China's economy has been growing at the most rapid rate in the world, and some futurists predict that it will be the world's largest within several decades.
- Vast differences between geographical regions and urban and rural environments make China an extremely challenging marketplace for foreign firms.
- Rapid growth rates and burgeoning employment opportunities in China's major cities have made long-term retention and development of employees a vital competitive issue.
- Strong local players with global ambitions have emerged in key Chinese industries such as computers, automobiles, or telecommunications; these enterprises can be key customers, alliance partners, or competitors for non-Chinese enterprises.

Introduction

China accounts for one-fifth of the world's population, but to most Chinese the concept of diversity as it is known in many western countries today is entirely alien. Since the word *diversity* implies a deliberate departure from a norm or standard, its meaning is consistent with the Western notion of individuality. But China comes from a very different tradition, where the group has always been more important than the individual, and hence the term has different implications.

While the notion of diversity that is current in other countries today is unfamiliar in China, diversity does exist there in the form of striking variations across the Chinese physical and human landscape. After all, China is a big place—its total area is greater than all of Europe and about the same as the United States. There are marked variations in China's physical geography, demographic characteristics, language, customs, dress, and diet that are consistent with its size and history.

China's vast population includes striking ethnic diversity. There are approximately 55 ethnic minority groups, the largest of which include the Zhuang (15.5 million), Manchu (8.8 million), Uighur (7.2 million), Yi (6.5 million), Mongols (4.8 million), and Tibetans (4.5 million). In total, however, these minorities comprise only about 8 percent of the population, a relatively small number when compared with other large nations such as India, Brazil, or the United States.[1]

For both demographic and political reasons, ethnic diversity is not a prominent feature of contemporary Chinese society. The other 92 percent of the country's population consists of Han Chinese, a group that originated along the Yellow River and later spread throughout China.[2] Han Chinese today thoroughly dominate nearly every aspect of Chinese society: government, military, schools, and business. The pervasive influence of the Han Chinese is further reinforced by political considerations. Because a number of minority groups, notably the Tibetans, Uighurs, and Mongols reside in contested border areas with a long history of conflict, the Chinese government is unlikely to embrace diversity in a way that would support any form of political autonomy.[3]

Aside from ethnic differences, there are other forms of diversity that are more prominent in the everyday workplace of most Chinese. In this chapter we will take a look at several aspects of China's diversity that are evident to contemporary Chinese themselves, and draw some practical conclusions. Astute business professionals will understand that China's own distinctive brand of diversity is much more than a curiosity, as it has profound implications for business. Themes covered will include:

- Regional Origin
- Socioeconomic Status
- Language
- Educational Background
- Age

Regional Origin

Two important geographic lines divide the People's Republic of China (PRC) (see Figure 2-1). The first runs from north to south approximately

FIGURE 2-1. Map of China: the East-West and North-South Divides

1,000 miles inland from China's east coast, dividing China into an eastern part accounting for about one-third of China's area and a western part accounting for the remaining two-thirds. The second line runs from east to west along the course of the Yangtze River. It roughly bisects China into northern and southern halves.

A third, more subtle line separates Chinese who grew up in the PRC from their fellow Chinese who currently live in the PRC but who were born in different regions and countries including Taiwan, Hong Kong, Singapore, and the United States. The PRC Chinese, in fact, use different names to refer to these Chinese communities: those from Taiwan or Hong Kong are called "compatriots," whereas those from other parts of the world are called "overseas Chinese." For simplicity's sake, we will refer to all Chinese who were not born in the PRC as overseas Chinese. Though they are relatively few in number compared with the PRC's enormous native population, overseas Chinese are an important part of China's professional class, as they are often valued by global corporations for their knowledge, expertise, and bicultural perspective. In spite of their strengths, however, they also present a set of unique problems for companies.

Each regional distinction between different subgroups of Chinese can lead to broad stereotypical characterizations that may not apply to individuals. However, such images are sufficiently widespread that they do shape the perceptions and behaviors of Chinese themselves. It can be useful for foreign businesspeople in China to understand local counterparts on their own terms in order to work together more effectively with them in shaping the country's evolving workplace environment.

The East-West Divide

Nearly three-fourths of China's population resides in the eastern third of the country. It is concentrated in major cities such as Beijing, Shanghai, and Guangzhou as well as in densely populated farm communities. This eastern third of China is its heartland: here one finds the national government, major institutions, and a culture that we might broadly call typically Chinese. This is the fastest developing area of China, and it is here that we find the booming economy that has propelled China to prominence as an economic powerhouse. In fact, income has risen so rapidly in the eastern part of China that a large and potentially destabilizing gap has developed between this area and the western interior. So great is this gap that eastern cities now must manage a mobile population of tens of millions of migrant workers who come from China's western interior in search of employment.

The geography of the western two-thirds of China is much different from the eastern heartland (see Figure 2-2). Generally speaking, it is far more mountainous: Gansu, Xinjiang, Sichuan, and Qinghai provinces all have mountains over 15,000 feet, and Tibet (the Chinese name for historic Tibet is Xizang) shares Mt. Everest, the world's tallest mountain at 29,028 feet, with Nepal. There are large deserts, too, including the Taklimakan in Xinjiang and the Gobi in Inner Mongolia. While Sichuan province lies in the west and has a very large and dense population, it is the exception: in general, the western part of China is more sparsely populated and much poorer than the east. This accounts for the Chinese sense of their western

FIGURE 2-2. Map of China with Neighboring Countries

interior as a frontier. Most Chinese today see the action in China as happening in the east, view the eastern cities as the model of the new China, and feel that the western interior is something of a hinterland.

Generally speaking, the Chinese who live in the coastal eastern third of the country consider themselves more sophisticated and cosmopolitan than their fellow citizens in the western part of the country. Besides the relative economic weight of Eastern China, its people have also experienced greater contact with people from the other side of the globe since the late 1500s, when Europeans first arrived at the beginning of Europe's Age of Exploration. For example, in cities like Qingdao, Shanghai, or Tianjin one is likely to find citizens who are comfortable with foreigners from around the world, are likely to speak a fair amount of English, and who genuinely welcome the growing presence of non-Chinese in their communities. In addition, these cities draw Chinese from the interior who are more cosmopolitan in outlook and who are attracted to the best job opportunities. Chinese from the eastern third of the country are much more likely to stay abreast of world news and are particularly aware of China's rapidly evolving role in international relations and trade. Both men and women from the east tend to spend more on luxury items to the extent that budgets and income allow, and they are apt to be more fashion conscious than their fellow citizens in the interior.

The rising incomes of the eastern coastal cities have led to a rapid rise in the material standard of living to a degree unthinkable 20 years ago. For example, the lifestyle of a young, well-educated electrical engineer who works for a foreign multinational in Suzhou would have utterly astounded his or her counterpart from the 1980s. The color TV, stereo system, dishwasher, dryer, air conditioning, two or three attractive bedrooms and, most recently, car owned by the engineer's small family represent a level of wealth that even the communist elite could not attain in the relatively recent past. Today this level of material wealth is increasingly the norm and is expected among successful, well-educated corporate employees in major eastern cities.

By contrast, citizens of Western China tend to be more conservative in their outlook, are still sometimes unaccustomed to foreigners, and are materially less well off than their eastern neighbors. This is partly because physical distance has separated them from the coast. Although it is improving rapidly, China's transportation system has not made it easy for people from the interior to travel east cheaply, nor has it made economic sense for many foreign multinationals to locate their operations deep in the western interior.

In addition, since the interior cities have not undergone restructuring and privatization of industry as rapidly as those in the east, state-owned enterprises, or SOEs, are the more common employers in the west. Although many SOEs have undergone wrenching reform, SOE employees still cling to the socialistic norms of guaranteed employment, shared wealth, and modest but secure wages and benefits for all. Consequently, many in the west, especially older Chinese, tend to be less comfortable with the market-driven free-for-all that is so much a part of the "new China" in the east. And many may even quietly long for a simpler, more secure past where no one was rich, but most could earn a comfortable, if austere, living by sharing the wealth.

Because the interior cities are typically less developed than their coastal counterparts, their pace tends to be a bit less hectic. Many of these cities still have a kind of provincial charm and a more relaxed atmosphere that have long disappeared in the east. The number of cars in Shanghai, for example, has grown to the point that traffic is horrendous; this traffic, coupled with urban sprawl, has made it much harder to get out of town for a weekend. By contrast, it is relatively easy to leave the interior city of Xi'an for a tour of the surrounding cultural sites or a walk in the countryside or nearby mountains. Thus, though they may be more remote and lack a modern infrastructure, interior cities can often offer a quality of life for Chinese and expatriates alike that has advantages over that of the developed east.[4]

The East-West Divide: Workplace Implications

Business professionals should know that China's central government has established a policy to create incentives to attract companies to invest and establish operations in the western interior. This policy has a name: *Xi Bu Da Kai Fa,* or "Western Region's Grand Opening," more popularly known as the "Go West" campaign. While most businesses will be attracted to the eastern coastal areas, with their better services and more cosmopolitan environment, they should not overlook some of the advantages of a move to the west.

First, there are many excellent technical colleges and universities in the western cities. Xi'an, capital of Shaanxi province, is a good example, with over 17 technical colleges and universities that annually graduate thousands of well-trained, if inexperienced, young people eager to work for Western companies. In addition, labor rates in the western part of China tend to be lower than those of the eastern cities. The price of labor in Shanghai, for example, has risen so dramatically that much of the original cost advantage offered by China's workers there has disappeared. In contrast, interior cities like Xi'an and Chongqing in Sichuan province offer labor rates as low as one-half of those in eastern cities.

Whether one's corporate operations are located in the east or in the west, the east-west divide in China leads to a kind of stereotyping among Chinese that is common to other large, continental nations. In China, easterners think of themselves as the sophisticated, urbane leaders of modern China's transformation, and sometimes look at their fellow citizens in the west as backward country bumpkins. For example, a group of young corporate professionals in Beijing enjoying dinner at a restaurant in an upscale shopping center might overhear tourists from Gansu, a very poor province in the west, notice their strong accents and less-than-fashionable clothing, and comment about "hicks from the west coming to the big city." Such attitudes also find their way into the workplace and may cause some employees raised and educated in the east, for example, to disregard or undervalue the ideas or suggestions of a colleague from a far western location.

This cultural snobbism sometimes has an amusing side when viewed historically. For example, the Shanghainese are very proud of their status as leaders in China's modernization and integration with the rest of the world. They see themselves as the New York or Paris of China and frequently compare themselves to other Chinese cities, like nearby Suzhou, with long histories of cultural brilliance. But Shanghai has not always been in the lead: in fact, as recently as 1800 Shanghai was a poor fishing village near the mouth of the Yangtze River and a cultural backwater if ever there was one.[5] The east-west divide is more socioeconomic and psychological than it is ethnic or demographic. Nonetheless, the diversity is real and accounts for a major element of differentiation in China's national makeup. A foreign multinational, whether it is located in the eastern or in the western part of China, may find that its workers from different parts of the country hold preconceived notions of one another, including a sense of superiority or inferiority that must be overcome in order for them to work effectively as a team.

The North-South Divide

The second great dividing line of China is the north-south divide, usually defined as the course of the Yangtze River. North of the river the climate becomes progressively colder, so that winters in Beijing, 1,000 miles to the north, are extremely harsh, with temperatures in February sometimes falling as low as minus 20° Fahrenheit (minus 29° Celsius). South of the river the climate becomes much warmer. Kunming, the capital of Yunnan province, for example, which borders Vietnam in the south, is so mild that it is known as the "city of eternal spring."

The change in climate as one heads north also accounts for the shift from rice to wheat as the staple crop. In the north, one sees noodles and buns made from wheat flour more often than in the south, though improved internal transportation of foodstuffs has blurred somewhat the former dietary distinctions between north and south.

Northern Chinese tend to be slightly taller and fairer in complexion. It is not clear what accounts for their greater height, but a lighter complexion undoubtedly reflects less exposure to sun. It is worth remembering that a significant part of China's southernmost provinces of Yunnan, Guangxi, and Guangdong lie below the Tropic of Cancer at a latitude similar to that of Calcutta, the Sahara Desert, or Cuba. Because Chinese who live in these lower latitudes are exposed to a fierce sun for half of the year, darker skin is probably a protective adaptation to the environment.

An amusing aspect of the north-south divide involves perceptions of seasonal temperatures. The north shore of the Yangtze River, for example, is officially "in the north," and houses have traditionally had some form of heating in the winter because "everyone knows that the winter is cold." But houses on the south shore of the Yangtze, typically no more than a half-mile away, traditionally have had no heating because "everyone knows that in the south of China, winters are mild." The Chinese themselves are fond of pointing out how silly this logic seems: that one family in north Nanjing would have to bundle up in all its clothes to stay warm on a cold winter day, while another family across the river in south Nanjing could enjoy the same day in shorts and T-shirts, is ridiculous. But at the same time, this example demonstrates the very different states of mind of people who live in China's northern and southern regions.

The north-south divide also has cultural and political ramifications. Beijing, for example, lies to the far north of China (its name means "northern capital" in Chinese). Because it is China's capital, it is the home of China's government, its ponderous bureaucracy, and some of its best universities. Southerners tend to view their cousins in Beijing as conservative, inflexible, rule-bound, and often a bit full of themselves. Because Beijing in the north is the center of political power, which has at times been administered quite heavy-handedly, southerners have traditionally harbored a mistrust and even resentment of their countrymen from the capital.

But residents of Beijing see things a bit differently. They tend to be proud of the status that comes from living in the capital, and often regard southerners as either hicks or slick businessmen who can't be trusted. The latter stereotype is particularly strong with respect to southerners from Guangdong province, adjacent to Hong Kong. Chinese from this region have a venerable merchant tradition, in part because of their close ties with the vibrant trade of the southern coast, and also in part because of their proximity to Hong Kong, an important entrepot and the center of China's trade with the West for much of the past two hundred years. (It is important to note that Shanghai is rapidly replacing Hong Kong as the focus of China's trade and contact with the West, a point of great pride to the Shanghainese, and one of considerable distress for many Hong Kong Chinese.)

More generally, southerners are inclined to agree that their countrymen in the north possess a frankness and directness that one does not find in the south. Southerners typically admire this trait: they find it refreshing that northerners will seal a business deal over dinner and drinks with a simple, direct "sounds good—let's do it." Southerners will admit freely that they tend to "always have the calculator running in their heads"—that is, they are constantly calculating costs and benefits and worrying about who might be cheated in a deal. Furthermore, many southerners admire the way that northerners "say what they think, and do what they say"; southerners will tell you that, by contrast, they are more likely to think one thing, but say another—and then act differently still. Although any of these characterizations are certainly not true for all the inhabitants of a particular region, they do have some basis in real behavioral differences.

The North-South Divide: Workplace Implications

Businesspeople should also be aware that there is a certain conservatism in China's north, especially in Beijing. One should be prepared for a more bureaucratic attitude and a slower and more cautious approach, especially when dealing with the central government or any of the large SOEs in the north. Although there is corruption everywhere in China, northerners will tell you that they are more trustworthy and willing to play by the rules than their southern counterparts, and there is a grain of truth to this claim.

Commercial interactions in the north of China also tend to be more measured than in the south. For example, in northern cities like Beijing or Dalian, one often finds a certain reflectiveness—almost a philosophical streak—when educated professionals get together. This is not to understate the economic hustle and bustle in the north that is a defining characteristic of all of China today, but the usual intense focus on making money is somewhat tempered in the north by greater interest in other aspects of life: for example, art and film, as well as political and social concerns.

In the south, by contrast, one typically finds an accelerated tempo of life and a more single-minded focus on business and the pursuit of wealth. Southerners tend to speak faster than their northern counterparts (more on language shortly), and this adds to the northerner's sense that people from the south are perpetually in "business overdrive." Add to the frenetic tempo of life the intense, muggy heat of the summertime, and southern cities like Shenzhen and Guanzhou become tropical hotbeds of relentless economic activity in the view of northerners.

It is in the south, moreover, where one is more likely to encounter a freewheeling mentality and a great deal of creativity in circumventing or disregarding rules. Southerners have a saying that goes, "Heaven is high above, and the emperor is far away." Interpreted broadly, this means, "To heck with the government's rules . . . and besides, they are so far away, who is going to catch us?" In the south, therefore, a foreign company can take advantage of the greater speed and flexibility it is likely to find, but its managers should also exercise caution and be sure that its partners are reliable and that any flexibility in the business plans they propose does not expose the firm to trouble from the authorities.

These differences, like the differences between east and west mentioned previously, also lead to regional images that are voiced and perpetuated by the Chinese themselves. Northerners at times will view southerners as somewhat uncultured, overly concerned with money, and lacking cultural breadth and even a sense of humor. Southerners, by contrast, tend to view northerners as stuffy, slow-moving and, at their worst, arrogant and effete, especially if they come from Beijing.

Overseas Chinese in the PRC

As noted earlier, the term *overseas Chinese,* strictly speaking, refers to ethnic Chinese who live outside of Greater China, where Greater China refers to the PRC, Taiwan, and Hong Kong. Here we will use the term more broadly to include Chinese from Taiwan and Hong Kong as well as those from Singapore, other Southeast Asian nations, the United States, Europe and, in smaller numbers, other parts of the world. It is worth noting that Taiwan, Hong Kong, Singapore, and the United States account for the vast majority of ethnic Chinese who were not born in the PRC.

Overseas Chinese have come to China to work for multinationals chiefly because they bring several advantages that enable them to find ready employment both as managers and as individual contributors. First, they usually speak one or more Chinese dialects fluently, although in the case of Chinese from Hong Kong and some from Taiwan their Mandarin may be heavily accented. Second, they are already familiar to at least some degree with Chinese cultural norms, as they have grown up with these norms in Chinese families overseas. Finally, they typically have educational and professional backgrounds that are quite valuable in China today. Many overseas Chinese have graduated from excellent universities: Hong Kong University, Taiwan University, Singapore University, and U.S. schools such as UCLA, Stanford, and MIT. Many of them also have long years of experience working for major multinational corporations in industries that have strong growth prospects in China: electronics, telecommunications, consumer products, automobiles, and so on.

With their many advantages over non-Chinese professionals, overseas Chinese have viewed the PRC as a land of opportunity, particularly since they have found well-paid jobs in management at top-ranked companies. It is worth pointing out, however, that PRC nationals who return to the PRC after many years of professional study and work overseas now compete directly with overseas Chinese for competitive advantage in the PRC labor force. Because overseas Chinese are typically more expensive to employ than returned PRC nationals, the advantage of hiring them has diminished somewhat compared to ten years ago.

Overseas Chinese: Workplace Implications

Although overseas Chinese are ethnically Chinese, it should come as no surprise that since they have grown up in other countries they are, in fact, quite different in many ways from Chinese born in the PRC; in this regard they bring a remarkably rich element of diversity to China today.

First, the behavior and values of overseas Chinese usually reflect strongly their countries of origin: for example, a Singaporean Chinese might reflect aspects of the Anglo-Saxon value system left as a residue of Singapore's colonial experience under the British; she might thus be relatively direct and candid in speech. Similarly, a Chinese person born of Cantonese immigrants to the San Francisco area might be relatively friendly, open, and democratically minded—all traits of the United States, even though he has grown up with Chinese parents in a Chinese household.

Insofar as overseas Chinese bring a layer of culture from their home countries outside of the PRC, they are a kind of hybrid in the PRC professional population. On the one hand, they are likely to feel very familiar with the behaviors of their professional counterparts from the PRC that stem from a shared and enduring Confucian foundation. A good example of this shared Confucian heritage would be the strong emphasis they place on personal relationships. But, at the same time, since they have not experienced the uniquely turbulent recent history of the PRC or grown up under communist rule, overseas Chinese often neither share nor understand many of the assumptions and attitudes of PRC nationals.

For example, overseas Chinese from Singapore and the United States tend to be better team players than PRC nationals. Even though the Chinese communist ideology has emphasized sacrifice for the communal group, the single-child policy of the PRC has engendered a self-centered, "me-first" attitude. In addition, the social chaos and economic hardship created by twentieth-century political movements like the Great Leap Forward of the 1950s and the Cultural Revolution of the late 1960s and 1970s has left a lingering tendency to focus on personal survival and gain even at the expense of others.

Overseas Chinese tend to be more cosmopolitan in their attitudes and thinking than their PRC counterparts as well. Taiwanese or Singaporean managers in their mid-forties will often have done graduate work abroad, started their careers with a multinational, and worked in several different countries. Such managers will therefore have far more education and global experience than their counterpart PRC nationals of the same age. But while their experience has great value, at the same time they may be inclined to view their PRC national counterparts as backward or unsophisticated. If an overseas Chinese manager reveals such an attitude, he or she will likely cause offense and quickly establish a reputation as an insufferable snob and a lousy boss.

The overseas Chinese living and working in the PRC today bring an unusual dimension of diversity to Chinese society: as ethnic Chinese, they are uniquely positioned to navigate easily within PRC society and its norms; yet as outsiders bringing different cultures with them, they exert an important influence on China's development into a more cosmopolitan and sophisticated player within the world community that is simultaneously valued and resented. The influence of Taiwan and Hong Kong is particularly strong in shaping the PRC's popular culture as well as commerce: PRC pop music, fashion, foods, and even manners of speaking are all influenced by offshore cousins in Taiwan and Hong Kong.

Socioeconomic Status

China's vast regional differences are reflected on a smaller scale in the differences between urban and rural settings throughout China. One of the remarkable features of China's traditional form of human settlement has been the abrupt change from city to countryside. Until the twentieth century, most of China's cities were walled, and the wall marked the boundary between urban dwellers and the surrounding farm communities that sustained the cities. Before the rapid development that began in China in the 1980s, this boundary was particularly striking: even in the capital, Beijing, a few miles' drive away from the center would bring the traveler to an invisible line at which, suddenly, an urban concentration of houses, shops, and factories gave way to open farm fields.

Today, the pattern is changing as cities acquire adjacent agricultural land and develop it for industrial purposes. Nowhere is this change more evident than in the Lower Yangtze region that stretches from Shanghai upriver through the cities of Changzhou, Suzhou, and Wuxi. Here innumerable factories—many of them owned by well-known global enterprises like Hitachi, Siemens, Matsushita, and Nokia—now occupy former farmland next to the Shanghai-Suzhou highway as it makes its way inland.

Although cities and their suburbs are expanding rapidly outward, the line between city and farm that used to be marked by city walls can still be witnessed today in socioeconomic terms. Between 60 and 70 percent of China's people still make their living as farmers, and land that is not being developed for industry remains extremely important as a source of food for the world's largest population. This is why many Western executives working in China find rows of cabbages or beans planted a mere 50 feet away from the factory entrance where they go to work every day.

The White-Collar vs. The Agricultural Workforce

There has always been a great difference between the lives of China's educated elite and the farmers who have traditionally been the bedrock of China's economy. This difference has its roots in a view of the world that dates back to the time of Confucius, more than 2,000 years ago. Confucius viewed society as consisting of four traditional classes: scholar-bureaucrats, farmers, artisans, and merchants. Scholar-bureaucrats typically served as civil servants in the imperial government. They attained this coveted position through a series of extremely demanding examinations, and one's placement in the imperial government depended directly on how well one scored on the imperial exams. Since such a great reward came from an investment in education in traditional China, there developed over time a deep respect for learning and education that directly reflects the Confucian placement of the scholar-bureaucrat at the top of Chinese society.

China's society and economy today are, of course, far more complex than they were during imperial times, but we can see aspects of China's Confucian past in the thinking of white-collar workers today, who are in many ways the inheritors of the scholar-bureaucrat tradition from imperial times.

First, today's white-collar professionals still value education above everything else. In fact, the perceived value of education in China goes beyond the Confucian value system and reflects the simple law of supply and demand: owing to a relative scarcity of colleges and universities in relation to China's enormous population, there are far fewer college openings every year than there are applicants. Those who do win acceptance are viewed as the fortunate elite.

A second way the high value of education is apparent among white-collar professionals is in the way new college graduates assess potential employers. To a remarkable degree, these recent graduates will favor companies that are committed to ongoing professional education, and will even accept a lower salary and fewer benefits if they can see tangible evidence that an employer will give them opportunities to continue their professional development on the job.

Once on the job, the primary aspiration of China's white-collar workers is rapid promotion and advancement, primarily because promotion confers increased rank and status, along with higher pay. Taken together, these are the governing values of China's modern professional workforce today. But, to a remarkable degree, the Chinese today tend to see the quickest pathway to promotion as more education instead of consistently strong job performance; in this respect their view is quite different from U.S. Americans, for example, who might want to earn an MBA on the job but who, for the most part, view the path to promotion as mainly dependent on their work performance results.

The situation for China's farmers is more complex. Farm families that work near a major urban center like Shanghai will typically benefit from better elementary, middle, and high schools than their cousins in the more remote regions of the country. Accordingly, it is not uncommon to find parents in such farm communities doing everything they can to encourage their children to excel at school, in the hopes that they may gain admission to college. These families reflect the same Confucian value system as their white-collar, urban counterparts and believe that it is possible to escape the rigors and economic insecurity of farming life by doing whatever they can to ensure entry for their children into the white-collar workforce.

For these farming parents, there are multiple payoffs if their child can get a higher education. First, there is a huge boost in status within their local community. Second, if the child succeeds professionally, there is the likelihood that he or she can move from the farm to the city, where it is possible to enjoy a more comfortable standard of living. And finally, the higher earning power of a successful child in the white-collar workforce is added retirement insurance: farming parents know that their child will feel China's traditional obligation to care for aging family members, and if their child is successful financially, the odds increase that their retirement will be comfortable and worry free.

For farming families in the poorer parts of China, however, things are quite different. There, the local standard may consist of little more than elementary education, with few, if any, prospects for attending high school. Furthermore, if the family is financially pressed, there can be considerable pressure for children to leave school early to help with work on the farm. The result is that families of China's rural poor typically view attaining a white-collar standard of living as completely out of reach. And although as inheritors of the Confucian value system they will likely still maintain a respect for education, they may not place as much emphasis on education as their farming countrymen in wealthier parts of the nation simply because there are far fewer opportunities available to them.

The children of China's poorer rural areas often take another route toward economic advancement, which has its tragic side. Lacking education, but attracted to the glitter and riches of the big cities, young people from the rural poor areas who are in their late teens and twenties have migrated in large numbers to look for work in China's urban areas in the hopes that they can find manual labor that pays good wages—part of which they can remit to parents and relatives back home. Unfortunately, wage rates for manual labor in urban areas are very low. In order to save anything at all, these migrant workers must make extreme sacrifices. This usually means living in rudimentary shacks, possibly provided by their employer, and eating meals that, while not starvation rations, are likely to be meager.

One can see these migrant workers in any large city in China today, particularly in the wealthiest cities such as Shanghai and Guangzhou on the east coast. A few minutes' walk away from the tourist areas with their posh hotels and a turn down some back alleys will almost always reveal crude shacks with roofs made of plastic sheeting and a lack of cleanliness that defines the living environment of many of China's rural poor who have left the hard labor and grinding poverty of farm life to search for better employment and a higher standard of living.

There is an additional aspect of the working rural poor that is particularly distressing in China today: widespread prostitution. For many young women who may only have had a very basic elementary education and who are from China's poorer areas, the quickest way to boost their incomes is through prostitution. While officials in China are loath to admit it, there is a thriving sex industry in China today, and it reflects the fact that large numbers of young women from China's poorer agricultural areas feel that prostitution is their only opportunity to earn a living and, if they are lucky, to save enough to send back home to help support their families.

Private Companies, Hybrids, and State-Owned Enterprises

The second noteworthy socioeconomic gap is the one between SOEs and both private and hybrid companies. Before discussing this gap and its many manifestations, it is worthwhile to define some terms.

A private company is a firm that is owned by independent individuals in China. For example, a group of bright graduates from Beijing University might form a software development company called East Cloud. All of the capital for forming the company comes from the founders, and they are free to pursue a business strategy with very little government interference. There are, of course, regulations that govern a private company. These have chiefly to do with registration of the company with local authorities, compliance with labor laws, and payment of taxes. But it is in fact remarkable how much freedom the private sector in China has today. Compared with the mountain of regulations with which a European or U.S. company must comply, the private company in China today represents a strikingly pure form of capitalistic enterprise.

A hybrid company in China is a firm that has mixed ownership. Lenovo, formerly known as Legend, is China's best-known computer company and is a good example of a hybrid company. Typically, the hybrid's largest shareholder is a state organization that serves as the parent company and is often the source of startup capital and support from the government. But there are often a number of private shareholders as well. A hybrid company's founders, for example, usually hold a significant number of shares. Moreover, after becoming established, hybrid companies will often create a listed subsidiary and offer stock of this subsidiary on a public exchange (usually Hong Kong) to raise additional funds. As a rule of thumb, the publicly owned portion of a hybrid company will not exceed 50 percent, and the parent company is typically the majority shareholder of the listed subsidiary. Like private companies, hybrids enjoy substantial freedom to operate free of government meddling; but unlike private companies, hybrids can turn to the government for a measure of support if they encounter difficulties.

A state-owned enterprise (SOE), by contrast, is a company that is completely owned and managed by the state; SOEs are a relic of the Soviet-style planned economy adopted by Mao Zedong after his communist victory in 1949. The central organizational principle behind the SOE is to provide cradle-to-grave employment for workers in an independent, freestanding productive unit, or *danwei.* The typical SOE is situated on a large piece of land, or on several large pieces of land, and in addition to factory employment, it provides housing for workers' families, schools for workers' children, one or more dining halls for communal meals, a hospital, recreational facilities, and sometimes even a cemetery. Because the SOE was designed to serve such an important social function, and because China's economy was a planned economy until 1978, the SOE was not designed or equipped to be economically competitive or profitable in the Western sense. In fact, as long as an SOE met its production quota, it did not matter if it overran its costs or produced products of such poor quality that they were of little use.

The harsh reality in China today, however, is that its SOEs are in severe distress. The vast majority of SOEs are unable to compete effectively in an open economy, and many are technically bankrupt; they survive only through large loans from the state. But the central government's ability to prop up failing SOEs is limited, as the level of nonperforming debt in China continues to grow and banks are not able or willing to offer new loans. China's leaders, therefore, face an extremely difficult social problem—namely, what to do with the millions of workers in the SOEs who do not have the skills or experience to survive in the new, highly competitive free-market economy. China today can be described as a bimodal society, in which a new, healthy, and growing private sector is proving to be highly successful in the global economy, while an older China, that of the SOEs, is an aging dinosaur, heading for extinction but still alive and a burden to the rest of society.

In thinking about SOEs, it is natural to wonder why the state can't simply let them go bankrupt in order to rationalize the economy. The answer is that the SOEs employ such huge numbers of workers that the unemployment caused by massive bankruptcies would likely lead to considerable social instability and the possibility of widespread protest against the government, civil disobedience or, worse, revolution. Revolutions in China's past have been extremely bloody and destructive; this is why the mere possibility of revolution induced by massive unemployment is such a nightmare for China's senior leaders. Moreover, the SOE workforce is a greater threat to the government than the agricultural poor: the SOE workforce is generally better educated, urban, and includes the leadership and management resources necessary for organized and potentially highly threatening protest.

China's leaders would, of course, like to find as many creative solutions to the problem of noncompetitive SOEs as possible. One such solution is the joint venture. In this arrangement, an SOE with some productive assets, a salvageable workforce, and perhaps a good national reputation is "married" to a Western firm. The non-Chinese company then provides capital, training, and operational knowledge in return for market access and various forms of government support, betting that the joint venture will be able to compete and that a significant number of the original SOE's workers can keep their jobs after retraining.

Some SOEs have potential as promising joint-venture partners for Western firms. Joining with the right SOE—one with a valuable manufacturing plant, equipment, and knowledge, along with a trainable workforce—can be a good way for a Western business to gain quick access to a manufacturing base with existing channels for distribution that would require a strong network of relationships and substantial infrastructure expenses to build independently. SOEs are often backed by senior officials who are eager to do everything they can to promote the success of a joint venture; their behind-the-scenes support can confer substantial competitive advantage in the China market.

The unfortunate fact, however, is that joint ventures have met with only mixed success in China, and most of the better SOEs that are good candidates for joint ventures have already found partners. The remaining distressed SOEs today typically offer few attractions to Western firms, which explains why so many Western companies today prefer the wholly foreign-owned enterprise (WFOE) structure, in which a company operates independently, without any formal connection to an existing Chinese enterprise. The lack of suitors for the remaining SOEs is an additional problem for the government, as the chance of joint venture is now increasingly remote for them.

Hybrid and Private Companies vs. SOEs: Workplace Implications

The tremendous differences in structure and purpose between the SOEs and the more modern hybrid and private companies lead to equally large differences in the attitudes of their respective employees. For example, in the typical modern private company one finds a strong work ethic, and most employees are willing to work very long hours in order to succeed. This is often amplified by the use of stock options and generous performance-based bonuses as rewards. Furthermore, since the government is unable to fund retirement pensions for even their oldest workers, let alone younger workers in the private sector, workers in private companies today know that they must provide for their own retirements and support their aging parents—both of which tend to increase their willingness to work hard and sacrifice for financial success.

Like their counterparts in private companies, employees in hybrid companies must work hard to succeed, and their careers are determined largely by their performance. Although it may be somewhat harder to fire employees at hybrids, and this type of organization may be more reluctant to downsize precipitously than private companies, employees at hybrids are not guaranteed a job. Moreover, although a hybrid will typically contribute to its employees' retirement, much like a Western firm, employees of hybrids are not guaranteed a retirement pension.

By contrast, workers in SOEs traditionally learned that there is no incentive to work hard: typically, salaries were paid on a fixed or seniority-based system, with no connection to output or quality. Furthermore, most managers in SOEs found little to do to occupy their time productively; reading reports and newspapers, drinking tea, and idly chatting with colleagues became the norm. Managers set a poor example for their workers, and, in fact, workers aspired to management as a way to continue to draw a salary without having to do much work at all. The socialist promise of full employment and the inability of an SOE to fire any worker evolved into a view of work called "the iron rice bowl." This fitting image refers to a rice bowl that cannot break and that will always be filled—implying a job for life whether one works hard or not.

While pressure to reform has wrought some changes in the employment culture of SOEs, the fact remains that workers who have spent their entire lives in SOEs typically have a noticeably different attitude toward work when compared to their counterparts at hybrids or private companies. SOE workers tend not to be as motivated; they are less concerned with quality, since the state was traditionally much more concerned with output quantity than with quality; and they tend to have an entitlement mentality—it is assumed that one will keep one's job, regardless of the economic climate.

In the event that workers of a privately held foreign firm are thrust together in the workplace with former SOE employees through a joint venture or other means, there is potential for considerable workplace friction. The employees of many Chinese SOEs often have interests that lie at odds with a Western partner, and this difference in interests may unfortunately remain hidden until it is too late. For example, senior leaders in an SOE often are primarily concerned about preserving jobs, with profitability a secondary concern: they know that jobs are Beijing's biggest worry, and their own bureaucratic success may depend on showing that they are keeping workers employed.

Rank-and-file employees, too, might resist the introduction of new technologies and production techniques if they feel that these could possibly threaten their jobs. Chinese employees of foreign multinationals and employees of SOEs who must coexist in a joint venture structure often encounter obstacles to cooperation because of widely differing values and skill levels. Again, the best path for employers to address these problems, albeit a long one, is through intensive workplace education and training. This strategy will take time to yield results; but it has the more immediate advantage of the potential for government support.[6]

Language: Linguistic Diversity and Its Consequences

Another important factor that contributes to diversity in China is the Chinese language itself. Although all Chinese today learn the national language, called *putonghua,* and known in the West as standard Mandarin, most Chinese grow up speaking one of more than two hundred local dialects. Unlike most English dialects, where one's accent may be strong but there is little difficulty in comprehension, the dialects in China diverge in pronunciation and vocabulary to the extent that they are often not mutually intelligible. For example, without study, a citizen of Beijing will not be able to comprehend the Cantonese dialect spoken by someone from

Guangzhou, and a citizen of Shanghai will not understand the Minnan dialect of his compatriots in Fujian province.

What makes the dialectical variations of spoken Chinese so fascinating is that the Chinese sometimes deliberately use dialects as a way of regulating whom they choose to include in a conversation. For example, in a negotiation involving a business from Beijing in the north selling to a customer in Guangzhou in the south, the two parties would naturally begin their discussions in Mandarin—all one would notice is that the southerners speak with a distinct accent. But should the southerners wish to begin a side discussion in private, perhaps to respond to a sticky point in the negotiations, they would probably switch into their local Cantonese dialect. At this point, the Beijing team would be left in the dark, unless, of course, one of them spoke Cantonese, which is unlikely. The Guanzhou team would thus have a convenient tool for continuing the conversation in private, without having to leave the room.

The ability to shift into a local dialect represents a powerful communication tool used to regulate social interaction. The Beijing team would not feel insulted by this behavior, but would certainly feel excluded and, in the case of a negotiation, would fully understand why their Cantonese counterparts had shifted to their native dialect.

Common local dialects are sometimes used for another purpose, namely, to emphasize that the two speakers are from the same region and are therefore more akin than any outsiders who cannot speak that local dialect. This separation of China into a mosaic of dialect groups exerts a subtle but powerful effect making the country more an agglomeration of regional communities rather than a truly unified national community. One's sense of identification with a specific region of China through a local dialect is therefore a very important element of China's makeup.

Use of Dialects in Everyday Business

The business implications of China's linguistic diversity are several. First, there is a subtle tendency for Chinese to prefer to deal with individuals who speak their own regional dialect. This is certainly not to say that a southerner would harbor deep suspicions about a northerner based on language; but it is to say that a Cantonese speaker will feel more comfortable dealing with a fellow Cantonese speaker than with someone from Liaoning province in the northeast.

Such linguistic preferences can influence sales efforts. Although it is perfectly possible for a sales team to market and sell its product or service anywhere in China using Mandarin, it is much more effective if the team can speak to its prospects and customers in their local dialect. Speaking the local dialect brings a sense of closeness, community, and linguistic kinship that helps build trust and confidence in the product or service. All other things being equal, it is considerably harder for a Shanghainese salesman who did not grow up speaking Cantonese to sell products in Guangzhou than a local salesman there who is a native Cantonese speaker.

Another business implication of China's linguistic diversity is related to the negotiation scenario mentioned above. A Chinese team that can speak both Mandarin and a local dialect will have a slight advantage over an opposing team of negotiators that can only speak Mandarin. This is because the first team can easily switch to their local dialect and exclude their Mandarin-speaking counterparts. Not only does this instantly convert the conversation into a private one, but it also tends to throw the members of the other team somewhat off balance, as they realize that the more linguistically versatile team is in control of the conversation.

Therefore, it makes sense for a business to have a clear sense of its linguistic diversity in China and to ensure that key Chinese managers in each region are able to speak the local dialect. This will confer a huge advantage in a variety of areas from motivation and development of local staff to negotiations with local officials. The easiest way to ensure this linguistic match is, of course, to hire locally. But with increased mobility in China today, qualified candidates for a job—for instance, people from Chengdu who speak the Sichuanese Chengdu dialect—might be found in cities as far away as Harbin in the north or Kunming in the south. So it pays during the interview process to ask where a candidate is from and what dialects he or she speaks as a way to ensure the best possible match of talent, business need, and geography.

Educational Background

As mentioned in the Socioeconomic Status section, China's historical emphasis on education as a key determinant of social standing is still very much in evidence today. Although the country's educational policy guarantees every citizen an education through high school; in fact, many children in rural areas complete at most an elementary education. There is also a distinct hierarchy among Chinese educational institutions: beginning with high schools, each city in China has a very clear understanding of which are the top-rated schools, the mid-rated schools, and the lower-rated schools.

As a result, gifted students who attend the best high schools have an advantage in being admitted into the top-ranked universities. And it is striking how much a degree from a top university carries real clout, both

TABLE 2-1 TOP-RANKED CHINESE UNIVERSITIES*

University Name	Rank	Location	Reputation
Tsinghua (Qinghua) University	1	Beijing	Strong science and math; good political connections
Peking (Beijing) University	2	Beijing	Strong humanities; good political connections
Zhejiang University	3	Hangzhou	Large comprehensive university with long history
Fudan University	4	Shanghai	Good science and math; political connections in Shanghai
Nanjing University	5	Nanjing	Strong research faculty with nearby Nanjing University Science Technology and Industrial Zone

*Other schools commonly found in top-ten lists for Chinese universities include Huazhong University of Science and Technology, Shanghai Jiaotong University, Wuhan University, Jilin University, and Zhongshan University.

from the standpoint of one's personal reputation and status and from the standpoint of one's job prospects.

For businesses, this emphasis on education and the hierarchy of schools within China creates both opportunities and costs. The chief opportunity is, of course, that China's emphasis on education means that graduates from the best schools are China's elite, and they are likely to be extremely intelligent, gifted individuals. The chief problem today for most multinational companies is that such a small proportion of China's population has the opportunity to attend a college or university at all. The result is that demand for talented new graduates far exceeds supply.

Education: Workplace Implications

A consequence of the imbalance between supply and demand is that graduates from China's best schools expect, and will often demand, a premium in their compensation; this is especially true if such graduates speak good English. They have been repeatedly told that they are "the cream of the crop" and they want this reflected in both pay and status. Unfortunately, sometimes their attitude can go beyond a healthy self-confidence to become an offensive arrogance. Even some new hires will expect to have a level of responsibility and a title far greater than what is realistic given their actual work experience; if they don't get it, they may feel insulted and look elsewhere for work.

Another challenge is that, once on the job, top graduates from the best schools may feel entitled to a greater say in the business than is warranted by their level of experience or capability, and may, as a result, become a real irritant to managers with their constant criticism and second-guessing of management's decisions. Further difficulties arise when elite graduates feel they are socially superior to their subordinates and are entitled to an autocratic management style. Their demanding behavior often has an adverse and sometimes severely negative effect on morale. Having graduated from the best schools, top graduates feel entitled to give orders. But because they are young, recent top graduates often fail to see that with respect to managerial competence, a degree from a first-rate university is not the same as many years of business experience and that only the latter can serve as the basis for wise, informed leadership. The chief complaint from subordinates when they encounter this kind of elitist behavior from their hotshot bosses sounds like this: "My manager is always ordering me around and never takes the time to listen. He may think he knows it all, but he doesn't. He may come from a top-ranked university, but in my field, I am far more of an expert than him, and I wish he would acknowledge it."

A final and costly consequence of the wide variation in China's educational system is the tendency of China's top graduates to switch jobs frequently. While they may be very attractive candidates for all the obvious reasons, once on the job many of them become restless and convinced they are not being promoted quickly enough. Soon they begin looking for new jobs, making the most of their current position and responsibilities to jump to a position with higher pay and status. If they jump to a competitor, the loss to a business is even greater.

It is therefore essential that businesses be aware of the diversity of China's pool of human talent and understand both the benefits and the costs of hiring graduates from China's elite institutions. It is wise to keep in mind that although top schools like Beijing's Tsinghua University or Shanghai's Fudan University do indeed graduate China's best and brightest, there are many other fine schools—second- and third-tier universities—that graduate capable students who may actually be easier to manage and in the long term constitute a more stable workforce.

Age: China's Generation Gap

Two factors are at work in creating a substantial generation gap in China today, and as this gap widens, it is creating an additional, dramatic kind of diversity within Chinese society.

The first factor is China's one-child policy, which mandates that couples in China today may only have a single child. Since its inception in 1980, this policy has been remarkably successful in curbing China's population growth rate. But there are a number of important sociological and cultural consequences that stem from this policy. To understand these consequences, we have to recall that the Chinese have traditionally viewed the family as the center of their universe and the basic building block of their society. Indeed, in traditional China there was no concept of the individual: one's identity was completely defined through one's relationship to family members, and one's life was governed by a complex web of obligations within the family network. In return, the family, at its best, was a source of emotional and financial support and, in old age, social security.

Because family is such an important concept to the Chinese, it is not surprising that children have customarily been viewed as the greatest blessing of all. And the mark of true prosperity in the traditional family was not so much money itself, but a big family and the ability to support it. A husband and wife therefore traditionally hoped to have more than one child; ironically, poverty actually was a spur to have more children, since children and their earnings, meager though they might have been, were the only source of support to parents in sickness or old age.

Consequently, there has long been a Chinese tendency to dote upon children—mothers have traditionally been extremely protective in China, more so than in the Anglo-Saxon tradition that seeks to develop independence in children and therefore avoids lavishing too much attention on them (recall, for example, the tradition of the English boarding school and the Victorian notion that "children should be seen and not heard").

A second factor in China's current generation gap is a dramatic rise in material wealth since 1980. Prior to the economic reforms that began in 1979 and have since unleashed an unparalleled rise in material wealth in China, most Chinese—including urban dwellers—were extremely poor by Western standards. As a result, the children in a traditional family could expect affection and nurture, but not a surfeit of toys, clothes, or other material trappings. Hand-me-downs and sharing were the norm.

Today, however, the situation is radically different. Parents and grandparents are more inclined than ever to dote on the family's children because one child is the limit: the one-child policy has thereby intensified an existing Chinese cultural trait. But with their much greater disposable income, many families express their affection for children by buying them an unheard-of quantity of material belongings including toys, electronic games, stereo systems, TVs, and videos, to name but a few.

The result of this indulgence, as the Chinese will themselves admit, is a new generation of "little emperors"—that is, the spoiled children of China's growing middle class. Thoughtful Chinese observers, particularly educators, point out in conversations and opinion pieces every day throughout China that today's children reflect nothing of past generations' willingness to work hard, save, sacrifice, and, in a particularly evocative phrase, "eat bitterness" (*chi ku*). They worry that something of the soul of China's hardiness and durability has been lost, as the next generation of spoiled children is growing up to expect everything they want with no effort of their own required to get it.

Age: Workplace Implications

There is an additional element of this generation gap that is of particular importance to multinational businesses in China: since the new generation of young, bright, ambitious Chinese corporate workers are the product of the one-child policy and have grown up without siblings, they tend to be poor team players. It should be emphasized that this is not their fault; it is the sociological outcome of a necessary national family planning policy. But these employees' lack of understanding of teamwork can be a tremendous headache to Western managers who wish to build strong teams in their Chinese operations. Instead of teamwork, Western managers quickly find that in spite of their best efforts and often a large investment in training programs, their young Chinese managers are ferociously territorial and unable to view their peers in the organization as anything other than a competitive threat. This phenomenon reflects what anthropologists and specialists in child development have known for a long time: teamwork is not hard-wired into the human DNA; instead, it is a skill that must be learned through one's upbringing.

In addition to a lack of teamwork skills, young workers in China today are often quite unrealistic with regard to how fast they will be promoted, what title they will acquire, and how much they will be paid. In part this is because they have seen in their own childhoods a rapid increase in material wealth and have come to expect it as professionals. In addition, they are part of a labor market for white-collar talent in which demand far exceeds supply. Consequently, this generation of young workers has made a habit of job hopping and parlaying their most recent job into a new position with a grander title and a bigger compensation package. Furthermore, they compare their progress quite explicitly with their peers: friends and colleagues think nothing of directly comparing their current positions and salary levels, and those who perceive that they are not advancing as quickly as their peers feel tremendous pressure to look for a new job that will accelerate their advancement, or else risk losing face in their peer group.

Younger Chinese workers who display the "little emperor" attributes often come in conflict with older, more mature employees when they work together in the same company. For example, a Western multinational may have hired some seasoned engineers, general managers, or human resource (HR) professionals from an SOE or other government organization. While these workers may not have the same entrepreneurial fire as their younger colleagues, they are likely to be much more mature in their judgment and people management skills. This is because they are typically quite a bit older—they are more likely in their late forties or early fifties, rather than their thirties. Younger workers may look down on older workers and feel that they are stodgy, conservative, and risk-averse. While this may to some degree be true, what younger workers often fail to see is that their older colleagues bring balanced judgment to business operations along with people management skills that are the product of their greater experience. Conversely, older workers will often find their younger counterparts to be full of themselves, at times outright rude and disrespectful and immature. They will typically acknowledge the value of a degree from a top university and the energy that comes from relative youth, but they know clearly that a degree alone does not confer organizational wisdom.

Thus, whenever younger and older professionals work together in China, with their diverse backgrounds and perspectives, they will almost always generate an internal tension that must be managed carefully or else teamwork and morale can suffer. Knowing the background behind this generational gap, and working to bring into play the strengths of both older and younger workers—in short, managing generational diversity—is an important challenge in China today.

Managing the "Little Emperor" Generation

Foreign managers in China today face a daunting challenge in retaining a first-class workforce: the demographics of the labor market combined with the consequences of China's one-child policy and the generation gap have created in China's top young talent an extreme case of high expectations and a corresponding proclivity to change jobs frequently with little or no loyalty to any one employer. As a result, annual turnover rates in many multinational organizations operating in China today exceed 20 percent.

While a corporation can do nothing to change the external circumstances that create this problem, it can take steps to reduce its effects. For example, a firm can make an investment in an extended, multipart orientation and training process of a year or more, particularly for younger employees who have no prior experience working for a multinational firm. If this process contains carefully designed components reinforcing the idea of the company as a family and the benefits of company loyalty and teamwork, it can measurably increase employee retention; if such a program is followed with additional training in teamwork over a three-to-five year period, retention can increase even further. Companies that commit to a systematic career development program in which white-collar workers are given the opportunity to learn new skills and earn advanced degrees with certification through an exam are likely to both attract the best candidates and also to improve retention of their top talent.

In addition, a company can insist on management practices that require all managers to spend time with their Chinese employees as mentors and teachers, focusing on their long-term career development. At first glance, this recommendation may seem contradictory: after all, an investment in career development would seem to equip employees with precisely the skills that will make them more attractive to another employer. This is undeniably true, but there is another factor at work that acts as a strong counterbalance: Chinese society remains intensely relationship based; consequently, a strong relationship between manager and employee acts as a powerful inhibitor to employee defection. The model manager in this relationship is seen by his or her employees as both competent and caring, much like a dependable parent. With these two conditions in place, a manager can, in fact, be quite demanding and still retain happy employees.

Applying Global Diversity
Hiring a Key Factory Manager

Regional Origin

SITUATION:

A Western-owned manufacturing company with a factory located in Wuxi is facing the challenge of finding a good candidate for the plant's director of assembly operations. There are currently three candidates to choose from, each of whom has a mix of perceived strengths and weaknesses as identified by the recruiting team:

Xu Tang-jun: External Candidate from Beijing

Strengths: Elite educational background from a top university in Beijing; extremely bright and a quick learner; solid operational experience and a proven track record; self-confident and willing to take big challenges

Weaknesses: Aloof and not a natural "people person" or team player; may have a "Beijing is best" attitude that will not be so palatable in Wuxi; could be perceived as a snob by local employees in Wuxi; might be inclined to jump to a new job quickly if he disagrees with the expatriate factory head

Franklin Chen: External Candidate from Wuxi

Strengths: Good understanding of manufacturing based on thirty years of experience; cheerful attitude; team player with excellent management skills; positive role model; SOE background could help in dealing with government officials; seniority and local connections will be a plus in working with rank and file employees; willing to train to learn new skills

Weaknesses: Lacks technical understanding of latest assembly processes; at times a bit cautions and slow; may need to acquire more of an entrepreneurial spirit; could be seen by younger managers as out of step

K.S. Lau: Internal Candidate from Singapore

Strengths: Solid professional training and thorough understanding of the assembly process; knowledge of company culture and management philosophy; academic credentials and seniority within the company; young managers are likely to be impressed with his fast-paced work style and professional knowledge; strong work ethic and good role model

Weaknesses: Possibly impatient, especially with less experienced staff; could find daily operational challenges too frustrating to want to stay long in Wuxi; possible "culture gap" between him and general employee population due to his Singaporean background—at risk of being seen as an outsider; may retreat to Singaporean "ghetto" in Wuxi; limited language skills in local dialect and hard for employees to understand; does not read Chinese well

POSSIBLE SOLUTION:

Although Xu Tang-jun has many appealing qualities, his lack of people skills, sense of rivalry with other managers, and tendency to withhold information all suggest that he might be a divisive figure in this new role. Franklin Chen has a number of strong qualities, but his lack of up-to-date technical background and his history as a manager of an SOE could put him at a significant disadvantage with the managers who will be reporting to him immediately. K.S. Lau is a hard-working and technically skilled employee, but he and his family may encounter major difficulties in adjusting to life in Wuxi. There is also a danger that differences in language and style based on his Singaporean background will cause him to be isolated from the factory's employees.

The best choice might be to ask K.S. Lau, who is already an employee, to work on a transitional plan that will enable the factory to run efficiently for the time being. In the meantime, Franklin Chen could be brought on board and given time to get to know the corporate culture and to learn any essential technical skills he may be lacking. Time in the Penang factory and at headquarters could give Franklin the background he needs, and also burnish his credentials in the eyes of his subordinates. Longer term, he has a much better chance of establishing positive and productive relationships with workers in Wuxi than K.S. Lau based on his background as a PRC national, his regional ties and dialect, and his strong combination of hands-on factory experience and management skills.

Summary Recommendations

We have seen that although Chinese today do not share the concept of diversity as it is understood in the United States and other Western countries, variations in physical and human geography lead to a diversity in China every bit as great as that found in the West. This diversity in turn creates both opportunities and perils for Western businesses operating in China. Below are five summary recommendations for companies that will help them to both adapt and prosper through understanding and leveraging the remarkable diversity of the Chinese workplace:

1. Know China's north-south and east-west divisions between **regions** as well as the gaps that separate citizens of the PRC, their Taiwanese and Hong Kong compatriots, and overseas Chinese. Learn the implications of these regional differences for business and for workplace interactions, and avoid the disadvantages, for example, of having a mixed sales force with members from many different regions competing with a rival whose sales force consists entirely of local employees.

2. Be alert for distinctions in **socioeconomic status** because of the differences between urban and rural environments, or between SOEs and both hybrid and private companies. Reduce the effect of such status distinctions among employees through intensive training, development, and a sustained emphasis on teamwork. Capitalize on the Chinese government's strong desire to alleviate the hardships of its agricultural population and the burden of distressed SOEs.

3. Ensure that **language** does not become a barrier to good business by paying attention to the linguistic capabilities of employees and ensuring both that key employees speak and read Chinese, and that they can speak the dialects of the locations where they work.

4. Understand the intricate hierarchy that stems from China's system of **education.** Build a corporate culture—starting with fundamental values—that allows you to hire and retain top employees while preventing destructive elitism; invest in additional workforce education to reduce educational gaps between employees.

5. Remember how **age** affects the outlook and values of China's workforce. Develop, encourage, and reward good teamwork early as an antidote to the "little emperor" syndrome. And remember that in China, as anywhere else in the world, age brings wisdom, which is a priceless asset.

CHAPTER 3

Diversity in Egypt

Graziella Figi

Why Egypt?

- Egypt has the largest population of any country in the Middle East, with slightly more than both Turkey and Iran; the number of Egyptians will continue to increase rapidly due to high birth rates.
- The country has experienced relatively rapid economic growth rate of 4 percent or more per year, with recent expansion in areas such as telecommunications.
- Egyptian expatriates work in key roles in many other Middle Eastern nations, both as professionals and as laborers.
- Egypt has long held a central position in the Middle East; it exerts considerable political influence due to its size and its role as home to the League of Arab States.

Introduction

One's first experience in Egypt usually starts in Cairo. There is no better place to hear and see African-Mediterranean diversity than in this world capital and crossroads city. It has a day and night cacophony that exists nowhere else: high-volume classical and popular music and Qur'an recitation emanate from apartments, stores, and taxis. At regular intervals, these sounds are amplified by the simultaneous *adhan* (call to prayer) from over 500 mosques. Add to these the constant honking of car horns in an unremitting traffic gridlock of cars, combis, donkeys, and tour buses and you have placed yourself in the throng of 15 million-plus Cairenes moving along the city's pulsating streets. Go beyond the city limits, and you will feel the energy of another five million inhabitants; the population of Greater Cairo, including Giza, is estimated to be closer to 20 million people.

Egypt is the most populous country in the Arab World and the second largest in Africa after Nigeria. Total population figures vary from 60 to 77 million—the physical complexion of people on the streets ranges from blonds with blue eyes of Greek or Italian heritage, to the distinct features of the descendants of the pharaohs, to the classic Arab and Afro-Mediterranean residents and visitors, to the elegant height and ebony skins of the Nubians. To what does Egypt owe this variety?

Ethnically, Egyptians are a mixture of races that have intermingled at various times over the past 6,000 years. In terms of cultural identification, they consider themselves to be a dual mix of Arab and Egyptian. Egyptian culture and tradition have survived centuries of non-Egyptian rule, whereby the waves of humanity that have entered the country and mingled with its preexisting peoples and cultures have created the Egypt that tourists explore en masse to this day. Based upon this centuries-long tradition of dealing with both visitors and invaders, Egyptians are known for embracing new ideas and learning.

Another more recent influx of people who are neither tourists nor invaders can be found in Egypt's cities. Some stay for extended periods as representatives of international agencies, resident archeologists, or heads of foreign cultural centers; there are also children of expatriated Egyptian parents who seek to rediscover their heritage by returning to their culture of origin. These people bring the unique perspective of outsiders who come to know Egyptian society well. A number end up staying as permanent residents and maintain the legacy of integration within the proud and secure Egyptian culture, while making contributions that immigrants with a fresh perspective can bring to an already diverse population. Multinational organizations can tap into these more recent arrivals as a valuable asset.

Key Locations

Cairo is the center of Egyptian life (see Figure 3-1). In the spoken dialect of Egyptian Arabic, it is common to refer to Cairo as *el masr* (Egypt), rather than its Arabic name, *el kahira*. Businesspeople rarely venture outside

Cairo unless it is to visit a factory in Helwan, a military base in the desert, a branch of an Egyptian company in Alexandria, or if they take a break at a tourist destination in Upper Egypt or a beach resort in Sharm El Sheikh or Hurghada. If they travel among the 26 governorates, they will feel a marked change in the pace as they move from city to town to village.

Egypt's second largest city is Alexandria, an ancient urban center with

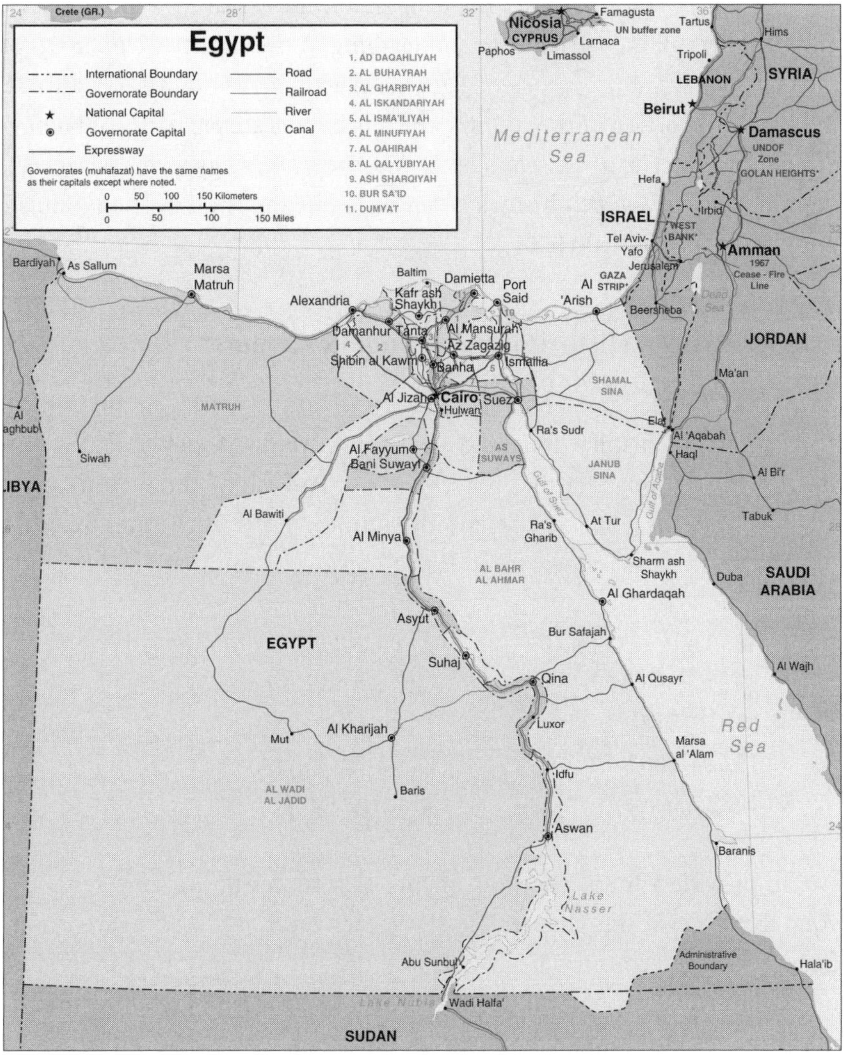

FIGURE 3-1. Map of Egypt and Its Political Regions

4.5 million people on the Mediterranean Sea whose culture is influenced by residents of Greek, Italian, Lebanese, and Armenian origin. Cooler than Cairo, it is a summer destination of many Cairenes; the population swells significantly during the summer months, impacting the availability of hotel and conference space for businesspeople. Other important locations include Port Said and Suez, both key commercial centers due to their location on opposite ends of the Suez Canal.

The Nile Delta comprises the lush area from Alexandria to Port Said, and supports all the agriculture and farming in the country. Upper Egypt includes the breadth of Ancient Egypt and actually lies south of Cairo. In the southern portion of the country, the inhabitants are primarily of Nubian origin, and refer to themselves as *El-Masri-Sudani* (Egyptian-Sudanese), an indication of Egypt's historical ties with Sudan. The Egyptian Nubian population is about 300,000.

Historical and Economic Context

Egypt has the longest recorded history of any country in the world. Throughout its history, this land has been governed independently by a succession of foreigners that reflect the rise and fall of the region's great empires: Persians, Greeks, Romans, Byzantines, Arabs, Turks, and British.

There are six main periods in Egypt's history as a unified state:

3000 B.C. – 332 B.C.	Ancient Egypt
332 B.C. – 639	Greek and Roman Egypt
639 – 1517	Early Arab Egypt
1517 – 1882	Ottoman Egypt
1882 – present	Modern Egypt

To provide a full account of Egypt's rich succession of empires is beyond the scope of this chapter. However, each layer of history exerts an influence over the country as a whole and the self-perception of individual inhabitants. The strongest influences are the most recent, including the administrative and Islamic heritage of Ottoman Egypt, the influence of

British colonial rule and control of the Suez Canal, and the pan-Arab nationalism movement begun by Gamal Abdel Nasser after he led a military coup in 1952 that toppled the former king. Egypt's history of the last half century is also inseparable from the Arab-Israeli conflict, in which the Egyptians have played the roles of both combatants and later peacemakers.

Since it became independent, Egypt has struggled to take on a role that reflects its history as a vital part of the Arab world and a link between the Middle East and other nations. Egyptians take seriously what they see as their country's position as the center of Middle Eastern art, culture, media, and publishing, and as the political capital of the Arab world. Egypt is also a center of education: Al-Azhar in Cairo is the oldest university in the world, founded in A.D. 972.

Although Egypt is still working to establish its attractiveness to the international financial markets, Cairo has indeed achieved the status of a prominent world capital. It hosts numerous international conferences, donor agencies and their projects, and an increasing number of multinational enterprises and their employees. Cairo, Egypt, and Egyptians are growing into a notable new role as a part of the "neighborhood" in the Middle East, promoting and exemplifying stability and taking on special responsibilities in dispute resolution.

The Economic Context

Egypt's economy has expanded steadily in recent years, although its growth rate of approximately 4 percent is insufficient to provide jobs for a rapidly increasing population—there are an estimated 800,000 new job seekers each year, and unofficial estimates of jobless rates range from 15 to 25 percent. Life expectancy in Egypt continues to rise, with its current level at 70.4 for females and 66.3 for males; literacy rates of 44.8 percent for females and 67.2 percent for males are also increasing, according to statistics of the United Nations Development Program. The combination of population growth, longer life expectancy, and improving education makes Egypt a significant exporter of workers, especially to other countries in the Middle East. The movement of workers abroad has made Egyptians an important factor in the economy of the entire region, and has produced a segment of the workforce with international skills.

Privatization of former state-owned enterprises has also brought about significant change; about 40 percent of such enterprises have been transferred to private hands. The country has benefited from higher oil prices and also recent discoveries of natural gas.[1] The main sources of hard currency represent a blend that is unique to Egypt: tourism, oil exports, remittances from expatriates abroad, and Suez Canal tolls.

Despite these sources of income, Egypt continues to need foreign aid. The United States provides $3 billion a year, and other development projects are funded by the Swedish International Development Agency (SIDA) and Japan. Arab countries provide significant amounts, but the figures are not available. Funding is available from multilateral donor agencies and those of other countries for development and other projects.

The fastest Egyptian technology growth is in telecommunications. Three of the four Egyptian companies among the Top Companies in the Arab World annual list are in that sector; the top four include Orascom Telecom, Orascom Construction Industries, Mobinil, and Vodaphone Egypt. The rise of Orascom Telecom is an Egyptian success story. In true multinational form, its owner, Naguib Sawiris, manages risk well and has a presence in Asia, Africa, Europe, and the Middle East, including Iraq.[2]

Egyptian companies are avidly pursuing joint ventures and consortia partnerships with other companies, not only in the Arab World but from other world regions as well. People from the Arab Gulf states who formerly came as summer tourists have become year-round residents, creating new jobs in the private sector—primarily in the service industry—and bringing foreign direct investment. Egyptians now share their workplaces with many Arabs from other countries, establish new personal and business relationships outside of the country, and are exposed to the depth and breadth of other Arab cultures.

Diversity Dimensions in Egypt

The Arabic word for diversity is *ihtilaf*, meaning differences, although without a negative connotation. There are many factors that define diversity in Egypt, not the least of which is its unique history as the world's largest open-air museum of the oldest living civilization on the planet.

Aspects of diversity that are particularly relevant for conducting business in Egypt today include:

- Family Background
- Socioeconomic Status
- Job Function
- Gender

Family Background

Business and family background are closely connected in Egypt, and successful business is often very much a family affair. In Egypt, family refers not only to the core family, but also to the extended family of aunts, uncles, cousins, and those related by marriage. Almost every Egyptian can say that he or she comes from a "good family" because within the extended group there will be at least one person of distinction—a general, judge, or other person of rank and title. The family is each person's support system. It is normal and usual to live with or have as part of the household one or more relatives and to spend leisure time with family members. In challenging times, it is the family who will offer emotional and financial support, while relying heavily on a religious foundation as moral guide.

The family is usually the first source of *wasta,* from the Arabic *wisata,* "mediation," or *muwasata,* "intercession." *Wasta* means personal connections, which one needs for meaningful socioeconomic status. It has also been called a form of affirmative action in the sense that it provides access to government or business connections for individuals who lack other forms of power or status. Everyday functions of Egyptian life, such as applying for a passport, a driver's license, an apartment to rent, and especially for a government document, cannot be accomplished in a timely and efficient manner without *wasta.* This term is also used for a class of professionals who fill out and expedite paperwork in exchange for a fee negotiated in advance.[3]

In a country with such a large population concentrated in Cairo and a few other major cities, family ties, profession, educational background, military service, and sometimes even the village origins of the individual and family are important for identifying *wasta*. These *wasta* identifiers represent and give important clues to a family's standing, including its social network and background. In a gathering where people meet others for the first time, family members may speak of family achievements in order to find common ground in an evolving relationship. The art of dropping names into a conversation is a means to establish status, serves to unify the networks of those who are getting to know each other, and acknowledges the long ancestral history of an Egyptian family.

As the family is the primary network, the home is a focal scene that reflects and promotes current and historical social status. At some point, business partners, employers, or colleagues may be invited to a residence, typically for tea or dinner. An invitation into an Egyptian home, and therefore an invitation to understand more intimately an individual and his or her family, is always considered an honorable occasion, and rarely refused.

In almost every home there is a proudly displayed exhibit depicting family highlights. Photographs dating as far back as the first cameras in Egypt, as well as sketches, mementos, newspaper clippings, and memorabilia are lovingly preserved. This visual narrative often portrays the relationships and storyline family members refer to for self-definition.

The experienced observer will note that in this exhibit, professional or educational achievements are either subtly or overtly displayed. In a family of judges, males will wear a sash that denotes the office. In families of professors, there will be photographs of them standing with their graduating classes. Other class photos will indicate the schools attended; private foreign secondary schools and universities enhance status. In families of Turkish origin, elder males will wear the fez, a hat that is worn by Turkish males and distinguishes their cultural background.

Military Service

Families with a military tradition will also display photos to commemorate their members' service to the nation, which is another important credential. Military conscription for males is mandated by the Egyptian constitution. The branches of service are the armed forces, the air force, the air defense force, and the navy, and it is believed that the total forces are around 450,000, with 250,000 reserves.[4]

Although Egypt's military has been a peacetime force for the past 30 years, military rank and branch of service are badges of honor, with special camaraderie and perks for each branch. Those who remain in the military as officers beyond their minimum time receive discounts on everyday necessities such as apartments and cars. Retiring officers with high rank are sought after by private companies as consultants for their connections and experience, and are afforded considerable power and respect.

Family Background: Business Implications

The foreign businessperson who becomes familiar with how and why families seek to establish their credentials, and who appreciates the remarkable history behind Egypt's political and educational institutions, will have a distinct advantage in understanding business partners or colleagues. Further, time spent getting to know the culture will pave the way for mutually trusting professional relationships. Being able to gauge the impact of family ties is another step toward a working understanding of how business is done in Egypt.

Socioeconomic Status

External perception of one's socioeconomic status is taken seriously in a country with a wide gap between rich and poor. With the growth of the formal private sector since the 1980s, such status has meant higher stakes as Egyptians compete vigorously for well-paying company jobs that in some quarters are viewed as status enhancing.

Class distinctions provide one kind of status label. This is not as simple as saying that there is an upper class, a middle class, and a lower class, as family background also plays a role, along with an individual's educational and professional training.

The population can be loosely divided into the following classes:

- The highest echelon: People of means gained through a family tradition of business, property ownership, or political power. A few have branched out internationally and achieved wider recognition.
- The nouveau riche: This category is used by Egyptians to define those who had no wealth and gained it rapidly, then ostentatiously acquired luxury items.
- Upper middle class: Those from "good families" whose members work as professionals, own their residences, and can afford to send their children to private schools and universities abroad. Included in this category are retired professionals and members of the military.
- Middle class: The majority of working Egyptians fit into this category. They are also from "good families." One or both spouses may have a government job or be retired and living on a relatively small pension, and one or both has another source of income from a second job. They struggle to maintain their families, put food on the table, and place a high value on their children's education in public schools and universities.
- Working poor: These people are primarily in the agricultural sector or labor in the service industry as maids, porters, and odd-job handymen. Many of the city dwellers come from villages and live during the work week in a space provided by their employers.

Another status label is the type of residence one can afford. A form of rent control, known as "old rent," is still in existence under the law. Apartment ownership, once out of reach, can now be financed with low down payments and affordable mortgages in the many developments springing up in the newer areas, especially on city outskirts and reclaimed desert, some of which include detached dwellings such as villas. Ownership of prime real estate in Cairo or Alexandria, country homes in the villages, or a resort area dwelling, is still out of reach for most Egyptians.

The Public Safety Net

In order to maintain or enhance their socioeconomic status, Egyptians often seek a social safety net. Sources of security are the family and the state. Pensions guaranteed through employment in the public sector—one of the last vestiges of the socialism of the Gamal Abdel Nasser era—are still desirable and reassuring to most Egyptians, as they are much more generous than pensions for private-sector employment. Average monthly pensions for government and public enterprise employees are more than double the amounts for private sector employees and many times the amount for the self-employed, so government employment becomes the ticket to a dignified and secure old age. Some professional Egyptians, such as educators, doctors, and engineers, and even those living out of the country, juggle their schedules to fulfill the requirements of the state in public institutions in order to guarantee their retirement. Many are often employed in both the public and the private sector at the same time. Private sector employees are not eligible for the full social safety net, and it is up to a company to institute its own benefits policies, and for the employee to see to his or her own future security.

After the July 1952 revolution and under Nasser, Egyptian social insurance became a state-run, universal public system under the National Organization for Social Insurance (NOSI), supervised by the Ministry of Insurance and Social Affairs (MISA).[5] It is considered one of the most comprehensive systems in the developing world. NOSI operates two funds, the Government Sector Fund (GSF) for civil servants and employees of government enterprises and the Public and Private Business Sector Fund (PPBSF) for other categories including the self-employed and Egyptian expatriates. Participation is officially defined as compulsory for everyone working in the country. It covers most categories of working Egyptians as well as non-Egyptians working in Egypt for at least one year whose governments offer reciprocal arrangements to Egyptians. The generous level of benefits—including death, disability, health care, maternity, retirement, and unemployment—represents of one of the finest safety nets in the world.

Most public-sector employees are insured, as opposed to the formal and informal private sector, where those employed pay contributions. It is a known fact that employers try to evade social insurance; contributions are not deducted in the same manner as with state employees.[6] In some cases, the formal and informal private sectors may offer their own plans and incentives for benefits.

Socioeconomic Status: Business Implications

Disparities between rich and poor and a keen sensitivity to social standing provide foreign companies in Egypt with numerous ways to attract and retain good employees. In addition to compensation, these opportunities could include providing access to better housing, support for advanced training or education, and more secure private pensions. Foreign managers should also remember that in the absence of a generous retirement plan, employees may be working at an extra job in order to ensure their future financial security.

Job Function

Public vs. Private

Recent breakdowns of public and private sector workers are found in Egyptian public census data.[7] The number of people employed is reportedly about 16 million, with agriculture the largest employer at less than 40 percent, followed by other job categories such as services, manufacturing, trade, construction, and transport. The formal and informal private sector share accounts for approximately two-thirds of the total, the government one quarter, and public sector enterprises the remainder (the latter includes, for example, the Egyptian General Petroleum Corporation). Work opportunities in the private sector are found particularly in growth areas such as business services, construction, finance, manufacturing, tourism, and transportation.

There are notable differences between public and private sector workplaces. The private sector has office buildings and apartments with many conveniences. Private workplaces in the cities can also be in apartments next to residences, where cooking smells mingle with the constant ringing of telephones, mobile phones, and fax machines. For a company or businessperson to have a more prestigious image, however, he or she must have an address in an office building. Meanwhile, the public sector is located in government buildings with standard-issue furniture that is generations old. Box files abound for lack of space for filing cabinets. A common factor in all workplaces, from ultra-modern office to government building, factory or hospital, from souvenir shop to showroom, is the coffee/tea man. He is everywhere and appears instinctively from nowhere. The workplace would not function without him.

Private sector employees advertise their accessibility by listing their mobile phone numbers on their business cards, keep up with and respond to e-mails outside of office hours, and work as needed. It is rare, except in ministries, to find this in the public sector because the same incentives are not there. Within both sectors, business moves at a slow pace, and the government sector is the slowest. It may take several weeks to accomplish a simple task. Historically, business decisions in Egypt have always been dictated by government rules and regulations. If the government is involved, decisions can take an unusually long time, while the participants are painstakingly embroiled in bureaucratic red tape, because ministers of several departments must give their approval. Getting government support requires networking with the right people, getting to know them, and demonstrating mutual benefits to your ongoing contact. Moreover, corruption in Egypt, which stems from insecure economic conditions, affects business transactions and progress at all levels and can add to labyrinthine processes and procedures.

A pronounced top-down hierarchy is a common characteristic of the Egyptian workplace. This is found in the Arab world in general. From the time of Islam, The khalif (or king) ruled over many regions. Current features of hierarchical organizations are overt, as in the public sector, with directors over managers over supervisors, where decisions come from the top and quality performance depends on following instructions. In more traditional companies as well, memos spell out what is expected, organization charts delineate stratified positions, timelines and deadlines regulate performance, and micromanagement is customary. There are other private firms, however, particularly those that are smaller or multinationals, which have a more informal and collaborative management orientation.

A few additional public/private distinctions include:

Competition: Civil service jobs are generally quite secure and career paths relatively predictable once employment has been gained. The Egyptian government formerly guaranteed employment for intermediate and higher education graduates, but this policy has been gradually phased out. The civil service has also been downsizing at approximately 2 percent per year with the privatization of some state-owned enterprises (SOEs). The competition for jobs in the private sector is thus becoming all the more pressing as youth who have left school, new graduates without jobs, and returning expatriates join the pool of job seekers. There is fierce, stressful competition for the higher-paying private sector jobs, even without the job security and the social safety net desired by the older generation. Job candidates who are recent graduates and returning expatriates have education, technical specialties, languages, international experience, and are willing to work long and hard to own those villas in the new developments outside the major cities.

Approaches to Absenteeism: Absenteeism in an Egyptian organization is often higher than in a Western workplace because of cultural differences. Both sectors take this into account so productivity is not lost. There is a longer leave for death or illness in the (extended) family, longer maternity leaves, and liberal sick leave. The public sector has an adequate workforce that can cover such absences. The private sector has to make its own adjustments through teamwork and alternate coverage of functions as well as outside access to the company intranet so that employees can work from home during a family emergency.

Termination: In the public sector, only an employee committing gross malfeasance would face demotion, suspension, or termination, and connections and family status would come into play. Separation policies differ in the private sector, and in some cases a company will negotiate a buyout of an employee if it is downsizing or for other reasons. Family and religious affiliations are very important when interpreting the law.

There are many workers who cross over between the public and private sectors. Egyptians working in the public sector with its lower salaries often need and want to supplement their incomes. Teachers by day are tutors after hours; hospital staff doctors by day have their private clinic hours in the late afternoons and evenings; salaried employees throughout the employment spectrum perform work in informal private sector enterprises or family businesses. Retired public sector workers or those in the military can be employed in the formal or informal private sector beyond retirement age, especially as consultants, if they have expertise in certain areas or if their contacts are valuable.

Egypt's Expatriates

There is a special category of Egyptians who work outside of the country. For many reasons, the foremost being lucrative sources of employment in nearby nations and the opportunity to build up their savings, Egyptians are willing to go abroad as expatriates, sometimes under difficult conditions and without their family support networks. Although they must live as foreigners, there is less competition in many professional specialties than in Egypt, and they can excel in jobs that are highly valued elsewhere. Among the roughly 10 million expatriates living in the Gulf countries, skilled and unskilled workers from Egypt constitute the largest category of Arab employees.[8]

Egyptian expatriates abroad number more than two million, with the majority working in the Gulf Cooperation Council (GCC) countries. Major destinations vary with the changing political and economic fortunes of the Arab world. Before the first Gulf War, Iraq hosted well over a million Egyptian workers; the number has dwindled to just a fraction of that as two wars have had a severe effect on the economy. Saudi Arabia has been host to a similarly large number of Egyptians. Other preferred destinations are Jordan and Libya.[9] In 2000, according to the Council of Europe, Egyptian residents in Europe totaled over 80,000, of which the majority was in either Italy or France. Another preferred destination is the United States, where tens of thousands have immigrated.

Although fewer than in the 1990s, there are still opportunities for Egypt's labor force to go abroad. Architects, engineers, doctors and medical technicians, lawyers, professors, and specialists of all types can be found in the Arab countries, Europe, and the Americas. Teachers are in demand throughout the Arab world and Egyptian teachers of both genders willingly pack their bags in August to work in the countries of the Arab Gulf. Agricultural workers and other laborers also continue to emigrate in large numbers.

Egypt treasures its expats, and the country's embassies and consulates abroad do everything possible to strengthen the ties that bind. The Egyptian government, inspired by the fact that expatriation eases unemployment at home and serves as a significant source of foreign exchange (expatriates send home several billion dollars a year) has instituted policies to encourage emigration. The remittances sent home by Egyptian expats are, in fact, the largest in the Arab world. They provide a crucial source of foreign exchange revenue that is as important as other pillars of the economy.

Egypt does not consider its departing expatriates to be a brain drain; rather, the expats are a reserve of both financial and intellectual capital. They are also investors in their home country because most do return to Egypt to live, purchasing real estate and other services. Many return with new skills and start small businesses with the money they have saved abroad, generating valuable jobs and contributing to the growth of the Egyptian economy.[10]

Job Function: Business Implications

The gradual shrinking of Egypt's public sector and the large pool of job candidates provides potential advantages to foreign employers. While the ponderous nature of the country's bureaucracies, along with a significant level of corruption can be impediments to private enterprise, changes in recent years have helped to diminish these negative factors. The hierarchical setup that is characteristic of many Egyptian organizations is balanced by a climate of trust and respect as well as a family environment. No matter what degree of hierarchy exists, trust and respect make all the difference when working with Egyptian employees. Egyptians tend to be extremely loyal to their bosses and will walk through fire if they like you. If mutual respect and trust exist, an employee will work long hours late into an evening, and even forgo compensation in order to be obliging and respectful. Employees are known to take cuts in salary and move to another company if there is more of a family environment. Promoting big-picture visions and a family-like culture alongside consistent and sincere interest in an employee's family and general well-being are components of effective leadership in Egypt. Foreign managers have to project themselves as a people who are going to make a difference not only through technical competence in their chosen professions, but as a caring and supportive people.

Gender

There is no doubt that the socially conservative society of Egypt is male-dominated. Some statistics indicate that female workers are paid for the same work at approximately two-thirds of a male worker's wages. Nonetheless, men and women in Egypt have greater parity than in other countries in the region.

By observing Egyptian tomb and wall paintings from Ancient Egypt in 3000 B.C., it becomes easier to understand possible reasons why some degree of gender equality exists in Egypt today. The life of an Egyptian woman then is similar to her life today in modern Egypt. Women were treated with respect and had some of the same rights as men. They could own property in their own names and engage in professions that gave them economic freedom from their male relatives. Although this era predated Islam, there are interpretations of the Muslim faith that also support such rights. An active feminist movement emerged in Egypt a generation ago. It originated from elite and educated women and attempted to address the needs of all classes; however, it has yet to attain the status of a popular movement.

The biggest social and gender issue has been reform of the Personal Status Law. The Personal Status Law is based on Islamic law and favored men in marriage and divorce. It was first codified in 1897 and has since been amended on numerous occasions. A 1929 recodification of the law gave women the right to divorce with grounds.[11] In 1979, then-President Sadat issued a decree law giving stronger guarantees to women. It was known as "Gehan's Law," after his wife, who lobbied him extensively for it. Popular folklore says that she saw the acclaimed movie *Aridu Hallan (I Want a Solution),* starring Fatin Hamama, the queen of Egyptian cinema and wife of Omar Sharif. The movie depicted a woman fighting for years to obtain a divorce and was a hit with Egyptian and foreign audiences in the Arab and Western world.

The decree promulgated by Sadat has gone through various legal and legislative permutations since his time. It was struck down by the Supreme Constitutional Court in 1985 on the grounds that Sadat failed to submit the decree to parliament; there have been subsequent dilutions and legislative amendments. A new law incorporating substantial reforms was finally passed in March 2004 after advocates enlisted the support of Suzanne Mubarak, Egypt's first lady and president of the National Council of Women and her husband, as well as Sheikh Mohammed Sayed El-Tantawi, the Grand *Imam* (religious leader) of Al-Azhar University. Among the provisions of the new law was the creation of a family court system and the right for women to seek divorce on the grounds of incompatibility. Despite legal gains, complex and challenging conservative, patriarchal, and stereotypical attitudes still affect the lives of Egyptian women.

Egyptian women are known for rising to the occasion rather than breaking the glass ceiling. They tend to have a quiet, calm approach to crises whether within the country or within the family. Beginning in the middle of the last century and inspired by their cousins in Turkey, they sought more formal education to add to the cultural upbringing provided by their mothers and grandmothers in the home. Customs passed on by women through the generations include those rooted in Egyptian culture, such as traditional foods and music, and those influenced by other cultures including European classical music and ballet. As more and more Egyptian women seek a formal education and enter the workforce, the continuation of cultural education remains a high priority for women of all classes.

During the last three decades, Islamic fundamentalism has swept through Egypt in many facets of life, from social protest in universities to political Islam to professional associations and syndicates as well as within popular culture. One aspect of fundamentalist Islamic approaches in other countries has been restrictions on the women's role outside of the home. Egypt has its own resiliency and maturity, and there are many devout Muslims who are not enamored of fundamentalist perspectives. Fundamentalism does appeal to those who are anti-Western, however, and it is fueled to some degree by a reaction to Western political and social policies that are born of a lack of understanding of the region's religion and culture as a whole.

Despite the spread of fundamentalism in Egypt, contemporary women in the workplace there have successfully contradicted the stereotype of what some see as the "slavery" of Muslim women. Estimates of the number of working women today range widely from just over 10 percent to nearly 50 percent, depending upon the criteria used for defining work. Most sources agree that the number has increased over recent decades, and there appears to be a trend toward more female wage and professional workers.[12] Employers are still advised to make accommodations for both formal traditions such as Islamic requirements for workplace prayer, dietary restrictions, and fasting during Ramadan, and to be prepared for more informal customs pertaining to leave for bereavement, sickness, or family events.[13] It is also best not to leap to conclusions about individual attitudes based on appearance. Girls and women may cover their heads and wear long dresses with the *higab* (veil or scarf) for many reasons, from faith to social mores to family tradition, and can be from open-minded families as well as highly conservative ones. Likewise, females who do not wear the *higab* may also be highly conservative.

Women's occupations range from the CEO of a company to a maid in a residence. They may be married or single, with or without children, supporting a nuclear or extended family, attending to meals, shopping, housework, and children's homework, sometimes continuing their own education in addition to holding down a job.

The reality of the contemporary Egyptian economy is that men are likely to be holding two jobs, and the second could be a continuation of one's day job, a second service job, or helping in a family business. Being out of the home from early morning until night, husbands are often simply not present except for a few insufficient hours of sleep. On their customary one day off, Friday, men who have children will typically take them on an outing or to a family gathering, watch a soccer game on TV, and catch up with family and friends.

Egyptian women are thus diversified themselves, becoming experts in time management while working in most categories of the economy, running a household, raising the children, and seeing to the needs of their husbands, parents, and both extended families. During the four wars with Israel, women were alone for extended periods of time, and a significant number became widows. Economic, social, and family pressures have also resulted in a relatively high divorce rate (to which women can now legally contribute more easily than before), with second marriages increasingly common. Single parents have become a part of the social fabric. The blessings of being part of an extended family were apparent during the war years, and are appreciated now by those who find themselves in need of that support.

There still exist gender-specific jobs and professions, driven by cultural considerations and tradition more than by gender inequality. Men still work jobs traditionally filled by males as drivers of trucks, buses, taxis, and donkey carts. Military service is still a man's world, although women are welcome in the National Guard. There are no female bartenders. In other areas, from agricultural workers to professors, from restaurant staff to doctors, from hotel room cleaners to tourist guides, and lately from computer graphics specialists to IT managers, women are working side-by-side with their male colleagues.

Gender: Business Implications

Egyptian women have successfully carved out for themselves a critical place in the country's workforce. They are increasingly ready and willing to take on jobs in the growing professional services sector. While Muslim fundamentalism is a growing force in Egypt, employers who respect and accommodate the common religious requirements of devout Muslims, male or female, for prayer and special religious occasions will probably not be affected by restrictions on the role of women outside the home. Companies that recognize and promote female talent are, on the contrary, apt to find they have access to an eager and capable workforce.

Applying Global Diversity:
Establishing a New Office in Egypt

Family Background

SITUATION:

Mohamed is 35 years old and was born in Cairo to Egyptian parents. He grew up in Saudi Arabia, where his parents worked as professors. After completing high school in Saudi Arabia, Mohamed went to the United States for higher education. He lived and worked in the Unites States until recently, when he accepted an offer to move back to Saudi Arabia as an expatriate for a multinational company.

Working for a western company in Saudi Arabia has been a positive experience for Mohamed. He has been successful in utilizing the personal network he established while growing up in Saudi Arabia to gain new contracts and develop the business. Based on his success in Saudi Arabia, his company offers him a position in Cairo to set up a new office and build the business in Egypt. Mohamed's employer is depending on his experience in the region and his linguistic and cultural background to get the job done.

In fact, Mohamed has never lived in Cairo except as a small child, and has limited recollection of life there except as a tourist in the many times he has visited his extended family still living in Egypt. He finds it very difficult to handle all of the new challenges he faces: corporate and personal banking, lease formalities and negotiation, the red tape of commercial registration and licenses, the procurement of visas for engineers of various nationalities, and the purchase of office and residence equipment and furniture. All the while he has to interview potential staff, make new contacts, and learn the business environment in Egypt.

Mohamed's company is unhappy with his job performance; his new job is in jeopardy.

POSSIBLE SOLUTIONS:

Mohamed has to face the fact that his professional life to date has been in the United States where there is a different work environment, and in Saudi Arabia where he has well-developed contacts. Even though he is Egyptian, he has made an error common to managers who are new to Egypt by failing to appreciate the importance of good personal relationships developed over a long period of time.

The fact that Mohamed has limited experience in Egypt does not preclude success there. The company will have to demonstrate more patience, giving him some time to get his feet on the ground and begin to make new contacts, and Mohamed will have to be more proactive in addressing his lack of business experience in Egypt. Mohamed can leverage his extended family network based in Egypt as a way to establish contacts and develop business relationships. In addition, he can utilize his extensive network of contacts in Saudi Arabia since so many Egyptians work there as expatriates and maintain contact with family back home. The same strategy that worked so effectively for him in Saudi Arabia can be applied to Egypt if Mohamed makes the important shift in mindset that he is starting over in Egypt as a newcomer, not as a local.

Summary Recommendations

With its long tradition of catering to foreign visitors and tourists who were at times the invaders, Egypt today easily accommodates the foreign businessperson with Western-style hotels, serviced flats, affordable cars and drivers, Internet dial-up with DSL on toll-free numbers, three mobile phone providers, and the yellow pages in English. Foreigners would be wise not to conclude, however, that such amenities mean that Egypt will be easily understood or that Egyptians themselves are a globalized lot who will know how to work with companies and individuals from other countries. Here are some recommendations for working with Egyptian colleagues in light of the nation's internal diversity.[14]

1. Knowledge of **family background** factors seen as important by Egyptians will enable one to recognize and demonstrate the appropriate level of respect toward family characteristics that are a source of pride for Egyptians. It also provides insight into how Egyptians are likely to assess one another as they are building a business relationship. Foreigners seeking to build their credibility in Egypt should consider how they will

reply to questions about their own families and how their responses will shape others' perceptions.

2. It is worthwhile for employers to consider the value Egyptian workers place on the link between **socioeconomic status** and having a secure retirement pension, and the fact that many people hold down more than one job in order to provide for their retirement. By addressing concerns about retirement security through their own employee savings plans, it is possible for private companies to build their image as an employer of choice.

3. In addition to the tendency for Egyptians to work at **job functions** in both the public and private sectors simultaneously, many leave the country as expatriates to work at jobs in other Gulf States and beyond. This pool of expatriates or former expatriates can serve as an excellent source of experienced talent for multinational enterprises seeking to do business in Egypt or in the region as a whole. However, it is best not to assume that Egyptians who have lived overseas for long periods are necessarily familiar with all of the business practices of their home country, or that they have already established the networks of key contacts that businesspeople who are Egyptian residents work so hard to cultivate.

4. Attitudes toward **gender** roles in Islamic countries sometimes restrict women's access to jobs outside of the home. Egyptian women, however, are able to work in most professional and service industry jobs; for many a bigger obstacle than social restrictions on the types of jobs they can do is the range of household responsibilities that they still bear in large measure. Employers who understand the readiness of women to work and who are willing to accommodate or provide assistance with women's multiple responsibilities are likely to find capable and motivated professionals in large numbers.

CHAPTER 4

Diversity in India

Bidhan Chandra

"The idea of India is not based on language, not on geography, not on ethnicity and not on religion. The idea of India is on one land embracing many."

—Shashi Tharoor[1]

Why India?

- India has become a key player in the modern global economy, serving as a significant global hub for knowledge-based economic activities, both as an "offshoring" destination but also through the growth of indigenous firms.
- The country has achieved a steady GDP annual growth rate in the range of 6 to 8 percent during much of the past decade. Factors such as reformed economic policies, large-scale privatization, the availability of an enormous talent pool, substantial foreign investment, and advances in communication technologies should continue to drive economic expansion.
- With a middle class estimated at 250 million people, India offers a large and growing market for goods and services.
- India holds incredible cultural diversity within its own borders that shapes the mindsets of Indian partners, vendors, employees, and other key stakeholders. Foreign companies that understand and know how to work with India's internal diversity are more likely to be successful in leveraging the country's economic potential.

Introduction

It is often said that there is no country on earth that offers the same cultural diversity as India. This is indeed a unique country when it comes to diversity, with 22 official languages, 29 states each with their own distinct traditions and character, and a population rich with diverse religious faiths, dress, and accents. Such a level of diversity could perhaps be found elsewhere in an entire region such as Europe; however, in India this diversity is contained within the boundaries of a single nation.

Not only is the country as a whole highly diverse, but the business environment within India is becoming increasingly diverse as well, as people are being drawn across regional boundaries by the growth of new jobs in manufacturing as well as knowledge industry services such as information technology (IT), business process outsourcing, R&D, and call centers. With job opportunities now being created rapidly through Indian private sector involvement as well as foreign investment in various sectors, it is becoming more common for people to move away from their home regions to take jobs in other states, where they join employee populations that include people from many different parts of the country. Within a team of Indian workers there may well be people who have difficulty understanding each other because of strong regional accents as well as other communication barriers and behavioral differences.

This chapter discusses internal diversity factors that have contributed to shaping India's present workplace environment. Diversity variables addressed will include:

- Language
- Regional Origin
- Religion
- Socioeconomic Status
- Gender

Understanding these dimensions is crucial for understanding the mindset of Indian colleagues and for being able to conduct business successfully in India.

Diversity in Language

India's diversity is perhaps most aptly symbolized by its profusion of languages. This is one of the world's most linguistically diverse nations, with 22 official languages along with English as an important associate language recognized by the Indian Constitution.[2] Add to these more than 300 less widely spoken languages and thousands of dialects, and it is easy to wonder how people from one part of the country can possibly communicate with those in other regions.

The degree of linguistic diversity in India is staggering not only for visitors but also for Indians themselves. Each of the country's 29 states (see Figure 4-1) has adopted one or two of the 22 official languages* for state business[3], yet several other major, as well as minor, languages could still be spoken in any state. India's linguistic barriers are compounded by the fact that each language also has a unique written form, with an alphabet that is unrecognizable to someone who doesn't know that particular language.

The linguistic diversity found across India stems from a history that saw numerous ancient kingdoms, each with its own language. These languages remained distinct to the area even after a kingdom was dissolved or merged with another one. State lines later drawn by the British during the colonial period often crossed former political and linguistic boundaries.

Hindi is one of India's official languages, and it is considered to be the single most widely spoken language, since it is the mother tongue of approximately 30 percent of the Indian people. It is used across parts of northern and central India, an area commonly identified as the "Hindi belt." Hindi is predominant in these territories, and is also the local official language in a number of other states: Bihar, Chattisgarh, Delhi, Haryana, Himachal Pradesh, Jharkhand, Madhya Pradesh, Rajasthan, Uttar Pradesh, and Uttaranchal.

India's prosperous film and TV industries have helped to spread the use of Hindi even in non-Hindi areas. The Indian film industry, centered in Bombay and often referred to as "Bollywood," is the largest producer of

*"Official" designation for languages means that they are listed in Schedule VIII of the Indian Constitution; these are also referred to as the "scheduled" languages. It is interesting to note that Hindi is not mentioned in Schedule VIII as the country's national language, but rather as just an official language.

full-length feature films in the world.[4] The films typically incorporate dancing, songs, and love scenes in imaginary settings, sometimes jumping from a dance scene at a hill resort to a love serenade at a palace or sea resort and back again. Crime and violence are other major themes in Indian films. Even though a majority of Bollywood films are in Hindi and are not always dubbed into a local language, the visual nature of the singing, dancing, and scenery makes these movies very popular among people of all language groups.

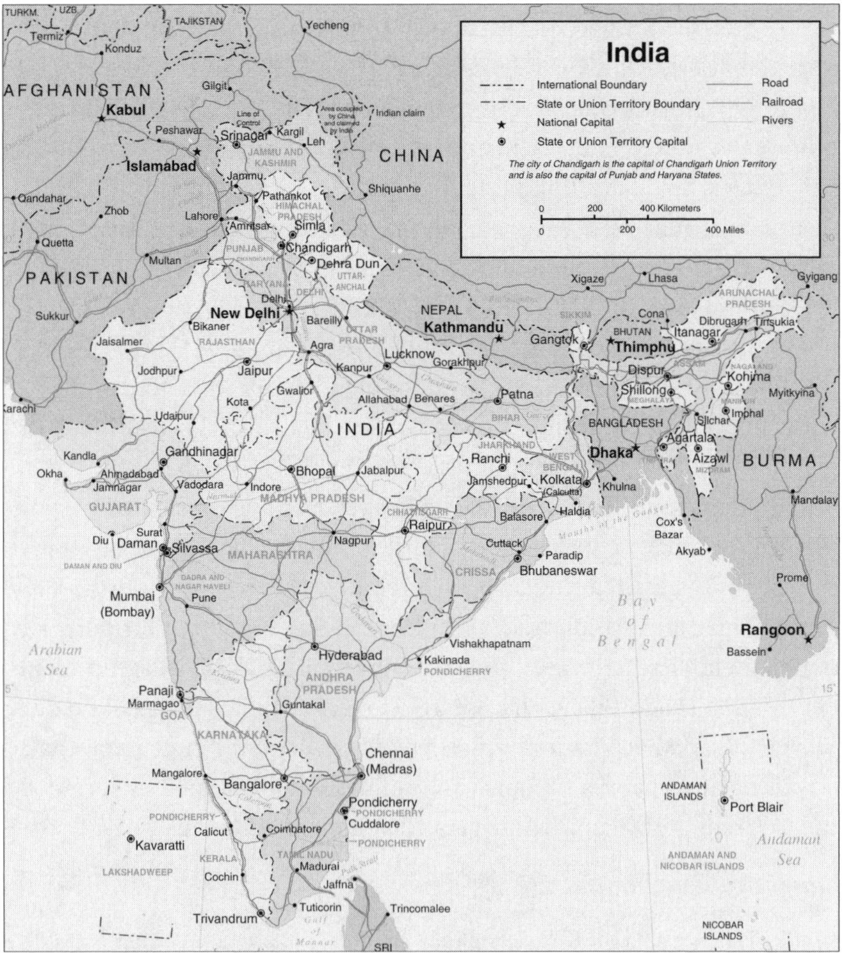

FIGURE 4-1. Map of India with States and Capitals

Compared with Hindi, English is used by a relatively smaller percentage of the country's population, but its use is more widespread in major urban areas. It serves as an important medium for higher education, business, and government. English also provides a communication bridge between people in the north and south, because North Indian languages are not commonly understood in South India (except in Bangalore and Hyderabad), and vice versa. It can be safely said that, while most Indians were glad to rid themselves of British colonial rule, the English language has served as a unifying force between different regions. The ability of Indian college graduates to write, read, and speak English fluently in comparison with countries such as China, Russia, and the Philippines has also been one of the major factors in the mushrooming growth of the IT and business process outsourcing industry in India over the last 10 years. Other crucial factors have been a well-functioning judicial system based on common law, a long-sustained democratic system of government, and the sweeping economic reforms started in 1991.

Indian Language Families

Indian languages belong to several families, but the two most dominant that divide the country are the Indo-Aryan in the north and the Dravidian in the south (Dasgupta, 1970). The Indo-Aryan language family has its roots in the Indo-European languages,[5] and there are many similarities among various Indo-Aryan languages.[6] The Dravidian language family of the south is indigenous to India and has very few similarities with the languages in the north. The historical significance of the Indo-Aryan and Dravidian language families is still reflected in the modern languages that have developed from these two families and the north-south communication barriers that they create.[7]

Language Issues in India

India's people are culturally separated from one another by language more than by any other factor. With such linguistic diversity, they are closely attuned to even the slightest differences in dialects and accents. People can often recognize an accent down to the detail of what part of the country and, in some cases, what district a person comes from. An Indian can glean a lot of information by simply hearing someone's accent or knowing what language he or she speaks, and often their first impressions of another individual will be based on what they consider to be the characteristics of people from that state or region.

The political reorganization of Indian states has occurred several times largely due to language issues. The country orginally had only 16 states after the momentous events of independence from the British rule in 1947 and adoption of the new Indian constitution in 1950. Several additional states were carved out in 1956, with accommodation of linguistic differences being a key rationale for the change. Bombay state, where Gujarati and Marathi were the two dominant languages, was split into the two states of Gujarat and Maharashtra in 1960 after a number of demonstrations and riots.[8] The city of Bombay (now Mumbai)—the crowded, fast-paced commercial capital of India and a major center of international business—was originally intended to be a union territory, but was given over to Maharashtra and the Marathi-speaking people in order to quell political unrest. Because of this distinct split, when meeting someone who speaks Marathi it is normally safe to assume he or she could be from Mumbai or the state of Maharashtra.

Language-related tribulations were particularly acute during the late 1960s. Instead of maintaining both Hindi and English as the two languages of central government business, the government was actively considering using only the Hindi language for this purpose. The south, led by the Tamilnadu state, declared a virtual war against imposition of Hindi in this exclusive manner. One implication of designating Hindi as the official tongue was that children from non-Hindi areas were also mandated to learn it. Moreover, all government buildings and properties were instructed to have signs in three languages: Hindi, English, and the state's official language if it was different from Hindi. The anti-Hindi stance of that period, however, did not last long and later became one of tolerance and understanding.

Table 4-1 displays the 29 Indian states and their primary languages.

TABLE 4-1. INDIAN LANGUAGES BY STATE

State	State Capital	State's Official Language(s) Chosen from Schedule VIII
Northeastern Region		
Arunachal Pradesh	Itanagar	English
Assam	Dispur	Assamese, Bodo*
Manipur	Imphal	Manipuri
Meghalaya	Shillong	English
Mizoram	Aizawal	Mizo
Nagaland	Kohima	English
Sikkim	Gangtok	Nepali
Tripura	Agartala	Bengali
Eastern Region		
Bihar	Patna	Hindi, Maithili*
Jharkhand	Ranchi	Hindi, Santhali*
Orissa	Bhubaneshwar	Oriya
West Bengal	Kolkata (Calcutta)	Bengali
Central Region		
Chattisgarh	Raipur	Hindi
Madhya Pradesh	Bhopal	Hindi
Northern Region		
Delhi	New Delhi	Hindi
Haryana	Chandigarh	Hindi
Himachal Pradesh	Shimla	Hindi
Jammu & Kashmir	Srinagar	Urdu, Dogri*
Punjab	Chandigarh	Punjabi
Rajasthan	Jaipur	Hindi
Uttar Pradesh	Lucknow	Hindi
Uttranchal	Dehradun	Hindi
Western Region		
Goa	Panjim	Konkani
Gujarat	Gandhinagar	Gujarati
Maharashtra	Mumbai (Bombay)	Marathi
Southern Region		
Andhra Pradesh	Hyderabad	Telugu
Karnataka	Bangalore	Kannada
Kerala	Thiruvananthapuram (Trivandrum)	Malayalam
Tamilnadu	Chennai (Madras)	Tamil

*The state's second official language was added to Schedule VIII of the Indian Constitution in 2004.

The Role of English in India

English is an "associate" official language for the central government and the official language for the states of Arunachal Pradesh, Meghalaya, and Nagaland. It remains a very important language for government, business, and higher education all over the country.

Language issues have always been an integral part of the Indian political and cultural scene. At the time of India's independence in 1947, the country's new national leaders faced the question of selecting the nation's official language and determining the status of key regional languages. They did not adopt English as one of the official and native languages listed in the constitution, as it represented the language of India's former colonial rulers. According to the Indian Constitution, adopted in 1950, both Hindi and English were to be used by the central government as official languages for 15 years. In 1965, the idea of making Hindi the only official language was again considered. Because of the opposition of several southern states mentioned above, however, the use of English as one of the official associate languages for the central government has continued, and it still plays an important role in the nation's life.

English alone is, of course, not sufficient for doing business within India. For example, many e-governance projects led by state governments must be implemented in the particular state's official language. Whereas it can be a challenge to deal with a number of Indian languages, having this local language capability also opens up vast business opportunities for large e-governance and educational projects.

The central, as well as state, governments have set the three-language formula with the expectation that every student in school must learn three languages—Hindi, English, and the native language. In the regions where Hindi itself is the native tongue, the student will often study the ancient language of Sanskrit, but may also choose one of the many other languages. In the national parliament, proceedings can take place in any official language. Thus, there is simultaneous translation into all other languages. The legal institutions at the State High Court and Central Supreme Court levels use English only for their proceedings as well as in all documents. Thus, any lower court documents in other languages have to be translated into English.

The relatively strong proficiency in English language skills among Indians who have had access to higher education has helped to draw many Western companies to India, and a number of these companies have been successful in achieving their goals for cost reduction and quality work. It is fashionable among Indians to read English newspapers and magazines, and the country's most influential newspapers are in English. However, there are significant differences, for example, between Indian English (which resembles the British English) and U.S. English sentence structure, speech patterns, and technical as well as non-technical vocabulary. These differences can pose some significant challenges in meetings, e-mail communication, and teleconferences in a global virtual team setting.

English language skill also tends to vary by industry. Engineers and managers are especially well known for their good English language skills. Indians working in the IT, IT-enabled services (Business Process Outsourcing or call centers), or R&D centers are also more likely to have much better English language skills than those in traditional manufacturing or services sectors because of the higher frequency of interactions with their English-speaking clients or head office personnel.

Language Diversity: Business Implications

There are several implications of India's vast array of languages that are worth taking into account from a practical business standpoint.

- Some of the growing IT or high-tech centers such as Bangalore, Hyderabad, Mumbai, New Delhi, and Chennai offer a multilingual work environment because these centers have been attracting human capital from almost every region of the country. Employees in such locations will include many people who do not speak the same mother tongue and may, in some cases, use English among themselves as their common language. But their different accents, speech patterns, and sentence structures could mean that they are not always well understood by non-Indians. Office tension can be created when the majority of a team speaks one language and they exclude other team members by sliding back into their native language rather than switching to English, Hindi, or another common language.

- Many new projects initiated by multinational companies involve state governments, and negotiations or project coordination meetings must take place with state-level politicians or government employees. It is likely that the English language skills of many of these Indians may not be at par with those of their foreign counterparts, and this disparity can become a source of misunderstandings and conflicts.
- The language diversity could be a bonanza for companies in the document processing, creation, or translation business. Examples are Microsoft, which is creating the MS Office bundle in several Indian languages, and Adobe Systems, which is working in the e-government sector with several state governments to provide government documents in the local official language. In a similar vein, many technology products such as pagers and cell phones and Web services are beginning to provide a menu of service options in Indian languages.
- Since the Supreme Court and state High Courts use only English, foreign companies may not need any translation services in these courts; their contract documents with Indian companies are also written in English.
- Business cards are needed in English only. But a regional language version on the other side of the card may be very useful in creating strong relationships with locals.

Regional Origin

Regional Identity Is Based on Names

Indians are very proud of their regional or state identity. When two Indians meet for the first time, they often ask each other, "Where are you from?"

even before they ask each other's names. The reason is that each person immediately tries to do a quick cultural DNA scan of the other person and categorize his other personal traits based on the place of origin. The next step is to ask for a name. Very quickly, the last name or surname conveys some more cultural characteristics of this person. Indian last names, or surnames, more often than not, give away not only the likely state of origin but also the caste or sub-caste (not so much the class) background of the other person. The bulk of last names are specific to one state or the combination of a couple of neighboring states. Many first names also fell into this same category of identifiers until ten years ago. However, first names from one region are being utilized in other regions as well these days and have become less useful in identifying a person's place of origin. Table 4-2 attempts to list some common last names from the key regions. Any given state or region uses thousands of last names, so it is not possible to list them all.

TABLE 4-2. EXAMPLES OF SOME INDIAN NAMES BASED ON REGIONS

Region	Some Common Last Names or Surnames
Eastern	Agrawal, Banerjee, Bhattacharjee, Bose, Chatterjee, Chaturvedi, Chaube, Chaudhary, Das, Dubey, Dutta, Ghosh, Goswami, Gupta, Jha, Karan, Kujur, Kumar, Lal, Mahanthy, Mahapatra, Marandi, Mishra, Mukherjee, Munda, Ojha, Oraon, Prasad, Ram, Rath, Roy, Sahay, Sen, Sengupta, Shah, Sharma, Singh, Sinha, Srivastava, Thakur, Tigga, Tirkey, Trivedi, Verma, Yadav
Northern	Agrawal, Arora, Bansal, Bajaj, Bedi, Bhatia, Chaturvedi, Garg, Gill, Goel, Gupta, Jain, Kaur (only women), Kapoor, Kaul, Kumar, Malhotra, Mathur, Mishra, Mittal, Murarka, Pandey, Poddar, Ram, Saxena, Sharma, Singh, Singhal, Thakur, Trivedi, Yadav
Western	Amin, Bapat, Bhate, Doshi, D'Silva, D'Souza, Fernandez, Gandhi, Godrej, Gokhale, Jain, Joshi, Kulkarni, Marathe, Mehta, Mulgaonkar, Paranjpe, Patel, Pathare, Puranik, Shah, Surani, Tata, Tendulkar, Thakre, Wadia
Southern	Ayangar, Battu, Chari, Chetty, Iyer, Kottackal, Mathew, Mathai, Muthiah, Nair, Nayyar, Panicker, Perumal, Pillai, Putta, Ramani, Rao, Reddy, Setty, Subramaniam, Swamy, Thamboo, Varghese, Varma, Venkatramani

In addition, some Indians' last names are derived from professions their families were engaged in for a long time. Examples are:

Batliwala = dealing in bottles
Carpenter = carpentry
Daroowala = dealing in alcohol
Engineer = engineering
Hazam = barber
Mistry = repair person
Pandit = priesthood
Rangwala = dealing in paints
Supariwala = dealing in betel nuts

Regional Divisions

India is a large country, both in terms of its geographic coverage and its population. It currently has 29 states and five union territories. One can easily see significant differences from east to west and north to south, but most people think of India's vast geographic diversity primarily in terms of the North-South divide, with the southern region comprised of the four states of Andhra Pradesh, Karnataka, Kerala, and Tamilnadu, and the remaining 25 states forming northern India. This North-South archetype is based more on linguistic and cultural divisions rather than geography. The cultural North-South divide is extremely visible in language, food habits, and behaviors of the people who reside in the two major regions.

Although it occupies a smaller portion of the entire country, South India has received a great deal of attention and prominence during India's recent economic revolution. Bangalore, Chennai, and Hyderabad are representative cities of the South that have become the embodiment of the twenty-first century high-tech white-collar revolution in India. For almost 50 years after independence, India was regarded as a very restrictive place to do business. Even the most optimistic policymakers never imagined that the Indian economy would witness such a major paradigm shift from low-tech to high-tech or I-tech. Progressive economic liberalization, massive capital infusions from Indian and foreign private sector investors, technology transfer from overseas Indians, and the increasing recognition of Indian engineers as a highly skilled yet economical resource have contributed to the South Indian states' ability to benefit from the force of global economic change.

Encouraged by the new liberal policies of the central government in the early 1990s, the South invested heavily in initial infrastructure building for the IT industry, providing significant incentives to both domestic and foreign companies for setting up export-oriented offshore development centers. There were strong educational institutions located in these cities even before the recent growth spurt, though after the IT business began to grow, additional institutions were established to ensure a regular pipeline of engineering graduates. As a result, South India has given birth to many new companies solely devoted to offshore development work, creating a huge market for the software development and business process industry. These efforts have paid large dividends. While the northern states (except Delhi and nearby areas in adjoining states) have so far lagged behind in this miraculous twenty-first-century economic development process, more recently the marketing and entrepreneurial skills of Indians in the North have begun to bear fruit as well. Moreover, because of growing infrastructure constraints in the South, many prominent companies have begun to look for new investment opportunities in the northern states.

North-South Comparisons

When discussing regional differences, most Indians like to focus on social, cultural, and economic distinctions between North and South. Some of the prominent comparisons and contrasts most often made are the following:

- The southern states generally have lower population densities (except in Kerala), higher literacy rates, use English more, and have a larger number of educational institutions on a per capita basis.
- More rapid economic growth in the South to date has been possible because of its stronger educational initiatives, infrastructure development, and less visible corruption in business and government. The government and influential bureaucrats seem to be more readily accessible to business leaders.

- While similar levels of poverty exist in rural areas in both regions, urban poverty is more clearly evident in the North than in the South.
- People in the South are seen as more religious and traditional in their social customs. The influence of Islamic rule in India also had less of an impact upon them, as the center of Islamic rule was based in the North. Thus, they were better able to preserve their ancient culture and traditions.
- Residents of the South are reputed to show more politeness and less aggressiveness in social and interpersonal interactions, while those in the North are sometimes thought of as being more outgoing.

Other Major Regions and Their Characteristics

The northwestern region includes the states of Jammu and Kashmir, Delhi, Punjab, Himachal Pradesh, Haryana, Rajasthan, Uttaranchal, and Uttar Pradesh (UP). The majority of this Northern region is populated by Hindus, with the exception of Jammu and Kashmir, where more than two-thirds of the population is Muslim. Hindus in this region exert considerable influence over national politics because they form a large base of eligible voters. New Delhi is the country's capital and the main hub of the region. Uttar Pradesh (the word *Uttar* means "northern" in Hindi) is the Indian state with the largest population. With well over 160 million inhabitants, this one state has more people than all but a few of the world's countries.

The state of Jammu and Kashmir, located in the extreme north, has been in the news ever since its accession to India brought about by its Hindu ruler in 1947. A small part of this area was seized by Pakistani guerillas soon after the creation of Pakistan and is known as Azad Kashmir (Free Kashmir). India and Pakistan have fought several wars over the Kashmir issue. Religious conflict in the state plus the struggles over the control of border areas have ruined the local economy, which was formerly based on tourism.[9]

The states of Maharashtra, Gujarat, and Goa form the western region of the country. Both Maharashtra and Gujarat are highly industrialized and developed in comparison to most other states. Maharashtra is the biggest recipient of foreign direct investment in the entire country. Its capital of Mumbai (Bombay), in addition to having the world's largest film industry, tends to set the trend for business policies throughout the country. A bitter irony is that despite all the commercial and economic growth in the state and its capital city, Mumbai has one of the highest urban poverty rates in the world. This is evidenced by a large number of slums around the city; the most prominent one in Dharavi is considered to be among the largest urban slums anywhere in the world. Mumbai also has the unfortunate reputation of having the highest incidence AIDS in the country.

The eastern region is comprised of the states of Bihar, Jharkhand, Orissa, and West Bengal. Kolkata (Calcutta) is the main hub of this region. This part of the country has undergone a huge shift in its economic base and regional comparative advantage during last 50 years. As India's former industrial heartland from the 1950s until the 1980s, it featured primary industries dependent on natural resources extraction and processing. Areas around Jamshedpur, Bokaro Steel City, Ranchi, and Rourkela became prominent for steelmaking and heavy industries. Kolkata was a major industrial center with an array of light and medium manufacturing industries. The entire region has now become one of the most economically disadvantaged in the country, mainly because of its continued reliance on low-value added industries and a lack of serious government involvement in attracting newer industries, both domestic and foreign.

Regional Differences: Business Implications

Implications of India's regional differences for companies doing business there include considerations such as the following:

- Foreign companies interested in India should carefully assess the costs and benefits of locating in a particular region. Regional comparative advantages are changing rapidly, so it is best to avoid decisions based solely on generalizations about a particular city, state, or region. Beyond the immediate questions that a foreign firm is likely to ask about workforce availability, infrastructure development, and incentives for setting up operations, it is also wise to look closely at other factors such as the broader economic climate, likely employee retention rates, changing government regulations, and political corruption.

- Investors should examine not only the current social and economic infrastructure in large cities, but in smaller cities as well.[10] Companies in the IT or IT-enabled industries are facing the fact that major business centers such as Bangalore are beginning to suffer from pressures of rising labor costs and rapid growth with accompanying infrastructure nightmares.[11] Shortages of experienced human resources along with infrastructure limitations in large cities have spurred businesses to take an interest in new ventures in the second-tier cities where the overall costs of doing business are lower and employee retention rates could be higher. For example, cities such as Pune in Maharashtra, Gurgaon in Haryana, Noida and Ghaziabad in Uttar Pradesh, Vishakhapatnam in Andhra Pradesh, Pondicherry in the Union Territory of Pondicherry, Mysore in Karnataka, and Kolkata (Calcutta) in West Bengal are drawing increasing attention as newer centers of domestic and foreign investment.
- Compared to the pre-liberalization periods in Indian business history when only the public sector companies owned by the government were big employers, privately owned companies are taking the lead in creating large numbers of new jobs. A modern private sector company is less likely to experience tensions among employees who come from different parts of the country, although these are still present. Interregional tensions are more likely to exist in some state-owned enterprises where the majority of the employees belong to the same region and may be inclined to exclude others.
- Seventy percent of the Indian population still lives in villages or rural areas, while the remaining 30 percent live in towns, cities, or urban areas. Although this ratio did not significantly change from 1947 until the late 1990s, there is now a growing rural to urban migration trend to as people move to the cities in search of better em-

ployment opportunities. Smaller towns and cities also are losing college graduates because foreign or domestic investments in offshore operations are concentrated in major cities. Over the long term, many regions in India should still be able to offer a plentiful supply of workers with strong technical training as a result of high-quality educational institutions and trends toward urbanization.

Religious Diversity

India presents an extremely broad spectrum of religious faiths among its more than one billion people, and this variety shapes its business and social environment. Almost every world religion is represented in India. Religion is a very important element in the personal lives of most Indians. India is the birthplace of many ancient, as well as newer world religions. Its oldest religion, Hinduism,[12] is practiced by 80.5 percent of the population. Other primary religious groups are Muslims (13.4 percent), Christians (2.3 percent), Sikhs (1.9 percent), Buddhists (0.8 percent), Jains (0.4 percent), and others (0.6 percent), including Zoroastrians.[13] Each of these faiths has its own history, some having originated in India and others imported from abroad.[14] Scanning through India's TV channels today, it is easy to find programs that represent its diverse religious heritage, from a Hindu guru swathed in saffron robes, to an English-speaking Baptist preacher on the GOD channel to Sikh prayers televised from the Golden Temple.

Religion and Regions

The distribution of followers of India's various religious groups throughout the country has a direct bearing on the character of many regions. Himachal Pradesh, north of India's capital city of Delhi, is overwhelmingly Hindu. Just to the north of Himachal Pradesh is the predominantly Muslim Jammu and Kashmir, where border disputes between India and neighboring Pakistan have long simmered. The state of Punjab, to the west, on the other hand, has a majority of Sikhs. Table 4-3 illustrates some of the highlights of statewise distribution.

TABLE 4-3. SAMPLE INDIAN STATES AND RELIGIOUS GROUPS[15]

Religion (percent of population)	Sample States and Percentages of Religious Group Adherents	States with the Largest Number of Practitioners (millions)
Hindus (80.5%)	Himachal Pradesh (95.6%), Orissa (94.4%), Chattisgarh (94.7%), Madhya Pradesh (91.1%), Gujarat (89.1%)	Uttar Pradesh (133.90 million)
Muslims (13.4%)	Jammu & Kashmir (67.0%), Assam (30.9%), West Bengal (25.2%), Kerala (24.7%), Uttar Pradesh (18.5%)	Uttar Pradesh (30.74 million)
Christians (2.3%)	Nagaland (90.0%), Mizoram (87%), Meghalaya (70.3%), Manipur (34.0%), Kerala (19.0%)	Kerala (6.00 million)
Sikhs (1.9%)	Punjab (59.9%), Haryana (5.5%), Delhi (4.0%), Jammu & Kashmir (2.0%)	Punjab (14.59 million)

Another group, the Zoroastrians (also called Parsees), comprises a tiny minority in number but contains a very powerful and influential group of businesspeople in the Indian economy. Because they were not directly involved in the religious fighting between Muslims and Hindus leading up to Partition, the Zoroastrians were able to remain neutral and survive the transition with more of their belongings and businesses intact. Two Parsee families, Tata and Godrej, are very well known and highly respected throughout India. The Tata group in particular heads up one of the largest business and industry conglomerates in India and is very influential. It has been successful in creating a diverse range of industries (steelmaking, automobiles, locomotives, light engineering, consulting, telecommunications, and IT, to name a few) in the country and maintains a high standard of corporate ethics and social responsibility.

Indian Secularism

The Indian constitution has guaranteed religious freedom since its inception in 1950. Although the vast majority (82 percent) of India's inhabitants is Hindu, the constitution provides for a secular form of government. This secular stance does not mean a lack of faith in religion. The Indian Constitution stresses that religion will not interfere with the governance process and that followers of any religion will have the same civil rights guaranteed by the constitution.

One positive example of India's secular stance is the political governance system both at the state and center levels. Persons from the Hindu, Muslim, and Sikh communities have been elected to the highest office of the president, even though Muslims comprise only 13 percent and Sikhs less than 2 percent of the general population. Several Hindus and a Sikh adherent have served as prime ministers. People from all religious groups have functioned as cabinet ministers, state governors, chief ministers, and other lawmakers within India's robust democratic system.

Indian religions, for the most part, have placed their faith in coexistence and have lived in harmony with each other, and there is a general attitude of mutual tolerance. As a tribute to India's long-term policy of ensuring religious freedom to its people, the UNDP Human Development Report 2004 states that "the ethos of religious and other kinds of tolerance in India goes back to the era of Emperor Ashoka in the third century B.C." The report adds that the belief from this early point in India's history that "the sects of other people deserve reverence for one reason or another is certainly among the earliest political defenses of tolerance anywhere."[16]

However, there have been some very trying times in recent Indian history, with communal disturbances and even violent riots involving major religious groups. Some examples still vivid in memory are the Hindu-Muslim riots at the time of the partition of India and Pakistan in 1947, riots associated with the Babri Mosque demolition in Ayodhya[17] (UP) in 1992, and the recent Hindu-Muslim violence in Gujarat in 2002. Hindus and Sikhs clashed in a major riot after Prime Minister Indira Gandhi was assassinated by her Sikh bodyguards in 1984. When they do occur, these instances of religious violence disrupt business and normal life considerably, because they erupt in one place but spread very rapidly to other parts of the country.

Currently members of the various religions represented in the workplace normally work together without major troubles. This is despite the fact that some politicians still play the "divide and rule" game, particularly during election campaigns or periods of political controversy within the country. Some religious tension may be reflected in the workplace during times such as these.

Religion and Literacy Rates

Literacy is one of the most basic indicators of a country's development. India's overall literacy rate for people age seven and above is 64.8 percent.[18] However, there are wide discrepancies in the literacy rate among states and on the basis of both religion and gender. The literacy rate varies according to religious affiliation, as different religious groups have traditionally had contrasting levels of access to education. The Jain group has the highest literacy rate of 94.1 percent, followed by Christians (80.3 percent), Buddhists (72.7 percent), Sikhs (70 percent), Hindus (65.1 percent), and Muslims (59.1 percent). Muslims were considered to be outside of the caste system, and although they were not exactly considered "untouchables," they were often neglected by the dominant Hindu population, had less educational opportunities because of a higher poverty rate, and were therefore the least literate. Now that it is illegal to discriminate based on caste, literacy rates are rising, but the impact of India's historical background on modern-day literacy rates is clear. Regarding the Jain group, "It is likely to reach the goal of universal literacy for its total population any time now. It is also important to remember here that most of the Jain population lives in urban areas and its primary occupational activities are in the fields of industry, commerce, and professional services."[19]

Religion in the Indian Workplace

Religion is not a factor in the hiring practices of the private sector in general and multinational companies in particular. Professional track record and interpersonal fit are viewed as being more significant.[20] Generally speaking, Indian workplaces embrace religious coexistence as well. At the same time, companies observe certain common practices in order to avoid religious conflict in the workplace. For example, because beef is forbidden for Hindus and pork for Muslims, employers do not serve any form of beef or pork at the company cafeteria or for company functions.

Hindus dominate most parts of the country except in Jammu and Kashmir, Mizoram, Meghalaya, Nagaland, and Punjab. With the exception of Punjab, until now foreign businesses have not shown an interest in these non-Hindu states. Therefore, as far as workplace implications from religion are concerned, the largest part of India continues to be influenced by the Hindu way of life. Hierarchy is an important concept in the Hindu paradigm, and most Indian organizations, in the private as well as government sectors, display a span of organizational and interpersonal hierarchy greater than that in the West.

Religious affiliation affects the way that employees arrange their workspaces as well as their own personal dress and appearance. The visibility of these religious practices is in sharp contrast with the West, where religious symbols are generally kept away from the workplace. It is common in Indian offices and private cubicles to display pictures of favorite gods or goddesses; these images may also be used as screensavers on computers. Many employees may come to the workplace with a red thread tied around their wrists from a Hindu ritual, or with ashes on their foreheads and necks from the morning *puja,* or prayer. A red thread is used for all types of ceremonies, from a general blessing to a funeral, and this thread is worn on the wrist until it naturally falls off as a reminder of the ceremony. A man from the Brahmin caste or some of the highest castes may wear a thread (*Janeyu*) draped over one shoulder and tied at the opposite side of the waist. This thread is tied in the marriage ceremony and is worn at all times.

Married Hindu women from the North will often have red vermillion powder on the parting of their hair to show that they are married. Married women in the South and West will instead wear a black-beaded golden necklace. Hindu women also wear *bindis,* an eye-catching round mark, often in the form of a red circle or a flowery pattern, on the forehead as adornment. The area between the eyes is an auspicious energy point known as the sixth chakra, and placing a *bindi* there brings protective energy and good luck. The Sikh code of conduct requires Sikh men to wear a turban as a sign of honor and self respect. They are not supposed to cut their hair, including their beards. Hair is tied up on the top of the head and covered with a turban. Muslim colleagues may wear a prayer cap. This cap usually worn during prayer to show respect to Allah, but may also be worn throughout the day.

India's complex holiday calendar reflects aspects of its religious diversity as well as key secular events. Public holidays in India tend to be observed on a strictly regional basis. Only the secular national holidays of Republic Day (January 26), Independence Day (August 15), and Mahatma Gandhi's Birthday (October 2) are mandatory and universally observed. In addition, there are numerous festivals and fairs that are also observed in some states as holidays; their dates change from year to year. Muslim festivals are timed according to local sightings of various phases of the moon, so their dates also change. Generally, Indian employees are entitled to 10 scheduled holidays of their choice in addition to the three national holidays. The government sector may celebrate more holidays because it does not share the same practices as in the business sector.[21]

As a mark of respect for local customs and for better relationships, foreign firms should avoid scheduling critical work processes during key holiday periods when Indians are likely to go on vacation, or productivity levels may be lower. Employees in Business Process Outsourcing or call-center businesses may follow the holiday schedules of their client countries because their operations are synchronized with client schedules.[22] Although many Indians are likely to be flexible on the holiday issue, an opinion poll is generally taken for deciding on companywide observance of some of the holidays, particularly when these follow the Indian calendar.

Here are some other workplace implications of India's tremendous religious diversity

- New company projects may be launched with a token religious worship or ceremony; a local priest often performs this. The priest decides an auspicious time for start of the ceremony. Key managers, politicians, or government officials may be invited for launching an important project or a new venture.

- According to Indian traditions, parents and families arrange the majority of marriages, and the wedding ceremonies are finalized in a span of weeks rather than over a year or so. Therefore, Indian employees may request unplanned or sudden leaves of absence for weddings and other family ceremonies.
- In some southern parts of the country, traditionally minded employees may refrain from making any critical decisions or starting an important task during certain inauspicious times on a given day. This period is known as *Rahu Kala,* which means the time or the period of the evil planet Rahu.[23] Such practices may or may not be of critical importance to a majority of the employees. (In one instance in a multinational firm, concerns were voiced about planning the new hire orientation at an auspicious time to ensure that people would join the company. It was later revealed that it was only those in the Brahmin caste who were particularly concerned with *Rahu Kala,* and that there would be little impact if the orientation took place during an inauspicious time.)
- Depending on the number of Muslim employees in the workplace, the company may have to provide a designated space as a prayer room to allow Muslim employees to offer their ritual prayers. This is especially applicable during the month of the Ramadan and for Friday prayers. If the employer is not able to provide the space for prayers, flextime should be allowed so that employees can go a nearby mosque or another suitable place to pray.[24] During the fast of Ramadan, Muslims are not allowed to eat during daylight hours. It should not be a surprise if, during this time, Muslim colleagues leave work right at dusk to eat for the first time that day, possibly even returning to work again after the meal.

Socioeconomic Status

It is impossible to talk about India without mentioning caste, a social kinship-based system that has been continuously evolving over many centuries. Rooted in the Indian civilization, the history of the *varna,* or caste system, dates back more than 3,000 years. It was originally conceived as a division of labor based on ability and included four main *varnas*, or groups: *Brahmin* (priests, teachers), *Kshatriya* (warriors, rulers), *Vaishya* (traders, farmers, craftsmen), and *Shudra* (menial workers, servants).[25] Brahmins exceled in knowledge, and by virtue of being scholars, they gained proximity to the rulers and other upper castes and became very influential in society. Untouchables (also referred to as *Dalits*) were those at the very bottom of this social ladder; they engaged in lower-ranked occupations that were regarded as being less clean. In an effort to eradicate the practice of untouchability, Mahatma Gandhi embraced the untouchables and coined the term *Harijan* or "children of God." Subsequently, the cause of improving the situation for this disenfranchised social group was taken up by others.[26]

The caste system has undergone many different permutations over the course of Indian history, and came to include thousands of smaller caste groups (*jati*). In the past, a person's caste often determined his or her occupation. Occupations of untouchables (or *Dalits*) were traditionally limited to jobs such as leather workers, toilet cleaners, and sweepers. Caste discrimination has now been outlawed, and more opportunities to escape the fixed occupational system are made possible through education. However, castes still exist in the background of India's cultural landscape and greatly affect socioeconomic inequality. It is, for example, quite likely that the majority of arranged marriages still take place between partners from the same narrower caste group. The caste factor also becomes more prominent at the time of elections, when voters often select the candidate belonging to their caste without necessarily taking into consideration the candidate's qualifications or abilities.

Although positive socioeconomic changes occurred in India after its independence, the country continues to be bogged down by stark inequalities. Before 1947 India was a stratified society with many layers of caste and social classes. None of the socioeconomic issues emanating from these systems were adequately addressed by British rule. However, after independence in 1947, the founding fathers of the Indian constitution saw a great opportunity to tackle a number of burning issues. The new constitution adopted in 1950 guaranteed that every citizen will have equal rights and banned any exploitation in any form. The most significant change was that the new constitution raised public awareness about the plight of lower caste members. Significant legal reforms followed the constitution, including the abolition of untouchability and education for members of formerly oppressed classes. To improve the socioeconomic status of these people, the new constitution provided for reservation of seats in the national parliament and state assemblies, particularly for Harijans, so-called backward classes, scheduled castes, and scheduled tribe people. These steps delivered a major blow against the monopoly of the higher castes and created better opportunities for socioeconomic advancement of the people at the bottom of the pecking order.[27]

Reserving jobs in the government sector was critical for uplifting the economically and socially destitute in the post-independence decades. Good government jobs provided both job security and a sense of empowerment that came from an approach to governance in which the public sector played a prominent role. But the preference for government jobs is changing now, as managerial positions in the private sector have suddenly become more lucrative than comparable jobs in the government. Even if job security in the private sector is much lower, the salaries and perks are higher and the power base is shifting from government jobs to private sector employment, particularly in the multinational corporations. Therefore, some political parties are now beginning to demand job reservation in the private sector as well. Private sector leaders have not welcomed this demand, mainly because they fear that any government-mandated reservation will have a negative effect on the talent pool, workplace efficiency, and merit-based standards, and therefore the competitiveness of their firms.

Socioeconomic Status: Business Implications

India's socioeconomic environment, including the enormous gaps in living standards that persist as well as the impact of post-independence reforms, has significant implications for foreign employers:

- Reforms in India's traditional social system, along with more widespread access to educational opportunities, have created a massive pool of human resources that are increasingly available to foreign employers. By hiring and promoting based upon merit, foreign firms can both help to support the country's social reforms and leverage this talent base to achieve their own strategic global objectives.

- Corporate social responsibility programs to improve the socioeconomic status of the communities where a business operates are important because of the huge disparity that still exists between rich and poor and the legacy of the caste system. These programs also tend to increase loyalty and goodwill within an organization and the larger community, and are a unique way of retaining talent.
- Favoritism or special actions on behalf of a particular caste sometimes occur but are not a prevalent practice in industry these days. With an open company culture, a committee may review and nullify any favors given in an inappropriate manner. Most employment in the knowledge industry is finalized only after a written test and technical discussion.[28]
- Job reservations in the private sector for so-called backward classes and scheduled castes and tribes are mostly opposed by the private sector management because of serious concerns regarding their global competitiveness. If hired under pressure of the political agenda (or the feel-good factor), the favored employees are likely to be put in noncritical departments to fulfill a job reservation quota, thereby minimizing the impact on the business.

Gender Issues in India

"You can tell the condition of a nation by looking at the status of its women."

—Jawaharlal Nehru[29]

India has traditionally fostered a male dominant society, but expected behaviors for male-female roles in the workplace as well as in other segments of life are starting to shift. The status of women in India within the family, extended family, society, and the workplace varies greatly between rural and urban areas, and is often influenced by the level of education.

Women in the workforce today are often caught between traditional expectations and modern realities. Many Indians continue to live in extended families, so a new bride moves into the groom's house to live with her in-laws, including her husband's brothers and their families.[30] Often there is a generation gap between the mother-in-law and modern wives. Traditionally, the young wife would take over cooking for the whole household, but a career woman is unlikely to have the time or energy to handle these additional responsibilities. Her mother in-law may find it upsetting to have a new female member of the household who continues to work outside of the home or takes a new job. Indeed, the mother-in-law frequently puts so much pressure on her son and his new wife that the younger woman is forced to cut back on her work responsibilities or give up her job entirely. Women who have sufficient means sometimes choose to hire a cook as a way to keep the peace in their extended family and to allow themselves the time to work.

Even if others handle some household tasks, it is still very difficult for women to take on positions with heavy responsibilities and long hours without family support and flexibility. Men in managerial positions in offshore development centers can be at work late for calls to the United States or Europe, but this is difficult for women. The infrastructure in India is such that only larger corporations can afford conference call bridge lines; most employees have to travel back to the office, sometimes for over an hour, just to be able to participate in the late-night conference calls. The off-hour calls (mainly because of time zone differences) so common in a global business environment are particularly challenging to schedule for women professionals who have other responsibilities to their extended families—for many, taking part in these calls is nearly impossible. The exceptions are women who work in the call centers where the contractual expectation is that they will work during night hours only.

In a world where much business is done in social situations, women are also at a disadvantage because it is not appropriate for single or married women to be out in the late evenings with males outside of their own families. Even in the case of call center businesses, it is very hard for parents of single women and husbands or in-laws of married women to accept that these women are out of the house at night on a regular basis.

India is filled with contrasts, and the way women are treated in society, government, and business is yet another example. Many Westerners and Indians alike might argue that Indian women continue to be victims of various forms of discrimination. Dowry is one extreme example. As in other countries in the region such as Afghanistan and Nepal, the bride's parents are expected to offer a dowry (money, goods, or estates) to the husband's family. Although giving a dowry is illegal (according to the Dowry Prohibition Act and the Indian Penal Code) and the practice is declining, it is still prevalent in most parts of the country. On a daily basis in India, it is possible to find news about social incidents and tragedies related to the dowry custom: for example, female infanticide or abuse of brides by a husband's family members who claim that the dowry was insufficient.

Advocates for women's rights in India observe that women are still compelled to lead a substandard life that is far from equal in comparison to men. Most will also acknowledge, however, that Indian women have made great strides since independence and that they are now visible in all walks of professional life, including government at the highest levels.

Unfortunately, the number of women to whom greater privileges have become available includes only a small proportion of the total number of women in the country. There has been progress in some areas, and now, for instance, it is acceptable for a woman to become a software engineer. However, it is still not accepted in most cases for women to serve as civil engineers because they would have to work outdoors in construction areas. What is seen as permissible also varies according to the caste and class background of each social group.

There is a fundamental differentiation in career choices for women according to whether they live in a rural or urban environment. In the rural areas of the country, the preferred professions are teaching in schools, healthcare, government agencies, rural banking, and social work through voluntary organizations. The scenario in the urban centers is significantly different because of greater exposure to the global economy. Preferred professions here are medicine and healthcare, teaching in schools and universities, scientific research, airlines, service industries (such as advertising, banking, legal services, retail business, insurance, hospitality), administrative positions both in government and the private sector, software engineering and development, and a variety of jobs in the business process outsourcing industry. Some of the non-preferred employment categories in both rural and urban settings are law enforcement, restaurant staff, cab and bus drivers, and security guards.

Non-skilled women do find employment in a variety of jobs. The agricultural sector is still the main job source for women in the rural areas. In the urban areas, the major occupations for women with limited skills are construction work or household help. However, while there is hardly any pay differential between men and women in the skilled category area, women are paid anywhere from 25 percent to 50 percent less than men in the non-skilled category.

As in other parts of the world, women in India are still frequently treated as second-class citizens and must leap numerous hurdles to earn a true sense of equality. Other behaviors toward women, however, convey a seemingly contradictory level of respect for important female figures. For example, most Indians revere and accord high status to their female goddesses. The three most revered Hindu goddesses, Lakshmi (goddess of wealth), Saraswati (goddess of knowledge) and Durga (goddess of power) are considered to be very powerful, prevalent, and not at all secondary to their male counterparts. Indians are also respectful of their powerful women politicians. The most frequent reference is made to Indira Gandhi, a former prime minister of the nation, and her daughter-in-law, Sonia Gandhi, who heads the Congress Party and is one of the most powerful politicians in the country. At the state level, women occupy numerous higher political positions.

Women in India face many challenges, but the biggest one is a general sense of powerlessness across the many stages of life. There are still many communities in rural and semi-urban India where girls are not encouraged to attend school in spite of the fact that the Indian government has made education free and mandatory for children up to the age of 14. It is not only that India's overall literacy rate is much lower than in many other developing countries (China, for example); the female literacy rate is often significantly lower than male literacy in the same area or region. Other burning problems for women's rights in India include longer work hours, discrimination inside and outside of the home, and poor health conditions. These circumstances are most acute in rural and semi-urban areas, but they can be found in urban areas as well. HIV/AIDS raises an especially serious health concern for women if their husbands have AIDS. Out of India's population of one billion, 5.1 million people are estimated to live with HIV.[31]

Although complete equality for education, marriage, inheritance, property rights, and political franchise are guaranteed by the Indian constitution, this is far from a reality. Laws are not strictly enforced, and abiding by them is made more difficult by the indifferent attitude shown by most stakeholders, including in some cases the victims themselves. Moreover, key differences in Hindu and Muslim laws also make it difficult to treat Hindu and Muslim women in the same way. Many women feel unable to change practices that have been long reinforced by the weight of tradition, and suffer in silence without taking action to mitigate the issues.

Traditionally, Indian culture has reinforced women's role as that of housewife and caretaker of the family. While males hold the majority of both blue- and white-collar jobs, the percentage of women entering these positions is growing. An increasing number of women are graduating from technology and business schools, and are much sought after in the current employment market. With the economic security of their own source of income, women are no longer as trapped in unhealthy marriages because of a lack of options. In other segments of society, the condition of women has improved significantly where measures have been taken by the government and NGOs to improve women's economic independence. Some are even getting divorced, which would have been unheard of just a few years ago. Nonetheless, activism on behalf of women's rights and greater economic opportunity has yet to transform a broader environment of discrimination embedded in longstanding traditions.[32]

In spite of the sociocultural barriers in a society slow to change, the good news is that many Indian women have made huge strides in their professions. The current situation offers a far greater range of choices for women than were available even 10 to 15 years ago. For almost three decades after independence, there were almost no women at the top level of key professions. But the situation has changed significantly since 1990. It is much easier now to see a large number of women, although in the minority when compared to males, occupying positions in professions that are considered to be both prestigious and an important route to attaining full economic freedom.

Gender: Workplace Implications

Indian women were historically treated as second-class citizens, but the number of very well educated and skilled women in the workforce is growing steadily. This provides an opportunity for domestic, as well as foreign, companies to find skilled and talented women in many fields.

Indian women constitute about 20 percent to 25 percent of the workforce in the IT sector. They have received a great deal of attention recently because this field is comparatively new to India in general and for women in particular. There is hardly any gender-based salary differential in this field. The annual salary packages in the IT industry tend to be 60 percent to 100 percent higher than in manufacturing or other service industries, providing a level of income for a significant number of women that would have been unthinkable in earlier decades.

Lower attrition rates among female employees can lend stability to workplaces and work teams that have been plagued by high turnover. Employers are starting to recognize the value of this greater stability in an employment market where retention is one of the most difficult issues. According to Western employers, their female employees have proved to be excellent professionals, very good in meeting project deadlines, and create a friendly work environment.[33]

The Indian statutory practice is to provide women employees with 12 weeks of maternity leave with full pay. Requests for some additional leave are being granted liberally based on individual circumstances. Some companies are also offering one to two weeks of paternity leave to husbands of expecting mothers. Because nuclear families in urban centers are becoming more common and motherhood is a respected role in the social fabric of the country, these liberal benefits are very positive steps for recruitment and retention efforts. Satisfied female employees often refer their friends to the same company.[34]

Prevention of sexual harassment in the workplace is finally being taken up at the political level. New legislation by the Supreme Court of India is addressing this issue, yet there is a perception that many in the workforce are still not aware of what constitutes sexual harassment. Most companies have or are establishing women's councils staffed by senior managers, with at least 50 percent female membership in these roundtable councils. Foreign companies are advised to pay greater attention to male-female interactions in the workplace.

Many hindrances still exist for female employees with limited skills. Some of the issues are less pay for the same work, lack of childcare facilities, unsafe working conditions in construction and farming jobs, and daily wages with no guarantee of entitlement to statutory benefits, including medical benefits and maternity leave.

The Indian Factories Act rules that prohibited women from working in offices after 7 P.M. have been modified in some states to allow female employees in the IT-related industry to work later. In such cases, a company typically provides door-to-door transportation during evening or night hours. The central government is introducing new legislation that will allow women to work in all industries during night shifts.

Applying Global Diversity: *Ensuring Full Participation of Female Employees*

GENDER

SITUATION

You are the Director of Business Development at a major high-tech company providing software applications for computer-assisted education, e-business and e-governance projects. Your company recently established an office in New Delhi to take advantage of business opportunities resulting from the recent economic growth of India's knowledge-based industries.

In India, you manage a team of twenty-five employees: four senior managers, five junior managers, and sixteen other employees. Two of the managers and seven of the employees are women. After several months on the job, you have a few concerns related to the female employees:

- Your senior manager for new business development is Mrs. Sujata Roy. She is very qualified and has an impeccable reputation in the office. You once asked her to accompany your IT Director, John Davis, on a 2-day business trip to Kolkata to meet the IT Minister of West Bengal. She politely declined the invitation, saying that she could not travel with him unless another female employee also went with them.

- You once asked a female senior manager, Radha Swamy, to travel alone on a business trip to some of the state capitals in the northern region. But Radha notified you that it was not safe for her to travel alone.
- Some of the female employees are needed for late evening coordination meetings with American headquarters, but they are unwilling to stay late, saying that this interferes with important family responsibilities. This reluctance continues even when you promise them a car ride back home and allow them to start their next day later than usual.

POSSIBLE SOLUTIONS:

It is important to proactively address these issues so that you can fully utilize the talent of the female staff. Possible solutions include:

- Ensure that traveling female employees have appropriate companions if they express a concern about traveling with a male colleague or traveling alone. Peer female coworkers as well as more junior female employees are a good solution as travel companions. When junior female employees travel with female managers there is the additional benefit of professional development for the more junior employees.
- Organize remote conference calls for female workers so they can join late evening meetings from home. The infrastructure in India is such that conference call bridge lines tend to be expensive. However, this is an important alternative to traveling back to the office late at night, as sometimes the commute time each way can be more than an hour. Keep in mind that female professionals are typically juggling family and responsibilities with their work, so taking part in these phone calls, even at home, can create additional challenges.
- Provide door-to-door transportation for female employees when they participate in night meetings that must take place in a face-to-face context.

Summary Recommendations

India's cultural diversity will continue to surprise and challenge foreign companies for a long time to come because the impact of globalization on cultural change for the bulk of India's enormous population is slower than many may perceive. Whatever cultural change is visible to foreigners is taking place mostly in those large urban centers where foreign companies have established a significant presence either through their own Indian subsidiaries or through their Indian vendors. Moreover, even in these urban centers, the cultural change is slow and not uniform across all sections of the society and workplaces.

In India, there is a constant struggle between maintaining traditions that are uniquely Indian, and Western traditions, which look attractive. This is particularly true for the younger generation of Indians. On one hand, they have to adapt to Western practices in their current workplaces because of their everyday interaction with overseas counterparts; on the other hand, they are pressured by their families and society to adhere to their Indian roots and traditions. This tug-of-war is of great importance particularly to foreign companies, because they are likely to make mistakes if they ignore the diversity and the difficulty of working in the multifaceted Indian society.

Some relevant summary recommendations for those who choose to do business in India or with Indian counterparts are listed here.

1. Although the widespread use of English as an important **language** in Indian educational systems, business, and government will continue to grow in the future, it is still important to understand the diversity of languages in India. Many of the newer business opportunities within India will come from states where there is currently no significant presence of foreign companies. Since the local official languages in these emerging places may all be different, it can be useful for foreign companies to ensure that they have Indian employees who are conversant in these languages, and provide at least basic local language training to expatriate managers so that they can interact better with the local government and other stakeholders. Even a minimal knowledge of a local Indian language can be a door-opener to building a good relationship with Indians.

2. **Regional identity** based on internal cultural differences is likely to continue as a concern for domestic, as well as foreign, companies in India. This concern will be especially consequential where employees from different regions are asked to work on the same team. Any rivalry or unhealthy competition between members of different regions should be discouraged through appropriate team building and by inculcating a belief in unity in diversity along with pride in being an Indian and a global citizen above any single regional identity.

3. Respect the **religious** beliefs of all segments of the Indian society even though some of the religious practices may look odd from a foreigner's point of view. Challenging the religious beliefs and practices of your Indian employees, colleagues, or business partners can become a serious demotivating factor for them. You should also try to participate, even at a minimal level, in some of the local religious holidays and associated festivals. There are certain areas in the country where religious tensions may sometimes arise between Indians who engage in different forms of religious practice. It is advisable to keep an eye on the news and take precautionary measures to avoid any harm to your employees or yourself.

4. In comparison to India's rapid macro-level economic growth during this decade, its **socioeconomic** situation is likely to change much more slowly. The country's GDP has been growing steadily and many of the economic indicators are on the rise. Yet the major beneficiaries of India's globalization are concentrated in limited segments of industry and society, and the distribution of income continues to be uneven and is likely to remain so for a very long time into the future. Foreign companies can create a positive image and enhance their Indian involvement if they take their corporate social responsibility seriously and get involved in assisting a disadvantaged area or group. Some community projects in which their involvement thorough local NGOs will be greatly appreciated are better primary and secondary education for socially and economically disadvantaged groups, improvement in rural healthcare, provision of clean water, and sanitation.

    Foreign companies should understand the legacy of India's caste and class systems, as this will continue to create barriers for development. However, non-Indians are advised not to ask about anyone's caste or participate in a caste-based discussion because of the complexity and the sensitive nature of this subject. Do not confine yourself to five-star hotels, modern workplaces, and luxurious vacations while in India. It is important to immerse yourself into an average Indian's working conditions. Meet a variety of people from all walks of life, visit economically diverse neighborhoods in the city, and travel to rural areas in different parts of the country to acquaint yourself with the realities of India's socioeconomic differences.

5. The **gender** gap between Indian men and women, as well as disparities between urban and rural women, are not likely to disappear anytime soon. Helping to empower Indian women in all sections of society should be a critical agenda item for foreign companies doing business in India. This can be done through creating better access to education, more job training opportunities, daycare, and better healthcare for the existing and potential female workforce.

CHAPTER 5

Diversity in Japan

Ernest Gundling

Why Japan?

- Japan's huge economy is still the second largest in the world, and an important source of profits for many global enterprises.
- Companies such as Toyota, Honda, Canon, and Sony are global industry leaders in areas such as the automotive industry or consumer electronics.
- Japanese society, with the world's highest median age and a population that has actually started to decline in numbers, is undergoing fundamental changes both in the workplace and in many key markets. This transformation will make it a harbinger for other countries facing similar demographic trends.
- The 35 million people who live in Tokyo and its environs comprise the most populous urban area in the world; there is an enormous gap between Japan's urban and rural areas that employers and marketing strategists need to understand.

Introduction

Many people inside and outside of Japan view the country as being much less diverse than it actually is. A legacy of Japan's modern history is a dubious but lingering myth of national homogeneity, or the notion that all Japanese share the same racial heritage and view of the world. This concept of homogeneity was useful for political purposes in directing the nation's energies during both the pre- and post-WWII periods. However, the realities of contemporary Japanese society as well as considerable historical evidence suggest that Japan's people are not nearly as homogeneous as some might believe.[1]

Japan today is sorely in need of a new point of view that is better able to clearly acknowledge and to leverage the diversity that actually exists among the country's population. As Japan's citizens seek to redefine their position in an increasingly integrated world economy in which other countries such as China and India are growing at a more rapid rate, they will need to show their foreign business counterparts a more diverse and personalized set of faces in order to build lasting bonds of mutual respect and friendship.

There are, in fact, considerable differences among Japanese that are influenced by which generation they represent, the part of the country they are from, their gender perspectives, and the types of organizations they belong to. This chapter will focus on the following variables:

- Age
- Regional Background
- Gender
- Organizational Affiliation

Age and Diversity

Perhaps the single most important key to understanding Japan today is the country's demographic profile. Since the beginning of its modern period with the Meiji era in 1868, the country has undergone a reversal in the age structure of its population that should be complete within just a few decades. This reversal is affecting nearly every aspect of Japan's society and economy, and it also accounts for significant differences between the viewpoints of the various generational groups.

Up to and including the baby-boom era of the early postwar period, the age structure of Japan mirrored the pyramid shape of other rapidly growing societies in the world today. A large portion of the population was under the age of 20, with each successive segment of the population triangle above this group slimming to a peak that represented a much smaller proportion of people in their old age. The chart on the left in Figure 5–1 represents the population distribution in 1950; a gap in the male population in the 20s and 30s age brackets reflects the ravages of the World War II years.

A more recent age profile, from the year 2003, displayed in the middle of Figure 5–1, vividly displays the shift that has occurred in the space of just a few decades. In this graph, the largest bulge in the population is visible in the 50s age bracket—the same postwar baby-boom generation that was much younger in 1950. Another, smaller bulge below them for people in their late 20s and early 30s represents the children of the baby-boom generation. The profile for the youngest part of the population slims down rapidly, with the age cohort of the population from zero to 10 years of age being much smaller than the number of Japanese in their 60s.

The chart on the right in Figure 5–1 shows the projected population picture for the year 2050—this profile is largely predetermined based on the numbers of people who have already been born. The only potential changes could come from large-scale immigration, natural or manmade disasters, or a markedly higher birth rate. Note that the graph for 2050 almost reverses the profile for 1950 up to about the age of 80; this is evidence for one of the most rapid demographic turnabouts in human history.[2]

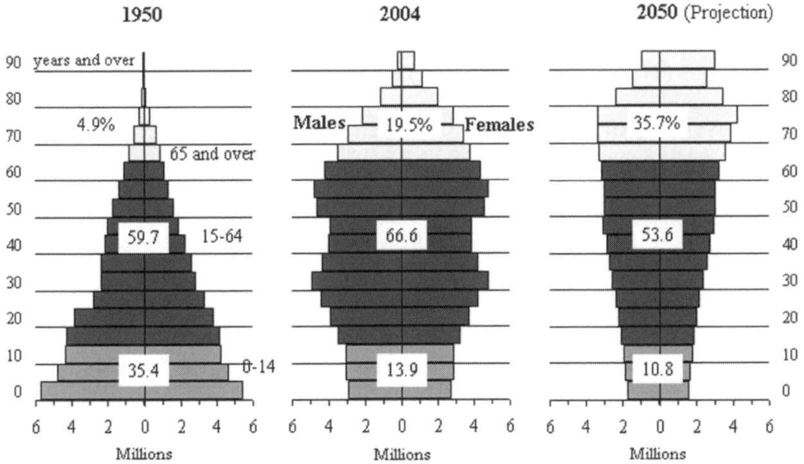

FIGURE 5-1. Japan: Changes in the Population Pyramid

Source: Statistics Bureau, MIC; Ministry of Health, Labour and Welfare. Used with permission.

Japan today is well on its way to becoming the world's oldest society. The birth rate is one of the lowest in the world, with fewer than 1.3 children born per woman. This is way below the standard replacement rate of 2.1 children for a stable population, and, together with the longest life expectancy for both men and women anywhere in the world, has created a rapidly aging nation. Approximately one-quarter of the population will be over the age of 65 by 2025. Japan's population has already peaked at approximately 127.5 million, and from this point is expected to actually *decrease* by 15 to 20 percent before mid-century unless significant changes occur.

What will it mean to have a society dominated by older people and declining in population? There are still many unknowns because this is a situation almost unprecedented in human history. Declining population has previously occurred only as a result of events such as war, famine, or disease, and these seldom spared older people. However, some of the implications of Japan's demographic reversal are already becoming evident. The government has begun to worry about how a smaller workforce will support such an enormous elderly population, and it is doubtful that the social security and medical systems in Japan will be able to withstand the ongoing changes in age distribution without further significant adjustments.

Age: Workplace Implications

Projected declines in the numbers of able-bodied workers are likely to drive up the cost of labor and make it more difficult for companies to find qualified employees. Japan has long since become a high-cost manufacturing location compared to Southeast Asia or particularly to nearby China—it is likely that such cost competition will continue. Pressures to allow increased worker immigration are increasing at both ends of the economic spectrum. Companies want to be able to import professional workers in areas such as information technology in order to compensate for a shortfall of workers with advanced training; at the same time, Japan has imported many legal and illegal immigrant laborers who are willing to undertake difficult, dirty, and dangerous work for comparatively low wages.

Meanwhile, industries focused on domestic markets must take into account the shifting demographics of their customer base. This may be good news for nursing facilities and pharmaceutical companies, but bad news for makers of children's clothing or products intended for young female buyers, as these markets are inexorably shrinking. Japan's exporters have continued to find buyers and growth prospects in overseas markets. On the domestic front, though, over the past decade companies even struggled at times with price deflation, an ominous phenomenon normally encountered only during economic depressions.

The Workplace Generation Gap

Opinion surveys suggest an emerging gap between older and younger Japanese that portends major changes for the future. When the attitudes of working adults were recently compared with student responses on measures of individual versus collective attitudes, the profiles were the reverse of each other. Scores for working adults mirrored the standard group-oriented portrayal of Japanese society, with more than two-thirds (67.9 percent) classified as collectivists versus less than one-third (32.1 percent) as individualists. Student profiles were the opposite, with more than two-thirds (70.8 percent) in the individualist camp versus less than one-third (29.2 percent) classified as collectivists.[3]

It can be argued that more individualistic student attitudes reflect the fleeting four-year interlude of freedom from social discipline between high school and the strict socialization process for new hires in the workplace. However, other statistics suggest that individualistic views are more and more finding their way into the workplace, and that these may be based upon profound changes in the upbringing of contemporary Japanese amidst a climate of material plenty, few or no siblings, and greater encouragement of self-expression. Younger workers are significantly less likely to report that they "try to do their best for the company," a measure of loyalty and willingness to make sacrifices on behalf of employers. Those in their 20s and 30s also express far greater support for merit-based compensation, with approval rates hovering in the 70 percent range for this type of system.[4]

Another expression of individualism on the part of young working Japanese has been the rapid increase of the *freeter*, or people who work in part-time jobs and avoid more permanent employment out of choice. *Freeter* is a Japanese-English term created through combining the words *free* and *time*.[5] These people comprise a significant percentage of Japan's younger workers, and the pundits predict that the ranks of *freeter* will continue to swell. There is a related and more socially worrisome trend toward the increase of the so-called NEET (not in education, employment, or training)—that is, younger people who have dropped out of the workforce altogether and are not looking for work, attending school, or in job training.[6]

Although startling, the marked contrast between older and younger worker attitudes is comprehensible based on the radical difference between the environments in which the two generations were raised. The older group grew up in an atmosphere of national fervor to regain prominence on the international stage, with an expanding population and economy; younger Japanese have known the fruits of their country's economic miracle while also seeing it plateau, and many come from small nuclear households where they witnessed the impact on their parents' lives of endless labor and self-sacrifice.

There are indications that Japan's economy is increasingly divided into older and younger industries and companies. When Japanese corporations encounter financial troubles, a common money-saving step is to stop hiring younger employees. Industries such as steel manufacturers or department stores, which have been in a chronic state of crisis over the last decade or more, have witnessed a constant rise in the average age of their employees because of the absence of younger workers. Companies in these industries run the risk of being dominated by an older generation of employees while the rest of the country moves forward. On the other hand, successful companies continue to employ young workers and to make changes in their internal systems and corporate cultures, while simultaneously reaping the benefits of a lower cost structure.

For employers, the changing perspectives of younger workers will probably mean a growing generation gap between these younger workers and more senior employees, with conflicts arising between the values, needs, and priorities of different age groups. This generation gap, with a preponderance of older workers in many companies, has several practical implications.

- **Balancing Teamwork with Individual Achievement.** Firms will have to master the tension between maintaining an environment that fosters good collective spirit and teamwork while also offering new opportunities for individual achievement. Striking an appropriate balance becomes particularly difficult when systems for promotions or rewards are considered; employees tend to want a different balance of teamwork and recognition of individual achievement based upon their age profiles. The business environment is changing quickly enough that periodic adjustments are necessary even for companies that temporarily achieve a satisfactory solution.
- **Dealing with Conflicts.** Younger workers are sometimes labeled as *wagamama* (selfish) by elders who expect them to be willing to accept instruction and to make sacrifices on behalf of the organization. There is a view of personal development common to the more senior generation that draws upon traditional forms of apprenticeship. A young person was expected to take orders and even verbal abuse with unquestioning readiness to serve on the assumption that one's seniors knew best. Unstinting effort and sacrifice on behalf of the group were thought to produce a mature adult over time. But among a newer generation raised in prosperous households with few or no siblings and having technological savvy that their elders may lack, many have no patience for the former system. Conflicts can arise when older workers expect a level of effort or individual sacrifice that is refused or seen as meaningless symbolism by their juniors.
- **Changes in the "Three Pillars."** At least two of the three traditional pillars of Japan's employment system, lifetime employment and promotion by seniority, are undergoing significant changes as the younger generation takes hold. It is reported that the number of firms offering lifetime employment, never more than one-third of the total anyway, has now dwindled to less than 10 percent.[7] The move away from such lifetime job security is typically accompanied by merit-based pay and promotion; even some of the largest Japanese manufacturing giants have announced that they will be placing greater emphasis on performance. The third pillar, the company

union, is being eroded as well by competitive pressures from the Chinese labor market—unions cannot afford to escalate their demands or entire facilities may be relocated to China.

- **Retirement.** A number of companies have already taken on the inverse pyramid shape predicted for the Japanese population as a whole in the years to come. This can mean one of two things, depending upon the nature of the business and the firm's degree of success. Some companies are concerned about an imminent large-scale exodus of skilled veteran workers as Japan's post-WWII baby boomers reach retirement age. They fear that vital skills and experience will leave with these people without being fully transmitted to the thinner ranks of younger workers. For such firms, the challenge is to transfer skills more quickly or to find capable replacement workers. Other companies that are in dire economic circumstances find the inverse age profile to be a recipe for high-cost labor; they also have the strongest internal pressures to resist change because existing systems for promotion, compensation, and guaranteed employment favor senior employees. It is a stark fact of the traditional seniority system that up to a certain age, older workers cost a company more. Many corporations have taken the drastic step of trying to shave off the cost-heavy top end of their age pyramid through attrition and voluntary early retirement programs. There are firms that unfortunately use coercive measures, encouraging the not-so-voluntary departure of employees who are seen as redundant or who are underperforming (coercive tactics include transfers to remote locations, removal of all responsibilities, assignment of trivial, mind-numbing tasks, or public embarrassment through workplace rebukes and remedial training programs). These approaches can have significant negative consequences, as there is a loss of face and the related social stigma associated with involuntary early departures.[8] Yet there have also been outstanding examples of firms that have accomplished early retirement programs in a truly voluntary fashion.[9] As Japanese society becomes more accustomed to this phenomenon, some people are discovering rewarding occupations that leave them better off than before, at least psychologically if not financially.

Regional Origin

There is a vast difference between Japan's urban environment and its countryside, with its major cities still vibrant centers that produce a tremendous array of goods and services, while some rural areas appear to be slipping backwards in time as their young people depart.

The Three Cities

Three large urban areas dominate Japan's national landscape. The Kanto plain, which includes Tokyo and Yokohama—Japan's two largest cities—is one of the most densely inhabited areas in the world, with a regional population of more than 30 million people and a volume of economic output that is larger than all but a few major countries. The Kansai area, encompassing the cities of Osaka, Kyoto, and Kobe, is another enormous cosmopolitan center, with close to 20 million people. Finally, the region around Nagoya, although less populous than either Kanto or Kansai, with only about seven million people, is nonetheless another major economic center—Toyota Motors, for example, is headquartered in Toyota City, not far away from Nagoya.

All of these urban areas lie on Japan's Pacific coastline (see Figure 5-2). More than two-thirds of the country's population is concentrated along this stretch of coast, which is blessed with a temperate climate and more fertile agricultural land than the other, mostly mountainous, regions of the country. In fact, nearly half of Japan's population lives in the narrow urban corridor just over 500 kilometers in length that runs from Tokyo in the east to Kobe in the west. Other large Japanese cities such as Okayama, Hiroshima, Kitakyushu, and Fukuoka lie further west along the Inland Sea coast or on the island of Kyushu.

The most striking regional differences between Japan's residents are related to the age factor already described. When the age distribution of the population is examined, it is readily apparent that the three major urban areas are also the youngest parts of the country. The average age in Japan's rural areas tends to be substantially higher than that of the largest cities. Some farming villages have been almost completely abandoned by younger people and are now primarily the home of the over-60 set. Indeed, Japan's agricultural population is rapidly aging, with people over the age of 60 accounting for more than half of Japan's farmers. The far southern islands of Okinawa hold some of the oldest people in the world.

The age imbalance between urban and rural areas contributes to strik-

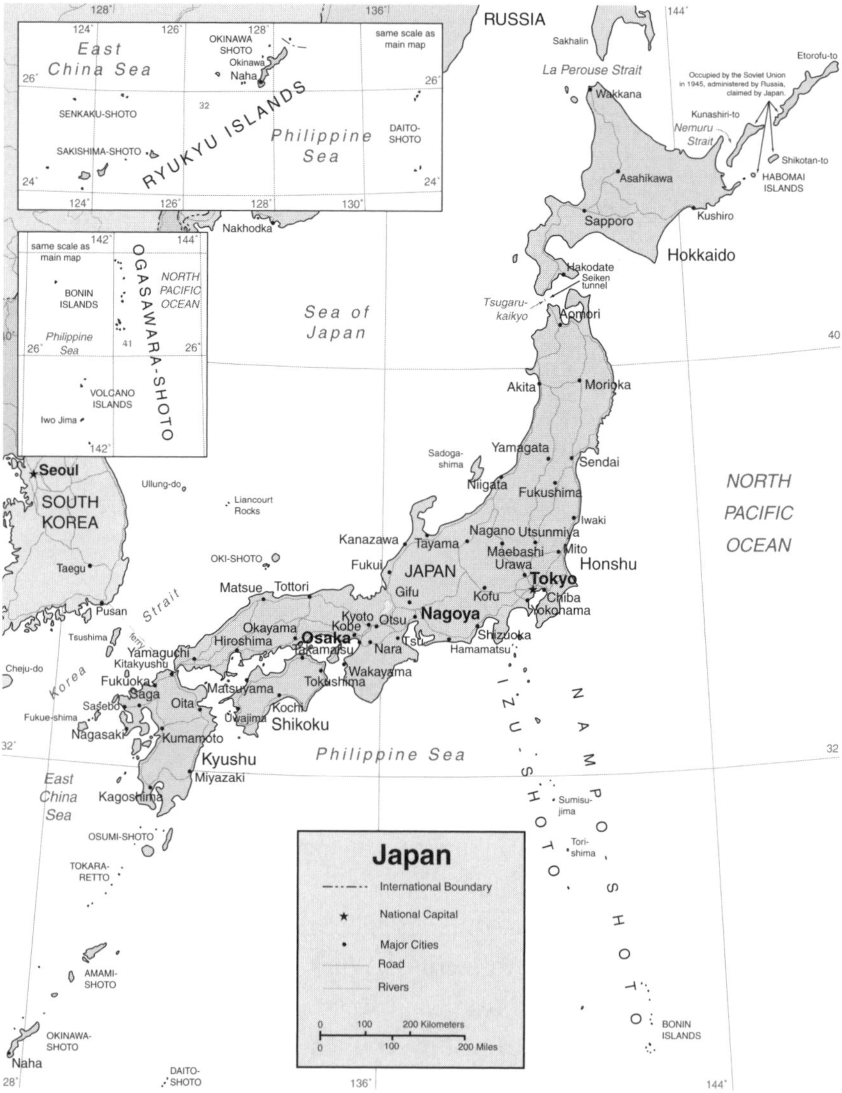

FIGURE 5-2. Map of Japan with Major Population Centers

ing gaps in perspectives. Travel into many smaller towns and villages in Japan is like a journey back in time. In a double-edged sense, both the virtues and the limitations of older generations are preserved intact in these environments.

Attitudes in Japan's rural areas tend to be less receptive to outside influences. For example, survey responses to a question about factors important to the growth and autonomy of young people demonstrate a gap between urban and rural residents; those who say that it is necessary to have direct contact with culture and ideas from overseas include 73 percent of big-city respondents, but just 61 percent of those from smaller towns. There is an overlap between this urban/rural contrast and the different scores for various age brackets. For instance, those in their 70s throughout the country support the same survey response at a rate of 60 percent,

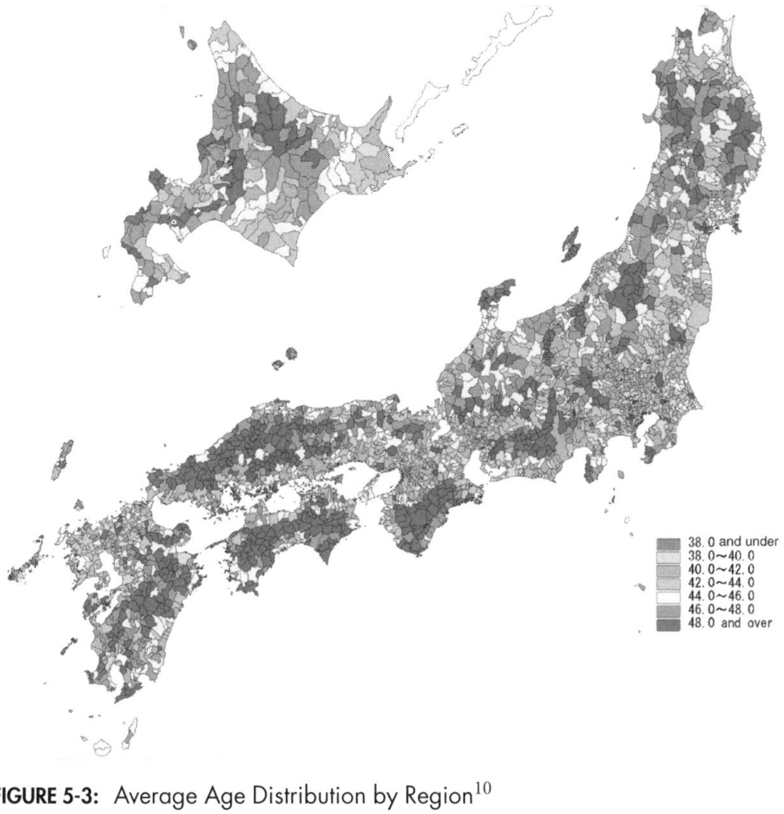

FIGURE 5-3: Average Age Distribution by Region[10]

nearly identical to the small-town number.[11] Rural areas are also more conservative politically, serving as strongholds for Japan's traditionally dominant Liberal Democratic Party.

Traveling "Up" to Tokyo

Tokyo is a remarkably livable big city that combines features of New York, Paris, and Washington, D.C. It is at once a center of finance, fashion, and politics. In addition to the entire central government, nearly every major Japanese corporation has either its headquarters or a significant presence in Tokyo, and most of the world's major multinationals are represented there as well. The Kansai region, with its several large cities and sophisticated industrial base, is Tokyo's only real rival as an urban center—Kansai itself has a GDP that would be among the top ten in the world if it were ranked as a country. Yet, from a business standpoint, the rivalry is very uneven; 80 percent or more of Japan's largest companies have their headquarters in Tokyo. Even firms such Matsushita or Sharp, which are based in Kansai, or Toyota, headquartered near Nagoya, have large offices in Tokyo. By contrast, organizations without a Tokyo presence are often relegated to second- or third-rate status.

Japanese based in Tokyo are quick to ask each other where they are from, and the accents of more rural areas, such as Toyama to the north or Kansai and Kyushu to the south, are often easy to detect. However, families that have resided in Tokyo for several generations are relatively rare, and the city's current inhabitants do not necessarily exclude people based on their place of origin, particularly if those who are originally from other places first came to Tokyo to attend one of its many universities. In fact, Tokyo itself has been called a "big country" town, a reference to the fact that so many of its people have migrated from other, more rural, areas in search of jobs or education. What does matter is that one is currently located in Tokyo or its environs—those who are not are regarded with a polite mixture of sympathy and slight disdain. Trains in Japan travel "up" to Tokyo and "down" to everywhere else.

From the perspective of other parts of Japan, there is an ambivalent attitude toward the capitol. On one hand, it is viewed with longing and envy as a stylish and civilized place to live, with myriad opportunities for personal advancement. At the same time, however, residents of Japan's smaller cities and towns see Tokyo as containing a somewhat frightening mixture of crime (although the crime rate is quite low compared with other global cities), exotic foreigners with their offices and embassies, and oddball or self-indulgent Japanese who dress up in eccentric costumes and frequent the nightclubs in hot spots such as Roppongi or Shibuya. Much as with other big cities, Tokyo's residents are also regarded by people elsewhere in Japan as more materialistic and less warm or generous than their relatives in the countryside.

Foreign companies that seek to do business in Japan, therefore, need to balance a presence in Tokyo with operations in other parts of the country. Having an office in Tokyo is a basic prerequisite for doing most kinds of business in Japan. Yet being there exclusively can convey a sense of estrangement—from the viewpoint of people living elsewhere on Japan's main island of Honshu or the other islands of Kyushu, Shikoku, or Hokkaido, Tokyo is a different world. Employees who are transferred from one place to another may choose not to take their families, as it is more difficult to transplant family members to a new location than it is for an employee to move to a different jobsite. Tokyo real estate is famously expensive; some families take out multigenerational loans in order to purchase a modest condominium.

Japan's Urban Foreigners

The number of foreigners in Japan is small in relation to the country's population, but their concentration in major cities adds to the urban/rural contrast. The approximately two million legally registered foreigners are equivalent to about 1.5 percent of Japan's total population. Even when another 200,000-plus illegal immigrants are factored in, the number remains below 2 percent.[12] The bulk of Japan's foreign residents are Asians. The largest group among Japan's legal residents consists of more than 600,000 people of Korean ancestry; their presence stems from the many Koreans who were brought to Japan during the war years to work as slave labor in factories and mines. Most of these Korean-Japanese, even those whose families have been living in Japan for several generations, are still not full citizens because having at least one parent with Japanese blood is a requirement for citizenship. Other predominant foreign groups represented in Japan include people from China, Brazil, the Philippines, Peru, and the United States. Their numbers are indicated in Table 5-1.

TABLE 5-1. FOREIGNERS IN JAPAN

End of year	Registered Foreigners in Japan (in thousands)						
	Total	Korea*	China	Brazil	Philippines	Peru	United States
1995	1,362	666	223	176	74	36	43
2000	1,686	635	336	254	145	46	45
2003	1,915	614	462	275	185	54	48

Source: Japanese Ministry of Justice[13]

*Democratic People's Republic of Korea and Republic of Korea.

There are several primary segments within Japan's foreign population.

1. **European and U.S. citizens:** This group is predominantly white-collar employees of foreign multinationals or of Japanese firms, along with students and academics. They are mostly temporary residents; a smaller number, including those with a Japanese spouse or an occupational specialty suited to Japan, may choose to live there permanently.

2. **Second- or Third-Generation Japanese:** During previous periods of labor shortages, Japan encouraged the immigration of people of Japanese ancestry who were citizens of other countries. The large number of foreigners from Brazil and Peru, which has continued to grow over the past decade, is evidence of this trend.

3. **Other Asians and Middle Easterners:** This group includes a mixture of students, white-collar workers, factory or construction laborers, and domestic workers.

Attitudes toward foreigners of course differ depending upon the individual Japanese and the group that a foreigner represents. People of Caucasian ancestry tend to receive the benefit of the doubt; many Japanese initially maintain a stance of politeness and may even be intimidated by the physical size of these visitors. Lack of adeptness with the Japanese language or perceived rudeness on the part of American or European visitors is often generously attributed to cultural differences. Underneath their polite surface, many Japanese have experienced a struggle between feelings of both inferiority and superiority. Based on a hierarchical view of the world, Japan's government and media have pointed to the country's status as an economic superpower and placed Japan near the top of the heap along with North America and Europe. In the heady days of the 1980s and early 1990s, when a more monolithic view of "the Japanese" still held sway over much of the populace, there was even serious talk of Japanese people somehow being innately superior to everyone else.

Other foreigners in Japan do not have the benefit of such positioning in a global hierarchy. Immigrant workers of Japanese ancestry from Brazil or Peru are often treated as poor cousins, working long hours for low wages under difficult conditions. Second- or third-generation Koreans in Japan are discriminated against in various ways, with Japanese citizenship still out of the question and a fingerprinting requirement widely loathed by immigrants in place until not long ago even for those who were born in Japan. Although recent reforms have finally brought about some changes, foreigners must still carry their alien registration cards with them at all times.[14] People from other parts of Asia, such as China or the Philippines, may receive a modicum of respect as students or white-collar workers, but employees in factories, on construction sites, or in "entertainment" professions can face a daily grind of exploitation and suspicion. Increasing crime rates in Japan have been popularly blamed with only limited justification on immigrants, particularly Chinese residents.

The greater foreign presence in Kanto, Kansai, and the Nagoya region underlines the distinctive identity of these areas in comparison with the rest of the country. Foreigners who receive startled, inquisitive, or suspicious looks elsewhere in the country are mostly shrugged off as part of the status quo in Tokyo or Osaka. Tokyo's financial district is peppered with workers of various nationalities, and its districts near the central part of the city host an alphabet soup of foreign embassies. It is not uncommon on weekends to see clusters of Iranian men in the city's Yoyogi Park or in certain train stations—many of these people came originally as construction workers. Indeed, Tokyo and its environs host nearly 40 percent of the legal foreign population, and fully two-thirds of all foreigners reside in one of Japan's three major urban areas.[15] This urban concentration has historical roots. During the early part of Japan's modern period, Westerners were mostly confined to the port cities of Yokohama and Kobe; prior to that there was only a single point of access for Dutch traders through an island close to Nagasaki in Kyushu.

Japan's ambivalent attitudes toward the rest of the world tend to fall to some degree according to the rural/urban divide. National surveys report that a significant percentage of the population would prefer to have nothing to do with foreigners. However, many urban dwellers actively savor and cultivate overseas languages, culture, and cuisine. Some even take on the trappings and behaviors of foreigners, albeit often in a safely predigested form that involves little contact with actual people from abroad.

Japan's Urban Gaijin Handlers

For centuries, Japan has had an elite cadre of experts on overseas countries and languages who both mediated the entry of foreigners (referred to in Japanese as *gaijin,* or "outside people") and their cultures while also interpreting Japan for their benefit. These people, too, naturally congregate in major urban areas.

An early set of such experts worked for the Tokugawa Shogunate and took on the task of studying and filtering Dutch knowledge of technology and medicine through the one window open to the outside world for trade in Nagasaki. Although small in number, their work was remarkably effective—Western observers in the late 1800s were surprised to find how much was already known in Japan about European practices in spite of more than two centuries of national isolation.

As Japan's economy developed in the modern period, distinctive institutions also emerged with it that took on a much more extensive interface role with the outside world. The trading companies linked with the large conglomerates, or *keiretsu*—Mitsubishi, Mitsui, Sumitomo—handled transactions with foreigners in a way that enabled enterprises with little overseas knowledge to engage in export and import. These trading companies came to include other famous names such as Itochu, Marubeni, Nissho Iwai, and Nichimen. Their employees were posted in far-flung locations around the world and became true veterans of global business. Trading company expatriates were increasingly accompanied by government representatives, bankers, and eventually manufacturing experts, who typically lived abroad on extended assignments of five years or even a decade.

Such overseas expertise, however, was not always welcome back at home, where Japan's "fifth column" of experts on foreign ways met with a lukewarm welcome upon their return. There are derogatory words in the Japanese language for those who have taken on too much of the odor of other cultures, and individuals coming back from long overseas postings were frequently passed over for top leadership jobs or confined to specialized roles in favor of people who had less of a foreign taint.

But with the Japanese economy looking more vulnerable over the last decade and the number of Japanese living abroad continuing to rise (see Table 5-2),[16] some organizations have begun to reevaluate the role that those with overseas experience can play. Companies and schools have deliberately begun to seek out candidates with overseas credentials, and firms are increasingly coming to regard an expatriate stay in one or more major foreign markets as an indispensable ticket to the top ranks. Among Japan's five leading companies, three of them are run by executives with extensive experience abroad: Hiroshi Okuda, the chairman of Toyota, and Fujio Mitarai, the head of Canon, both previously worked for many years in the United States; Carlos Ghosn, of Nissan and Renault, was born in Brazil and ran operations in the U.S. before he achieved superstar status in Japan.

TABLE 5-2. JAPANESE LIVING ABROAD

	Japanese Living Abroad (in thousands)				
Year	Total	U.S.A.	China	Brazil	U.K.
1990	620	236	8	105	44
1995	728	264	17	91	52
2000	812	298	46	75	53
2003	911	332	77	71	51

Source: Japanese Ministry of Foreign Affairs.

Urban/Rural Differences: Workplace Implications

The concentration of business in the capital makes it possible to have a face-to-face meeting with a representative of almost any major institution within an hour's subway ride of Tokyo Station. It is wise to extend this practice to customers and business partners in other locations outside of the city in order to personally bridge the gap between Tokyo and everywhere else. Japan's other large urban centers are still within a three-hour ride on the *Shinkansen*, or bullet train, and almost any part of the country can be reached by plane in little more than an hour.[17]

A corporate office in Tokyo, domestic or foreign, is increasingly likely to contain a mix of most of the people discussed in this section: Japanese from different parts of the country, foreigners of various extractions, employees with substantial overseas experience, and those with none. Employers have a number of opportunities that were much scarcer even a decade ago.

- High-caliber young Japanese with overseas experience are now more ready to consider a career with a non-Japanese firm as a viable option. There is a new openness on the part of many Japanese, particularly those based in the largest cities, to work styles that are more commonly found within foreign firms. Before the economic bubble burst, graduates from elite educational institutions who had bright job prospects would have felt a much stronger bias toward sticking with a traditional Japanese organization—a bank, trading company, or prestigious electronics firm.
- Mid-career employees and Japanese expatriates who have recently returned to Japan are more ready than ever to listen to recruiting enticements from foreign companies. Corporate headhunters report that the first six months or so after a manager returns from abroad is the best time to pluck him away from his old company, as upon his return he struggles with the pressure to conform to a more domestic mindset.
- A variety of well-qualified non-Japanese can be hired on a local basis, saving money in comparison with full expatriate packages. These include not only workers from Europe or North America, but

also Asians such as Chinese or Indians, many of whom have attended schools in Japan and speak the language.

- Leadership and management practices introduced by non-Japanese are once again an object of interest. Mediocre results in Japanese companies, the success of Japanese executives with many years of service abroad, and events such as the unexpected turnaround wrought by Carlos Ghosn at Nissan or the appointment of Howard Stringer, an Irishman, to head Sony, have shaken the insular self-satisfaction of the boom years.

Diversity and Gender

Japanese women face stark choices between personal and professional priorities. The traditional pattern, which some still follow, has been for a young woman to attend either a two-year or a four-year college, find employment in a clerical or secretarial function for a few years, and then stop working after marriage or the birth of a child. This pattern is seen as a valuable experience for future homemakers, and it is also very convenient for employers to pay low wages to energetic young workers without having to shoulder any long-term obligations. Women can choose to return to the workforce at a later time after their children are older, but normally only in lower-paying or part-time occupations.

The results of a recent Japanese national survey on gender equality demonstrate how such traditional attitudes have shifted considerably in favor of career or longer-term employment for women. The percentages listed reflect responses for the whole survey population, including both men and women. Female respondents, depending upon their own employment status, were particularly supportive of the choices to keep working or to reenter the job market after raising children.

Public Perceptions Regarding Employment for Women

It is better for women

- not to work (2.7 percent)
- to work before marriage (6.7 percent)

- to work until pregnancy (10.2 percent)
- to keep working (40.4 percent)
- to reenter the job market when their children grow up (24.9 percent)[18]

Over the past two decades or more, an increasing number of women have aspired to pursue a full-scale professional career, but they have faced many obstacles. For example, graduation from a two-year college puts a woman on a separate employment track at the outset that includes lower pay and much more limited prospects for promotion. This track is ostensibly based on the different type of education the person has received, but because the two-year colleges are typically all female, this generally means a separate career path for women. Those who do graduate from a four-year college are legally guaranteed the same promotion prospects as men according to Japan's equal opportunity laws, but the percentage of female managers in large firms is still miniscule relative to the number of male managers. During the economic doldrums of the 1990s, Japanese firms were quicker to lay off female employees, many of whom also conveniently tend to fall into temporary or part-time worker categories, and are seen as more expendable. Female unemployment is normally higher than male unemployment, and discrimination against working women is broadly recognized among the Japanese population by both genders.

TABLE 5-3. GENDER EQUALITY IN THE WORKPLACE

Men receive favorable treatment	*59.9 percent*
Men receive very favorable treatment	16.7 percent
Men receive somewhat favorable treatment	42.7 percent
Equal	*25.0 percent*
Women receive favorable treatment	*4.2 percent*
Women receive somewhat favorable treatment	0.5 percent
Women receive very favorable treatment	3.7 percent
Not sure	*11.3 percent*[19]

Not surprisingly, urban women in the 30 to 50 age bracket are most likely to respond that men receive favorable treatment.

There are a variety of social pressures that affect women as well. It was formerly all too common to hear of the "Christmas Cake" analogy, which suggested that a woman's value as a marriage partner decreases rapidly after the age of 25 (as in the price of the cake after the December 25). This notion has been largely superseded as more women have chosen to marry at a later age, but friends and family still remind unmarried women that delaying marriage and childbearing creates risks for both mother and child. Many women are still pressured both at home and at work to marry and retire (*kekkon taishoku*) once they are in their late 20s or have reached the age of 30, lest they be viewed as "losers" in the eyes of Japanese society.[20] Being a housewife and mother in Japan is seen a full-time job in itself, with some degree of status afforded to the position of *okusan* (homemaker). However, childcare resources are limited, and the ever-present neighbors in Japan's cramped living circumstances often frown on arrangements that do not involve care by immediate family members. Due to the demands of Japanese employers on male workers, married women are likely to face household and childrearing chores mostly on their own. While caring for their families, women face constant demands from schools, medical institutions, aging parents, and, for those who follow the traditional custom of moving in with the parents of a husband who is the eldest son, the exacting standards of a mother-in-law.

It is small wonder, then, that many women feel they must choose between a profession and motherhood, with these being mutually exclusive. One foreign financial firm with a large branch in Tokyo realized that it had a large number of female employees in key professional positions, including managerial roles. Some of these women were beginning to start families and have children, and the company was concerned about retaining these women as well as asking them to serve as role models for their younger female colleagues. As it cast about for positive examples in other organizations in Japan, the company concluded, regretfully, that there were few useful points of reference. It had to break new ground with its female employees to help them create a balance of work and family that had few Japanese precedents.

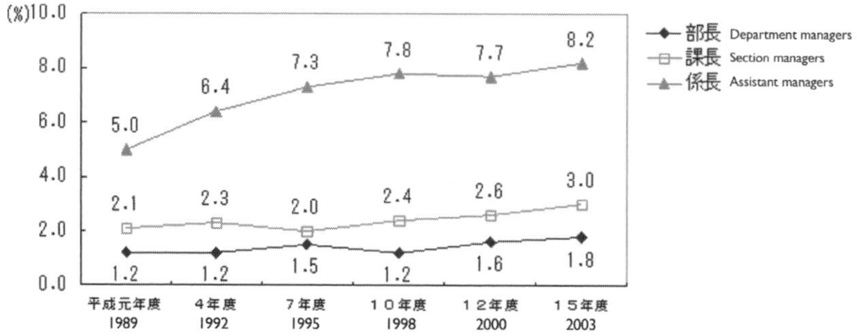

FIGURE 5-4. Percentage of Female Managers by Position[21]

Women who are not fortunate enough to obtain work with a progressive employer may still find themselves sidetracked into demanding but dead-end careers or encouraged in various subtle ways to move on as their male colleagues are promoted instead. Certain industries or professions such as medicine, social welfare, education, food preparation, hotels, and banking and insurance have been more open to female management than others. However, the overall number of women managers is still less than 6 percent of the total, and only 65 percent of enterprises indicate that they have female managers at all. Figure 5-4 shows a gradual upward trend in the numbers of female managers in three categories: assistant manager, section manager, and department manager. While there has been an increase in the number of assistant managers up to 8.2 percent of the total, section managers still number just 2 percent, and department managers 1.8 percent.

The major reasons offered by companies for the persistently small numbers of female managers seem to follow a circular catch-22 logic that raises questions about the future

- There are no female workers who have qualified knowledge, experience, and decision-making skills.
- There are female workers who may be promoted to managerial positions in the future; however, at this point, they have not worked long enough to be qualified for those positions.
- Female workers retire before they are qualified to apply for managerial positions.[22]

Keeping the limited prospects for advancement in mind, women may elect to postpone marriage indefinitely and work in less career-oriented jobs with the aim of maximizing opportunities for recreation, travel, and enjoyment. Given the custom of living with parents until marriage, which is reinforced by the high cost of urban housing, young women frequently have the luxury of using their own salaries as disposable income. Rather than seek satisfaction within the constraints of marriage or limited career prospects, they focus their energies instead on cultivating a pleasant and fashionable lifestyle in contrast to the steady toil of their parents' generation. High-heeled boots and less-than-enthusiastic attitudes toward marriage create an appearance of greater equality with men, even though the reality is still quite different.

There are practical impacts on Japanese society of changing women's lifestyles and attitudes toward careers and marriage. These include a later average age of marriage—now 27.6 years, as opposed to 24.2 in 1970, and delayed childbearing: the mean age of mothers at the birth of their first child is 28.9 at present versus 25.6 in 1970.[23] Laws designed to protect women and promote childbearing, such as providing extended leave for women who have given birth, can actually affect the employment prospects of women negatively, as companies realize that they will have to make allowances for women that are not necessary for men.

Gender: Workplace Implications

The disadvantages that women face in Japanese workplaces can be turned into advantages for employers who are able to understand and distinguish between the varying aspirations of individual female employees.

Foreign capital companies in Japan have found talented female employees to be a secret weapon in the local marketplace. Many women prefer non-Japanese companies on the grounds that they offer greater career prospects and more lifestyle flexibility. Firms such as Procter & Gamble have found that their female employees have keen insights into consumer markets along with excellent marketing and management skills. In some cases, traditionally minded male colleagues are reluctant to serve under women, but such attitudes can often be addressed by allowing men to observe global corporate norms in action, and reassuring them that merit-based standards will prevail.

Another contingent of female employees regards work primarily as a means to an end, and will happily leave their employers if a more attractive job appears elsewhere or if they find that they do not require the income. It is important for managers to be able to recognize both career-minded women and those who have other priorities, and to assist women who are still unsure about their future direction to sort out what potential options within the firm might exist. Women who have been socialized to be less assertive than their male counterparts may appreciate coaching, mentorship, and additional forms of support when stepping in to managerial roles. Others, particularly those with experience abroad, can overcompensate and become very aggressive in reaction to the conformist standards of the social context around them—it is important that they, too, receive feedback that is both honest and constructive.

Organizational Affiliation

Japan has traditionally been known as a society of group-oriented individuals and of institutions that demand the full energies and allegiance of their members. While many aspects of Japanese society are changing, people are still "branded" according to their institutional affiliations, and these brands, widely recognized within Japan, shape the social pecking order.

University Networks

Although there are various connotations attached to one's age, place of origin, and gender, the most defining stamp on a young adult's career is university affiliation. It has long been considered most desirable to graduate from a renowned Japanese four-year university, although time overseas is encouraged at other points in one's educational career. High school students travel abroad in large numbers for homestay visits, and many Japanese attend graduate school at foreign universities. Undergraduate diplomas from overseas schools, however, are frequently regarded as a possible sign that a person was not able to compete effectively in the Japanese educational system.

College ties are important to people in many countries, but in Japan they often last a lifetime, with Old Boy meetings of graduates from the same university class still occurring regularly 40 years after graduation. A ready-made network of connections in the workplace is created through university contacts, both horizontally across different departments and vertically through links to both seniors (*sempai*) and juniors (*kohai*) in the organization. Customers and suppliers may share the same university background as well and provide each other special access and consideration even if ultimately decisions are made based on what is best for the business.

In Japan, a university label immediately conveys a particular image. To say that someone is *Todai,* or a graduate of Tokyo University, places that person at the top of the educational hierarchy and labels him or her as a winner in Japan's rigorous competition for university entrance. Tokyo University graduates have often been designated for fast-track advancement toward upper management positions from the day they entered the company, based largely upon this school affiliation. In more popular terms, they are seen as very bright but also possibly deficient in social skills and awareness—a side effect of the intense preoccupation with study necessary to succeed on the university entrance exam. An unintentionally comic illustration of the power attributed to the *Todai* brand is narrated by a young woman: "I encountered a male student whom I had never seen before. He pulled out his student ID card from Tokyo University, held it up in front of my eyes, and asked me to go out for tea with him."

Kyodai, or Kyoto University, has a similarly prestigious connotation, except that it also marks one as possibly being from the Kansai region and perhaps having a special scientific or literary flair. Other university labels carry different meanings. Keio University, for example, is a famous private school in Tokyo with a liberal heritage and a strong economics and humanities curriculum; it is well known for producing graduates who are successful businesspeople. The archetypal Keio Boy is neat, snappily dressed in fashionable attire, and from a well-to-do family that perhaps provided him the chance to enter the primary school that is part of the

Keio system and offers a smooth path to admission to the university. The mention of Sophia University, a Catholic-run institution in Tokyo, brings to mind English-speaking returnees to Japan who have special insight into life outside of the country, but, for better or worse, may not have experienced a traditional Japanese upbringing.

Individuals who cannot claim affiliation to a university with a strong reputation are likely to want to avoid the question; when they do respond, they sometimes meet with a tactful but disappointed silence on the part of the questioner.

The list of top schools in Japan typically includes the following:[24]

Public Universities	*Private Universities*
Tokyo University	Keio University
Kyoto University	Waseda University
Osaka University	Sophia University
Tokyo Institute of Technology	International Christian University
Tohoku University	Meiji University
Kyushu University	Chuo University
Nagoya University	
Hokkaido University	
Tsukuba University	
Kobe University	

If public and private schools were ranked on the same list, probably only Keio and Waseda, among the private schools, would fall among the top ten. Other, smaller schools, both public and private, have strong reputations even though they are not listed with the biggest schools. Hitotsubashi University is one of the most prestigious among these, and ranks close to Tokyo University in the eyes of many. These rankings have changed little over the years—the universities at the top have remained there for decades. Tokyo University is strong not in just a few subjects, but has departments that are top-ranked in most areas.

Business: Reputation by Affiliation

As Japan moves beyond the circumstances that fueled its modern political and economic rise to world prominence, it is becoming increasingly important to understand how its enterprises and their employees differ, rather than what makes them similar. There are big differences in corporate culture and organizational systems that contribute to striking gaps in performance. Rather than a monolithic Japan Inc., with its legions of untiring workers formerly so feared and admired by foreigners, there has been a clear emergence of winners and losers among Japanese companies participating in the global economy. World-class enterprises such as Toyota or Canon are doing very well, while other entire industries such as retailing or construction languish.

The pecking order among schools is mirrored by the relative positions of different institutions or industries, by rankings within industries, and by positioning within major industrial families. Because of the tendency of Japanese organizations to become all-encompassing, demanding the full loyalties and energies of each individual, there may be little in the way of alternative affiliations that a person—particularly male employees—cultivates or is identified with. For many, the institution or company has become employer, social club, and church all wrapped up into one. There is little spare time for separate pursuits anyway.

Individual employees are labeled, in part, according to the type of institution they belong to. Until recently, top-ranking university graduates would enter one of the Japanese government's elite bureaucracies such as the Ministry of Finance, Ministry of Foreign Affairs, or the Ministry of Economy, Trade and Industry. Government posts have lost some of their cachet with the economic troubles of the last decade that have made them look much more fallible. Other occupations regarded as options for the elite include fast-track positions in trading companies, banking, electronics, automotive firms, or information technology. Each has its own image; for example, trading company employees are regarded as world travelers and astute businesspeople; the IT industry requires workers who are sophisticated and technical. Recently, it has become more fashionable for elite graduates to enter top foreign consulting firms such as McKinsey or Boston Consulting Group, and investment banking firms such as Goldman Sachs.

Joining a particular firm within an industry also influences individual perspectives and creates a series of associations in the minds of fellow Japanese about industry rankings, corporate culture, and career prospects related to business expansion. Each industry has its own relative positioning of different organizations. NTT (Nippon Telephone & Telegraph) heads up the telecommunications industry, Mitsubishi Trading ranks first among trading companies, NEC is the top computer firm, Toyota leads the automotive industry, and Sony is highly regarded for its innovative consumer electronics. The main industry players are remarkably durable. Over a period that saw the rise and fall of major U.S. computer firms such as Burroughs, Sperry, Wang, Digital, and Compaq, to name a few, the Japanese players continue to be companies like NEC, Fujitsu, and Toshiba. Relative market strength does shift among rival companies, but this tends to take place gradually, and social perceptions change even more slowly. Being employed with an industry leader lends prestige to its employees, while those who work with second- or third-ranked firms are also tagged with a label that reflects their employer's position. Corporate culture adds further character to the picture, even when employers are at the same level within their respective industries. For example, an individual who is part of NTT, the former government telecommunications monopoly and a secure, conservative employer, would be regarded very differently than someone employed at Sony, which is seen more as an organization of mavericks who have unique ideas for product development and marketing, although they may not always be commercially successful.

Within Japan's many conglomerates and large enterprises there is a hierarchy among member firms as well. An individual's sense of status and other people's attitudes toward him or her are further refined according to this internal hierarchy. In the case of the so-called horizontal *keiretsu,* with their maze of stock cross-holdings, giant banks and/or trading companies have normally occupied the central position, coordinating activities of hundreds of satellite companies. There have been other star firms in growth industries, such as NEC within the Sumitomo *keiretsu,* that take on prominent roles. Membership in one of these organizations, therefore, carries with it greater prestige than that afforded to a smaller, more peripherally positioned concern.

Vertically integrated *keiretsu* such as Toyota or Matsushita Electric have many layers of domestic and overseas branch offices and suppliers. Branch offices abroad typically hire people based upon local circumstances, and these are not regarded as core employees. Each successive layer of the supply chain, both in Japan and abroad, is likely to have not only lesser stature but also lower pay, reduced job security, and more part-time and temporary workers. Cutbacks in the work of lower-ranking members of this type of vertical organization serve as a safety valve for easing financial pressure during troubled times. In distressed firms, workers at the bottom of the social pyramid are subject to very difficult conditions, and foreign or illegal workers may be harshly exploited.

Challenges to Corporate Affiliation

Japan's organizational hierarchy in both education and business has been fueled by people's desire to join prestigious institutions and thereby receive the perceived benefits of such affiliations; this structure also depends upon at least tacit assent among people on the lower rungs of the system that the whole arrangement is fair and appropriate. However, the established system is being challenged from multiple directions by entrepreneurs and part-time workers who both reject more traditional corporate paths.

Until recently, entrepreneurship was not a fashionable career choice, with the most talented young workers generally opting for employment with large firms that provide the advantages of elite affiliation. However, the stunning success of youthful Internet entrepreneurs such as Hiroshi Mikitani, founder of the online shopping mall called Rakuten, has sparked the interest of a much wider group of people in joining startup firms. Employment in a small company once suggested that an individual had no other alternatives or was obliged to join a family business, but thanks to these kinds of business growth stories, entrepreneurial activity in industries with attractive future prospects is gaining greater prestige.

The *freeter,* or part-time workers, represent a whole class of younger

Japanese who have elected for various reasons to avoid or live on the edges of the country's corporate system. While working at jobs in the omnipresent convenience stores or fast-food chains, many of them live at home with their parents as "parasite singles" and thereby minimize living expenses. Their numbers have been growing rapidly, from approximately 500,000 in the early 1980s to anywhere between two and four million today—at least a fourfold increase.[25]

If the *freeter* and their more troubling dropout cousins the NEET are this generation's alternative to the diligent salaryman, their easygoing lifestyle represents a slap in the face to the work ethic and status consciousness of their elders. Older people without work have been known to don their work clothes and ride the subways aimlessly in order to avoid the shame of appearing to be unemployed. The goals of the *freeter* seem to include greater self-expression, more time with friends, and the freedom to define their own course in life without having it dictated by a suffocating institution.

One Web-based commentary provides an insight into the *freeter* mindset that seems to reject both Japan's quest for global economic prowess and the need to climb the corporate ladder, favoring individual self-expression instead:

> SMAP, perhaps Japan's most famous pop group, closed the show with last year's best-selling song, *Only One Flower in the World.* The song was popular among antiwar demonstrators, but more than anything else it struck a chord here by asking, "Why do we want to be No. 1 when each of us is different?"[26]

Japan's diligent Institute of Labor (no *freeter* employed there) has actually classified *freeter* into three types: the "moratorium type," the "dream-pursuing type," and the "no alternative type." Some prefer to put off entrance into the corporate world to avoid the pressures for conformity faced by more career-minded peers, others have plans for travel or hobbies that would not be possible in a full-time job, and still others do not have the skills or the education that selective employers desire. Delayed marriage, fewer children, progressively greater unemployability with age, smaller pensions, and higher social costs are all listed by critics as possible consequences of the *freeter* lifestyle.[27] At the same time, the average *freeter* work week of 4.9 days suggests that this is a relatively mild form of rebellion—it is hard to become overly concerned about the work ethic of a generation when even those labeled as slackers are working more than full-time employees in many countries.[27]

In truth, the *freeter* probably represent positive, as well as negative, impulses of Japan's younger citizens, and they no doubt have sympathizers even among employees of mainline companies. Their search for individual expression and affirmation of diversity could eventually serve as a welcome tonic for corporations and for fellow employees who have lost their way in a world where unlimited growth and Japanese economic leadership cannot be realistically expected to continue. But if the *freeter* phenomenon turns toward a narcissistic lifestyle that does not grapple with larger social realities in Japan and the rest of the world, it will ultimately not provide the solutions and fresh thinking that the country so desperately needs.

Organizational Affiliation: Workplace Implications

Here again it is necessary for companies to carry out a balancing act—in this case, between more traditional, status-minded employees and those with unorthodox backgrounds. Companies that can mix respectable positioning with youthfulness and innovation will not only have the best of both worlds, but also make a major contribution in helping to set Japan's future course.

- College graduates or mid-career hires with elite university backgrounds and experience outside of Japan have much to offer, including vital ties with customers and government ministries. Their university connections provide built-in business networks for those who know how to tap them.
- Companies that bring in mid-career hires from a variety of different enterprises may find that it is a challenge to meld these people into one group. Personal and social affiliations with a particular corporate culture or the status level of a previous employer are

difficult to leave behind, and organizations must consider ways to unify their employees around a common set of goals.

- There are undoubtedly gifted individuals among those working in entrepreneurial startup ventures or even people who are currently classified as *freeter.* If given a chance, such individuals who have previously resisted affiliation with more-established companies could provide unique ideas and energy when their work tasks are linked with their personal interests. Foreign firms that do not promise lifetime employment or follow the rigid processes for hiring, training, and development characteristic of Japanese corporations may be in a position to leverage the dreams and imagination of those who have worked in startup environments, along with former *freeter* who are ready to embark on a career. Tailoring of job descriptions to individuals has long been a strength in Western companies accustomed to dealing with strong personalities, and the human resource systems that support this, such as dual ladder promotions, flexible employment arrangements, pay for performance, and sabbaticals or voluntary leave without pay may find increasingly fertile ground in Japan.

Applying Global Diversity: *Reviving Subsidiary Operations*

AGE

SITUATION:

You have recently come to Japan as the head of your company's local subsidiary. The previous country president, Mr. Kuramoto, had a prestigious university background and several decades of work experience with a large Japanese firm in your industry; he personally hired most of the members of your management team. The subsidiary has unfortunately suffered through several years of mediocre results, and your own boss at headquarters has told you that it is likely the operation will have to reduce headcount in order to take out cost unless it can quickly begin to grow again.

You would like to kick off a new era in the company's history that will restore it to a healthy growth mode, and have spent the first month speaking with customers and with individual employees to get their ideas. You have heard complaints from inside the company that the former management structure favored people with seniority and a background that included ties to the "right" university or company as a previous employer. Junior employees have voiced ideas about products and services that you do not see reflected in the subsidiary's overall strategy, and they seem less than enthusiastic about the current direction, which they regard as overly conservative. You are becoming concerned that there are significant rifts between your senior and junior employees, and are looking for ways to create a greater sense of alignment and unity across the organization.

POSSIBLE SOLUTIONS:

There is not likely to be a single quick fix for creating a stronger sense of unity between different age groups within the company or a revival of the business, but here are a few steps that would be worth considering:

- Devote your first few months on the job to getting to know people at all levels of the organization as well as customers. Before arranging meetings with lower level employees, it is usually wise to ask their direct managers for permission to hold these skip-level meetings. Seek out people inside and outside of the company who have the experience and balanced judgment to offer good advice.
- Explain to your senior management team your desire to create greater organizational unity and receptivity to the ideas of employees of all ages, and request their cooperation and suggestions. It is best to get them involved and invested in proposing solutions.
- Participate in social events that involve employees of different ages, and promote informal communication on such occasions; respect the desire of some younger people to limit their company social commitments after hours by finding times and venues based on their suggestions.
- Initiate a company "change or die" effort that makes the formal business case for change very clear and incorporates ideas from all levels of the organization; give your highest potential leadership candidates key roles and pursue a focused set of objectives that become the top organizational priorities.

- Appoint teams of younger employees to work with markets or customer segments that they have the expertise to serve; encourage them to implement their ideas by having them report to one of your most flexible managers and giving them broad latitude to engage in low-cost experiments.
- Incorporate a "reverse mentor" program that taps younger people with specialized skills such as IT to serve as mentors to more senior employees who may lack these skills.
- Try to determine over time the extent to which each of your senior managers really adds value to the organization and is willing to support change, or if some have an inflexible authoritarian style and outmoded attitudes that are no longer a good fit. Tactfully ease long-serving but inflexible senior managers into honorary positions with a face-saving title and/or hold fair and honest performance management conversations that encourage underperformers to take advantage of a voluntary retirement package.
- Accelerate the promotion of younger people to management positions based on clearly recognized standards of performance, including their contributions to team efforts.

Summary Recommendations

1. Be aware of the **age** differences between employees. Find ways to ensure that younger people continue to enter the organization, and ensure that a youthful perspective is represented even if the number of younger people is smaller than that of older workers. Consider leveraging the diverse age groups within the company to determine what products and services are likely to appeal to their social peers.

2. Balance the requirement for a presence in Tokyo with business opportunities in other **regions.** Keep in mind that many rural areas are eager to have foreign company participation and are willing to offer incentives, although their residents may be more traditional in their outlook. Tap urban job markets to find Japanese with extensive overseas experience, as well as locally based foreigners familiar with both Japanese and non-Japanese business practices, to serve in bridging roles.

3. Beyond hiring capable, career-oriented women, there is a large opportunity for companies that are willing to work with their female employees to solve social dilemmas related to **gender** differences. Such issues currently force many women to leave jobs they enjoy in order to have a family or to conclude that placing a priority on one's career makes family life impossible. Because there are few successful precedents for firms that have been able to create a meaningful place for women in responsible roles from recruitment through retirement, those who make progress in this area are likely to reap large benefits as employers of choice for gifted women.

4. **Organizational affiliation** places a pronounced and durable stamp on people's lives in Japan. The public image of an organization can serve as a source of pride and a sign of success in the marketplace that helps to shape future achievements. It is also important to know that previous affiliations may become a source of divisiveness if people from many different backgrounds are gathered together to form a new entity. Companies should work toward enhancing the identity conveyed by their own stamp while bringing in new workers with fresh ideas. These could include people with entrepreneurial startup experience or perhaps even former *freeter* who are sufficiently independent-minded that they can offer a fresh perspective without being overly swayed by status considerations.

CHAPTER 6

Diversity in Mexico

Rossana Miranda-Johnston

Why Mexico?

- Mexico's economy ranks tenth in the world in terms of GDP; it is about 20 percent larger than the economy of Brazil.[1]
- Mexico attracts the third largest flow of foreign direct investment (FDI) worldwide and ranks number one in Latin America.
- With a population of over 100 million people, and almost a third of its people still under the age of 15, Mexico has a large and rapidly growing workforce.
- Mexico has trade treaties with more than 40 countries including its neighbors in Central America, the European Free Trade Area, Canada, the United States, and Japan; more than 90 percent of its trade is handled under free trade agreements.
- More than 25,000 foreign companies have affiliates in Mexico, the fifth highest number worldwide.

Introduction

The history and character of Mexico is a story of the blending of cultures and peoples: the indigenous population, Spaniards, blacks, and others. Pride in the country's heritage is often coupled with distress over the current economic situation for many of its inhabitants. People of mixed descent, particularly those of *mestizo,* or indigenous and Spanish background who comprise more than one-half of the total population, are the norm in Mexico to the extent that actual diversity is often overlooked or minimized. Mexico's diversity comes in a variety of forms that include:

- Socioeconomic Status
- Race and Ethnicity
- Gender
- Regional Origin

Each of these dimensions has an impact on Mexican society in terms of access to power, wealth, and opportunities. In this chapter we will examine the impact of these diversity dimensions on the day-to-day work life of a foreign businessperson who seeks to understand and work successfully within the Mexican business environment.

Socioeconomic Status

Mexico is a society dramatically divided by economic power. A businessperson visiting Mexico City will notice upscale houses and expensive cars along with makeshift tents and people living in the streets. Mexico City provides an extreme example of the coexistence between rich and poor, and yet it is also mirrors the rest of the country. With an estimated GDP per capita of $9,000, according to the indicators of the *Gap between Rich and Poor: World Income Inequality* report, Mexico ranks fifteenth on the list of countries with the highest degree of inequality. The report shows 57.4 percent of the nation's income concentrated in the top 20 percent of the nation's population, with only 3.5 percent for the lowest 20 percent of the population.[2]

A recent World Bank report indicated that in 2002 one-half of the population of Mexico lived in poverty, and one-fifth in extreme poverty.[3] Daily life for people at the bottom of the socioeconomic ladder is very difficult, with limited access to basic social services and infrastructure such as healthcare, housing, transportation, potable water, sewage treatment, or electricity. Despite the right to free education, educational opportunities for the poor tend to be limited due to isolation, the low quality of the public school system (principally in the elementary to middle school levels), and the need for young people to work to help their families survive. It is very difficult, although not impossible, to climb up the steep socioeconomic ladder. For many Mexicans at the lower economic levels, the way up the ladder is through emigration to the United States. Mexico is the largest source of immigrants to the United States, with 9.8 million Mexicans comprising 30 percent of the foreign-born population there (this number includes only first-generation Mexican immigrants).[4]

There is a significant difference between the lifestyle and opportunities of the lower class and those of the middle and upper classes. Typical higher-class lifestyles may include international travel, overseas study, servants and comfortable living, private schools, and luxury cars. Even though the life of Mexico's upper classes has been impacted by the country's economic crises over the past 20 years, there is still a wide gap between the "haves" and "have-nots." Members of Mexico's middle class fill the ranks of corporations and government ministries, and own or work in small- to medium-sized businesses. Many of them have struggled to regain financial stability and a return to a more comfortable lifestyle after years of economic setbacks. Social mobility for the middle class depends on contacts, opportunities, and, of course, education. Emigration to the United States, a drastic move that historically had been made primarily by Mexico's poorer residents, has been on the increase for this segment of the population.

The upper class is an elite segment of the Mexican population. Those seen as upper class are not necessarily the richest—although wealth is an important factor in social class level; they also have a distinct ancestry that can be traced back to Mexico's Spanish colonial days. A prestigious family background frequently provides more power than does money in the upper social circles. Many can climb the economic ladder and get very close to upper-class status, but financial assets alone are not enough to buy acceptance. Sophistication, education, and a well-known family name and history are the most essential traits. Over the past half-century or more, the Mexican upper class has accepted with certain reservations the new rich who have gained their fortunes through political positions and capitalist enterprises.

Members of Mexico's highest classes are likely to receive their education in some of the best schools in the world, speak at least French and English in addition to Spanish, and have a conservative ideological perspective that supports their affluent status. A premium is placed upon refined dress and etiquette. Upper-class Mexicans may choose to be involved in the family business, politics, the arts, or simply to administer the family fortune. Sporting pastimes are common and include golf, tennis, and polo along with other equestrian activities. People at this socioeconomic level frequently have second or third homes throughout Mexico, the United States, or in Europe. Certain surnames are immediately recognized as evidence of an elite family background. Some are double last names such as Sanchez Navarro, Rincon Gallardo and Garza Sada. Other current elite surnames that are immediately recognized in the upper circles are Carral, Terrazas, Azcarraga, Corcuera, Bailleres, Yglesias, and O'Farrill.

It is interesting to note the popularity of the famous Spanish socialite magazine *Hola* across all social classes in Mexico. Although it is an expensive purchase for many Mexicans, even many lower-middle-class housewives buy it regularly. What do struggling Mexican women of modest means see in a magazine that depicts the life of European royalty and the world's upper classes? They look at the colorful pictures attentively and admiringly. Later, some of them will go to a store and buy an expensive European brand product displayed in the magazine, while others will buy an imitation for a fraction of the price. There seems to be a link between famous brand names and personal aspirations that is important among Mexicans of different social levels. Such brands are associated with social class, and many want to be seen wearing a brand that raises their own image. Right or wrong, it is expected that this will help them gain admiration and respect from others.

Socioeconomic Status: Implications for Foreign Businesspeople

Mexico is a class-oriented society and, in turn, these classes shape economic opportunities and expected behaviors. Consciously or unconsciously, Mexicans visually screen each other using a set of social filters and treat each other according to those perceptions. Many international companies operating in Mexico and many mid- and high-ranking Mexican companies employ elite upper- and middle-class Mexicans in their executive ranks. Their level of education and lifestyle in many cases is beyond the experience of a middle-class individual from the United States, Canada, or Europe. The foreign businessperson may try to "do the right thing"—what would be appropriate in his or her own country—while inadvertently violating social class protocol and expectations.

The emphasis on social class level and status in Mexico can be uncomfortable for egalitarian foreigners who are used to more solidly middle-class societies where differences in status are not as obvious. A foreign executive shares this story.

> I was at a high-level business lunch in Mexico City, seated in the place of honor as the senior ranking executive from the corporate office, so I was very visible to the rest of the group. Unfortunately, everyone noticed my table manners, which were acceptable in the informal environment I was used to back in my home office, yet too casual and informal for the level of protocol required by this occasion in Mexico. I found out later that people were genuinely confused by the lack of consistency between my executive level and my behavior at that luncheon.

The foreign executive had not observed the proper meal etiquette that was expected of a person of his rank. He did not put his cloth napkin on his lap, he used his utensils improperly, he spoke with food in his mouth, and his clothing (casual pants and a shirt with no tie) was too informal for the occasion.

Protocol and manners are more than just social graces; they are interpreted as a window into a person's socioeconomic level and family upbringing. The terms used among Mexicans, *gente bien* (right people), or the *naco* (equivalent to unpolished), describe the extremes. Consistency between social level and behavior is important in the Mexican business environment and extends to proper dress and overall comportment. Attention to quality of clothing, shoes, and accessories all make a statement about who you are and where you fit into the hierarchy. Behavior that is polite and not too casual contributes to your level of credibility.

In the urban corporate environment, for example, Mexicans tend to rank each other by the quality of their clothing and the accessories they wear, the schools they come from, the companies they have worked at, the physical attractiveness of the person, the connections they have, the prestige associated with last names, and status and rank within the organization. The "haves" usually wear high-quality suits or dresses and accessories, come from recognized schools, may have good corporate and government connections and important last names (this is more important in the elite upper class), and have a high-ranking position at work. The "have-nots" do their best to achieve a formal appearance and demeanor within their means; they have a basic education, and usually occupy lower-level positions such as office boy, driver, or janitor. Members of the middle classes strive somewhat more successfully to maximize their status through emulating the trends set by those at the top. A Mexico City bank worker was quoted saying, "I spend almost a quarter of my monthly paycheck on work clothes. I am not a fashion victim. I would rather spend it on a car. I do it to keep up appearances, and that's the reality of our corporate society."[5] People at the middle levels in the manufacturing industry, advertising media professionals, and some IT workers usually have more relaxed dress standards.

U.S. executives often face a unique challenge, since they may frame their perceptions of Mexican businesspeople based on perceptions or experiences with Mexican immigrants in the United States. As stated earlier, the majority of Mexican immigrants in the United States come from Mexico's lower economic levels, and the ordinary profile of a Mexican businessperson in a managerial role is from the middle- and upper-economic levels. A U.S. businessperson must often shift his or her expectations to take into account expected behaviors among different social classes.

Foreign businesspeople might also notice the impact of social class on perceived levels of influence. In the Mexican workplace, people understand "who is who" in terms of social class and influence. Once people learn that a particular individual is upper class or is related to the owners, important executives, or directors of the company, this person will be treated with special deference. The opposite may also take place; a person without much influence could be ignored unless he or she stands out of the crowd for other reasons such as personality, hard work, or proven capabilities. The foreign businessperson without a Mexican cultural background may be better able to see the potential in people at all levels than Mexicans themselves. This can lead to difficult choices about whether to reinforce the status quo or to violate it in order to serve a different set of values. But knowledge of Mexico's social stratification can at least help to make this choice deliberate and strategic rather than accidental.

The foreign manager belongs to an intangible level of his or her own. As part of the global professional ranks, this unique status places the foreign businessperson at an upper level with all the implications and expectations that it entails. In part, this person is expected to behave according to upper-class Mexican standards, and, in part, anything can be expected from a foreigner. Generally, there is an ambivalent feeling toward foreigners who come to work in Mexico, and the way they behave will determine if they fall into the desirable or undesirable category. Demonstrating courtesy and proper manners and dressing in a manner that is appropriate for different occasions are ways to show commitment to the business relationship, while also earning greater tolerance for those times when the foreigner chooses to introduce a new idea or business practice.

Because personal relationships are such an important part of Mexican culture, the cordiality with which people treat one another is sometimes described as being *bien educada*—well educated is the literal translation, although the meaning is closer to well mannered. Social manners as part of education is something Mexicans learn at home and consider essential to human interactions. Many people, even those who have no formal education, yet possess the proper social graces, are still considered "educated" in the sense of being well mannered.

The gap between workers with different status levels and education may affect organizational performance. Plans that have been conceived at higher levels of an organization are often not implemented because instructions from managers and the steps necessary to put the plan into practice have not been clearly transmitted. The hierarchical nature of most companies in Mexico creates an atmosphere that can discourage individual initiative at the lower levels without management approval—employees at the lower levels of the organization may expect to be told what to do. If individual accountability is required, it is important to make that clear and put a system in place to support it.

Race and Ethnicity

Contemporary Mexico was created through the mixture of two distinct cultures, the indigenous and the Spanish. In this blending, these dramatically different civilizations created a new culture—*mestizo* (mixed). Yet despite the fact that four out of five Mexicans define their background as *mestizo*, race and skin color are complex and often taboo subjects.

In order to understand the dimension of race and ethnicity in Mexico, a historical perspective is useful. Prior to the arrival of European colonists, Mexico's indigenous cultures were sophisticated and highly developed. Two examples of the many indigenous cultures are the Maya and Aztec civilizations. The Mayan civilization developed a numerical system that led to advancements in engineering, astronomy, and calendaring. Mayan priests combined mathematics and astronomy to develop a solar calendar that was more accurate than that being used in Europe. The Aztec civilization and others who came before them realized tremendous achievements in architecture and engineering, which included building great pyramids.[6]

Mexico's indigenous cultures were devastated during the colonization by the Spaniards. Scholars estimate that the population of indigenous cultures in Mexico decreased from 25 million to one million following colonization.[7] For those who survived, the social hierarchy was completely changed. During the colonial era, there was a clear hierarchy of status and privilege directly linked to race, as illustrated in Table 6-1.

As captured in the paintings and readings of the era, Colonial Mexico had a rigid hierarchical system in which the people at the higher social levels were the white Europeans, or Mexicans closely related to Europeans, and the indigenous people were poorer and practiced lowly trades. The European standards became the ideal of power, beauty, distinction, and value that to some extent still apply today. Growing up in Mexico, one quickly learns that the lighter the skin and the more European the features, the better. One hears expressions such as *a pesar de ser morena es guapa* (despite the fact of being brown she is attractive); or mothers may urge children not to spend too much time in the sun because of the risk of getting darker. Middle-class *mestizo* families tend to be quick to point out their Spanish background

TABLE 6-1. COLONIAL ERA: MEXICO'S SOCIAL HIERARCHY

European-born Spaniards	Called *peninsulares* at that time, even though they comprised only 1 percent of the population, they had complete control over all of the top positions in the government, army, church, and universities.
Mexican-born Spaniards	Called *criollos* at that time, many were professionals: lawyers, physicians, teachers, and priests.
Mestizos	A mix of Spaniard and indigenous people, at that time they formed the lower middle class: a few had minor government positions, others were ranch, mine, or factory foremen, and some were shopkeepers and farmers.
Indigenous	Indigenous people formed the lowest level of society: manual labor.

Source: Miller, Robert Ryal. 1985. *Mexico: A History*. Norman: University of Oklahoma Press. 138–141. Reprinted with permission.

and avoid discussion of their indigenous heritage. The indigenous part of that *mestizo* identity tends to be excluded and denied despite its overt presence. One of the worst insults among Mexicans is to call each other *Indio* (indigenous person), a term loaded with discriminatory tones and contempt. Many people associate this term with backwardness, ignorance, and poverty.

The contrast between the glorious indigenous past and the stark reality of many indigenous peoples today in Mexico is tragic, yet pervasive. There is genuine pride in the remarkable cultures and civilizations of Mexico's pre-Columbian past, those great civilizations that are on display at the National Museum of Anthropology and History in Mexico City. However, the descendants of these great people often exist at the margins of society, begging on the streets or selling their goods barefooted. Mexican anthropologist Guillermo Bonfil Batalla writes, "The unavoidable presence of our Indian legacy is a mirror in which we don't want to see ourselves."[8]

The National Commission for the Development of Indigenous Peoples recognizes 53 indigenous groups and 62 languages dispersed throughout Mexico. Depending on the region of the country, you may hear one or several of these languages in areas where indigenous people live and work. Of the more than six million indigenous language speakers, the highest concentrations are found in the southern states (Oaxaca, Chiapas, Guerrero, Yucatan) and in the central part of the country: (Hidalgo, Estado de Mexico, Puebla, San Luis Potosí, and Veracruz).[9]

The World Bank reports that 44 percent of the indigenous population in Mexico falls in the country's poorest income quintile.[10] When employed, the indigenous tend to have the lowest rank of employment and remuneration, working mainly in the farming or service sectors as laborers or servants in private houses, or selling whatever they can on the streets in the informal economy.

The *Zapatista* movement in the 1990s brought to the national public conscience issues of historic discrimination based on cultural differences, race, and gender. This movement was named for a land reform rebellion headed by Emiliano Zapata during the Mexican Revolution in the early 1900s; Zapata and his followers sought the redistribution of land from the upper classes to the Mexican peasants who actually worked the land yet received minimum benefits for their labor. The *Zapatista* movement in the twenty-first century is now an indigenous movement based in the southern state of Chiapas that has forced the government to recognize that racial and economic discrimination still exist. This movement became highly visible to the public on the first day of the implementation of the North American Free Trade Agreement (NAFTA), making the point that this treaty could exacerbate the income gaps and increase the misery of the Mexican poor.

After years of difficult and unfruitful negotiations between the Zapatistas and the Mexican State, the Zapatistas have implemented their own community development initiatives under the watchful eye of the Mexican authorities. Although the movement has faded somewhat in the media and public consciousness, it marked a historic event in that a social resistance movement comprised of many indigenous peoples struggling for more rights and greater self-determination brought these issues to the nation's highest legislative chambers for the first time in the history of modern Mexico.

Black Mexicans

Africans arriving with the Spaniards as slave labor added another element of diversity to Mexico. The African slaves mixed with the indigenous populations and quickly became part of the dark-skinned people of the new country. Even today, African features are apparent in Mexicans throughout the country. The states of Oaxaca, Guerrero, Veracruz, and Tabasco still have large populations of Afro-Mexicans. The presence and impact that Afro-Mexicans have had in the development of the country are rarely acknowledged in the historic records or by the general population. Most Mexicans do not even know there are Afro-Mexicans who have been part of their country for as many generations as their own *mestizo* ancestors. In the last 10 years, Afro-Mexicans, scholars, historians, and anthropologists have begun different initiatives to document, revive, and narrate the contributions of Afro-Mexicans to Mexican culture. In the national population census there is no current data that tracks the Afro-Mexican population. However, the community-based organization Afro-Mexico estimates that around four million, or less than 5 percent of the Mexican population, has some trace of African blood. Most Afro-Mexicans have suffered racism, prejudice, and discrimination for generations from all levels of society. Their most common reality is that their existence is denied and their presence ignored.

Immigrants

During colonial times and after independence, migration to Mexico was primarily from Spain. In fact, many senior-level executives in Mexico can trace their lineage directly back to Spanish immigrant ancestors. Other European nationalities, such as German, Italian, and French, are also part of the historical immigration patterns in Mexico.

Throughout the last century, several small and diverse waves of immigration have added to Mexico's cultural mosaic. Currently, the last names *Chin, Helou,* or *Warman* (Chinese, Lebanese, and Jewish) reflect other ethnic groups that have made Mexico their home for generations. Although smaller in numbers, the Lebanese and the Jewish communities play a very important economic role in Mexico. Many of their members are well-known entrepreneurs and professionals. Lebanese-Mexican Carlos Slim Helou's fortune reached the *Forbes* 2005 list, and the Associated Press places him as number four among the world's billionaires; actress Salma Hayek is another well-known Lebanese-Mexican. The Jewish population has also established its own communities, with schools, clubs, temples, and other social infrastructure. In the last 30 years, immigrants from South America and Cuba have also made their home in Mexico. There are approximately one million U.S. nationals who have retired in Mexico as well.[11]

Race and Ethnicity: Implications for Foreign Businesspeople

In 1999, former President Ernesto Zedillo hosted a television documentary entitled *Mexico: A Centuries Old Creation.* In this historic summary at the end of the twentieth century, he acknowledged the ethnic, racial, and cultural diversity that existed in colonial days and downplayed the problems. He stated, "In Mexico, with painful exceptions, the rule was inclusion and mix, not exclusion and prejudice . . ." This commentary summarizes the general position of the government with regard to cultural diversity in Mexico. By mentioning exceptions, Zedillo indirectly acknowledged some level of exclusion and prejudice, yet minimized the overall impact.

This example provides a framework for the typical response to racial issues in Mexico. Many Mexicans take great pride in principle in the concept of *La Raza Cosmica* (Cosmic Race) that celebrates the mixture of races that has characterized Mexico since the 1500s. The more complex issues related to race tend to be taboo. Mexicans typically do not talk about racial issues with foreigners or even among themselves, and they can become defensive when foreigners question their racial identity or possible prejudices. This means that foreign approaches to racial and ethnic diversity, with their penchant toward open dialogue and discussion of behaviors that reflect bias, may fall flat with Mexican audiences.

Socioeconomic class and race are often (but not always) intertwined in Mexico. The upper class is still mainly comprised of white Mexicans, mostly of European descent. The lower classes are mainly the darker brown indigenous, although one can find whites as well (but in very low proportion). The proverb *El indio aunque se vista de seda, indio se queda* (The indigenous, even if dressed in silk, remains indigenous), illustrates the reality that even when one achieves access to economic affluence, his or her social and racial identity often remain the same.

Clinical and social psychologist Jacqueline Fortes de Leff writes in her 2002 article "Racism in Mexico: Cultural Roots and Clinical Interventions," "Discrimination within family members is often rooted in racism that is embedded in culture and history. However, racism is not only expressed in open behavior, but also in subtle and sometimes invisible ways." She refers to this type of dynamic as "intrafamilial racism" and states, "People often erase any Indian (indigenous) trait in order to appear as a powerful white figure."[12]

A first-generation Mexican living in the United States shares this story.

> My family from Mexico visited me in Chicago for my wedding. This was a good opportunity to ask them about my extended family background and create a more detailed family tree. I only got as far back as my grandfather—who I was very close to growing up. He had very indigenous features and was very dark-skinned. My relatives informed me that he was not really my grandfather; my grandmother had an affair with a Spaniard and that was my true grandfather. What was interesting to me was how they told me this story—which was confirmed by my grandmother as true—with much pride and excitement since my lineage was more Spanish than indigenous.

Given this deep psychological impact of race and ethnicity, the subject will probably not be discussed voluntarily with foreign businesspeople. Foreigners in Mexico may experience this phenomenon more subtly in the form of individual attitudes or reactions to outsiders. Although these are broad generalizations that will not apply in all situations, perceived status related to European background could serve as an advantage to European businesspeople, while foreigners with indigenous backgrounds of their own might experience prejudice. The historically difficult relationship with the United States may be a disadvantage to those from the U.S. for reasons having to do with resentment of the powerful giant to the north. On the other hand, the many personal ties between those of Mexican descent in both countries are a source of deep and lasting commercial bonds.

The most effective approach for foreign businesspeople is to ask questions and learn more about Mexican history, the country's great indigenous cultures, and the unique blend that makes up Mexico today. Mexicans often feel that their important contributions to history are overlooked by foreigners. Appreciation and openness may eventually lead to honest conversations about the current challenges in Mexico that are related to the issue of race.

Gender

Mexican women have played important roles recorded in history since the days of the Spanish conquest. La Malinche, the indigenous translator and wife of Hernán Cortés, was an important influence in the early days of the Spanish colonization. In 1650, Poet Sor Juana Inés de la Cruz, considered the first feminist in Latin America, was defending Mexican women's right to education and to attain intellectual prowess. At the time of Mexican Independence in 1810 and in the days of the Revolution from 1910 to 1920, important women intellectuals, such as Josefa Ortiz de Dominguez, and female soldiers known as the *soldaderas* played significant roles in building the nation. Within indigenous communities, a number of matriarchal societies have always existed. However, in the Mexico of the twenty-first century, much work is still needed in order to formally and fully integrate women's potential contributions into the workplace.

In Mexico, gender inequity has been discussed publicly since the 1950s, with a number of female scholars expressing their opinions in magazines and at feminist meetings. In 1953, women were finally recognized as full citizens equal to men. Since the 1960s female-related issues such as discrimination in the workplace, domestic abuse, and reproductive rights have been acknowledged and brought to a level of national dialogue but not resolved. The 1970s feminist movement in the urban centers made it more acceptable for educated women to pursue a professional life. In the 1970s, other constitutional reforms further improved female participation in public life, health, the workplace, and education. Constitutionally, the Federal Employment Law protects women's rights, but these protections are often ignored with no consequences. The administration of President Fox established the General Directorate of Gender Equity; however, the objectives of this directorate have yet to be translated into practice in the workplace.[13]

The number of women in the workplace has increased significantly over the past 20 years. In 2002, women represented 34 percent of the economically active population in Mexico, an 80 percent increase from 1980.[14] Mexican women face similar challenges to those faced by most women around the world with regard to gender inequality. Although they are slowly changing, gender roles are strongly influenced by Mexican traditions. Men still have more opportunities in the workplace and are paid more than women. According to the Inter-American Commission of Women, average net income for Mexican women is approximately 35 percent lower than for men, and the top 10 percent of male salaries are 50 percent higher than the top 10 percent of female salaries.[15]

The tough economic challenges of the last 25 years have made two-salary homes the norm, and these economic changes have presented women with new challenges. Those with education and opportunity have thrived in this environment, while others with basic education and skills have fallen victim to new exploitation and abuse by domestic and international manufacturing companies, or *maquiladoras.* The Inter-American Commission of Women has identified the *maquila* industry as a particular area of concern for working women, and recently signed an agreement with the National Council of the *Maquila* Exporting Industry and the Ministry of Labor. By signing the agreement, these institutions committed themselves to improving labor conditions for women in the *maquila* industry.[16]

Unfortunately, females are still not seriously considered for many opportunities based on their gender, marital status, or family responsibilities. Their emotional and hormonal "sensitivities" are frequently used as excuses to exclude them from new positions and promotions. It is normal practice during hiring interviews to ask both females and males if they are married or have children. The response typically influences the prospects of a female candidate more than those of a male.

The proportion of administrative and managerial positions held by women has increased slightly, from 15 percent in the mid-1980s to 19 percent in the mid-1990s. The numbers are still low and this indicator does not measure the actual decision-making power of women in these job roles, as the occupations include a range of responsibility levels. Women tend to be employed in jobs where the responsibility level is lower.[17]

Although Mexican males are not the copyright holders of *machismo* in the world, *machismo* is part of the daily dynamic between men and women. Some men define their maleness based on their capacity to seduce women or in their bravery and capacity to challenge other men; the workplace is no exception. Mexican society, including the workplace, has a high tolerance for sexually charged advances. It is not uncommon in an office environment to find that certain males are courting women and sharing their stories with one another in the lunchroom. But *machismo* does not have to have blatant sexual overtones only. In one *maquiladora* situation, a foreign manager reports that a senior male union representative refused to deal with a female representative and told him, "I don't work with women." This attitude can still be found mainly among the older generation of workers and in traditionally male job enclaves.

Machismo and discrimination against women differ in other ways by age and social class. Some middle- and upper-class people in the newer generation of professionals (20 to 35 years old) are more aware of the negative impact of these kinds of behaviors and are acting to change societal norms. Young males are becoming more involved in childcare and household chores when their wives have work-related responsibilities. The 2000

Census of the National Institute of Statistics, Geography and Informatics (INEGI) reported an increase in male participation in household chores from 39.2 percent in 2000 to 65.2 percent in 2004, with an average of 10 hours per week. Female participation in the same tasks has constantly been over 90 percent, with 96 percent participation in 2004 and an average of 31 hours per week.[18]

Occasionally, females are now earning higher salaries than men. This new phenomenon can bring tension to the traditional family dynamic, in which the man was expected to be the breadwinner. Some couples are able to reconcile this challenge, while in others the female has to step back when her professional advancement complicates her family situation. One can still hear working Mexican women say, "My husband allows me to work," an expression that reflects the prevalent attitudes between genders.

In contrast to the work environment, at home Mexican women are known for their power in the family. Women in the roles of wife and mother have great influence in family decision making, and men typically elevate women's position to a higher status in family situations. The wife of an executive, for example, is an important element of the success of the executive, as she is involved with social events related to business. Even though the role of women at home is stronger, females may still operate in a more indirect manner so that the power of the male householder is not challenged. It is suggested that Mexican women are more used to working behind the scenes than other Latin American women. In Mexico, a more submissive attitude exists among women at the lower economic and educational levels.[19]

As Mexican women carve their places in the professional world, many are following traditional male patterns as the path to success. Others try to establish a careful balance between their own job responsibilities and maintaining gender harmony. Mexican women often have to work harder than men to prove their capacity and experience. Concrete, positive outcomes must be evident for women to prove themselves and to establish leadership. Talking about his female boss, a Mexican executive was quoted as saying, "They know she delivers as much or more than any man, although many people fear her because she is tough. But that is why she is successful." Often, younger people lack role models and support networks for female success. Overall, current expectations of the role of women are slowly shifting to include more significant workplace responsibilities.

Gender: Implications for Foreign Businesspeople

Attitudes toward women are changing in Mexico, but the situation varies greatly depending on social class, age, industry, and region of the country. In the service, finance, and technology sectors and in urban centers such as Mexico City and Monterrey, women in the workplace tend to be more accepted. In manufacturing, women in senior-level positions are unusual and may be met with resistance; more rural areas may be less accustomed to women in business roles.

Many foreign businesspeople will encounter Mexican women in business. In fact, the female Mexican workforce is a huge asset for foreign companies. Because of the limits imposed on them through the nature of hierarchies in Mexican enterprises, Mexican women tend to thrive in foreign companies. Global companies managed by foreign expatriates are attractive avenues for the new generations of educated Mexican women who believe that these companies are more open and supportive of female development. Overseas opportunities with foreign firms are also good opportunities for Mexican women who see such experience as necessary to learn how to deal with current global trends.

One area of potential challenge for foreign businesswomen is sexual harassment. A foreign businesswoman recently observed that, "Actions that may be considered sexual harassment in some countries should be taken in stride in Mexico, a land where political correctness has yet to take hold." The Mexican *macho*-man image implies the ability to court and seduce women regardless of their social status or the context of the interaction. The same foreign businesswoman in Mexico continues, "Women in business in Mexico have to behave professionally and conventionally . . . It is a delicate boundary that she has to establish . . . She, and only she, can establish how far men can go." Men, on many occasions, may comment on a woman's good looks, open car or room doors for her, carry heavy articles, or escort her as she crosses the street. In Mexico, these are all considered courteous manners.

Regional Origin

Regional origin adds another element of diversity in Mexico. The World Bank indicates that 75 percent of the population of Mexico is urban and 25 percent is rural.[20] The economic and development model Mexico has followed concentrates the highest levels of development and economic opportunity in large cities such as Mexico City, Guadalajara, and Monterrey (see Figure 6-1). The General Agreement on Trade and Tariffs (GATT) in the 1980s, NAFTA in the 1990s, and other global economic trends have brought new economic development opportunities and challenges to the border corridors in the free trade zone with the United States and the southern cities that now house large manufacturing and high-tech industries.

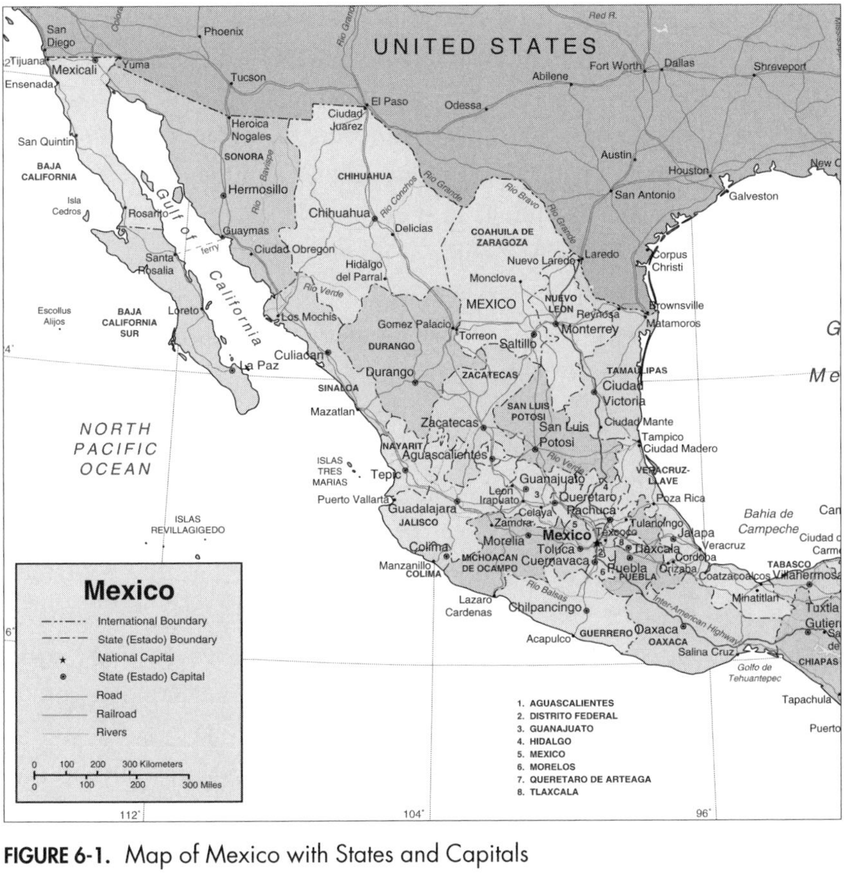

FIGURE 6-1. Map of Mexico with States and Capitals

The 31 states that comprise Mexico have different levels of development ranging from a high concentration of industrial activity in the northern part of the country—the state of Nuevo León for example—to less in the south—in states such as Oaxaca, Chiapas, or Yucatán. Centrally located, Mexico City, with a population of more than 20 million people, or 21 percent of the total Mexican population, has attracted millions of *provincianos* (people from the interior) from all walks of life, creating a metropolis of great complexity.

Personal introductions among Mexicans generally involve each person asking where the other person comes from, sometimes prompted by the different regional accents of Mexican Spanish. People from smaller cities or towns may have limited exposure to worldly realities of the big cities. Big-city people are perceived as sophisticated versus the more conservative *provincianos* (provincials) or the naïve and unsophisticated *rancheros* from the more rural areas. Depending upon the perceived level of sophistication, assumptions may be made about what to expect, or not to expect, from people based on where they were raised or what their place of origin is.

There are general perceptions about people from the different regions and, of course, many exceptions to these general statements. Northerners from the states of Chihuahua, Coahuila, Durango, Sinaloa, and Nuevo León, are sometimes labeled with the stereotypes of cowboys or drug smugglers. *Norteños* (northerners) are also known for their thriftiness, hard-work ethic, direct communication style, and lack of sophistication. The influence of the United States is strong, with many Spanish slang words derived from English that are not used or understood in more central or southern states. The Spanish language in the northern states has its peculiar accent, which varies from state to state. Among the northern states, Nuevo León is in a category of its own because its capital, Monterrey, is an industrious city nationally known as a business and educational center. Monterrey is the home of world-class companies such as CEMEX and Modelo, as well as the main campus of the best private Mexican university, the Instituto Tecnológico y de Estudios Superiores de Monterrey, better known as TEC de Monterrey.

In terms of religion, the growth of Protestantism and Evangelism is more predominant in the northern U.S.-Mexican border region and the southern and southeast Mexican states. As a whole, Mexico remains 76 percent Catholic, and Catholicism continues to be an important unifying force among different regions of the country.[21]

The central part of the country, which includes the States of Jalisco, Guanajuato, Querétaro, Aguascalientes, Michoacán, and Puebla is generally well developed and the people are known for their industriousness, skilled agricultural practices, and conservative Catholic beliefs. Mexico City and the state of Mexico are by far the most developed areas in the country. *Chilangos* (a slang word to refer to people from Mexico City) are often perceived as arrogant by people in other regions. *Chilangos Light* (in English) is used sarcastically to refer to people from Guadalajara, who purportedly attempt to imitate real *chilangos.*

During the year 2000, 62 percent of Mexico's GNP was generated by Mexico City, the State of Mexico, Nuevo León, Jalisco, Chihuahua, Veracruz, Puebla, and Guanajuato.[22] These mostly central and northern states year after year bear the heaviest weight of economic productivity in the service and manufacturing sectors. The state of Veracruz is part of the group of oil-rich states in southern Mexico together with Chiapas, Campeche, and Guerrero. These four states, rich in natural resources, score among the lowest in infrastructure and development and highest in poverty levels despite the fact that they house the largest company at the heart of the Mexican economy—Petróleos Mexicanos, or PEMEX. Since its beginnings, PEMEX has been filled with inefficiency and corruption and has been inclined to make political and nationalistic decisions rather than competitive ones. These realities have fueled the discontent of many of the indigenous peoples of these regions and has enticed them to participate in armed rebellions to protest their situation.

The southern states of Yucatán, Tabasco, Oaxaca, Chiapas, Quintana Roo, and Guerrero are known for their relaxed attitude and slow rhythm of life, although this is changing rapidly with the relocation of many manufacturing plants to lower-wage labor centers such as Yucatán. Due to their proximity to the Gulf of Mexico, states such as Veracruz, Yucatán, and Quintana Roo have a closer cultural connection with some Caribbean and Central American countries than the rest of Mexico, which is reflected, for example, in their cuisine and accent. *Tierra Caliente* (hot coastal lands) is a Mexican regional distinction that includes the coastal parts of the states of Guerrero, Michoacán, and Oaxaca.

There are certain light rivalries among the regions of Mexico, or between cities (Mexico City, Guadalajara, and Monterrey), but these are not significant and are normally at the level of jokes and soccer fan rivalries.

The *maquiladoras,* which initially in the 1980s were concentrated along the United States–Mexican border, drew tens of thousands of people north from the interior. Most of these jobs represented entry-level opportunities for Mexicans who, once they were next to the border, took the chance and entered the United States illegally for better opportunities. This transitory migration has brought its own challenges to the main manufacturing centers and to employers. There have been times when the strong demand for trained workers meant that for a few more pesos, workers would move from one company to another to find better pay and working conditions. Professional mid- and upper-level staff positions, however, have been more stable and are typically filled by a combination of Mexicans and foreigners.

The draw of the working population to the manufacturing centers, or to the United States, has had a significant impact on the rural development of the country. In many areas, farming has stopped altogether, or women are the primary workforce available to sustain local economies. However, over the last few years, the transitional draw of the workforce to the manufacturing centers in the north has diminished considerably with the migration of manufacturing to China and the elimination of at least 250,000 manufacturing jobs since 2000.[23] Yet migration into the United States has not diminished, and the money that approximately 22 million Mexicans send back home to their families has increased to more than $17 billion U.S. per year,[24] making this input in foreign currency into the Mexican economy second only to the oil industry and surpassing the traditionally strong tourism industry and foreign investment.[25]

Regional Origin: Implications for Foreign Businesspeople

Regional differences have an impact on business infrastructure and capacity. The scarcity of phone lines, limited high-speed Internet access, difficult roads, and lack of airports or professional services in some regions of the country, for example, need to be taken into consideration when planning. In general, and with many exceptions, the further north and inland near the center of the country you are, the easier it is to access services and the greater the availability of resources. The closer you are to the coastal areas, with the exception of tourist destinations, the less access to services and resources you will probably have.

Foreign businesspeople may experience quite different working environments that vary based on region. In Mexico City, for example, mid- and senior-level Mexican businesspeople tend to be well-educated, more conservative, and formal than in other parts of Mexico. In Monterrey, businesspeople typically operate in a fast-paced environment where a more direct communication style and quick results are valued.

In the *maquiladora* region, there is tough competition for qualified workers. Until recently, rival companies routinely tried to attract employees from other companies by offering greater benefits. Within the last few years, however, a truce of sorts has been reached. Today, most of the larger companies operating in the *maquiladora* region offer standard benefits, and employee retention starts with these. Such benefits typically include:

- In-house medical and dental care;
- Providing on-site meals to workers;
- Regular social functions hosted by the companies that involve the family. These are often connected with a Mexican holiday, but sometimes not. Typical activities include sports events, raffles, and always food;
- Transportation to and from work. Many Mexican employees cannot afford vehicles, and public transportation is often unavailable or unreliable. Most *maquiladora* companies provide buses for their employees.

In more traditional areas of Mexico (particularly the central and southeast regions, and to some extent the north), it is very common for companies to employ multiple members of the same family because of their trustworthiness. As competition grows in Mexico, the pressure to maximize productivity is also increasing. Foreign managers need to establish personnel policies that not only take into consideration the importance of family, but that also emphasize the necessity of job qualifications in hiring. Many foreign companies have established systems that allow family members to apply for positions while still making an effort to hire only the best-qualified applicants.

Because of the importance of family in Mexico, it is not unusual for skilled Mexican employees to decline job offers and promotions that might involve a move away from their family and support systems. In recent decades, the mobility of the Mexican workforce has changed for some segments of the population with the high rate of immigration to the United States, but even then, the goal is often to either bring the whole family along to live together, or to save enough money to return to Mexico and build a home.

Applying Global Diversity: *Implementing an Anti-Sexual Harassment Policy*

GENDER, SOCIOECONOMIC STATUS

SITUATION:

You have recently been named the personnel manager for the Northern Mexican operations of a Dutch consumer goods company. After several months on the job you are quite surprised by the level of what you consider to be sexual harassment that is routinely accepted by Mexican women and by your own company's management. You also notice that, although the women are sometimes promoted to middle-management levels, they are clearly not represented in upper-management positions. To start, you think there is a need for a rigorous anti-sexual harassment policy in the office and plant facilities; once that is in place, you can start working on ways to open upper management positions to female staff.

However, when you bring up the sexual harassment issue at a high-level staff meeting, you are gently ridiculed by your Mexican colleagues – even the one Mexican woman at that level, an upper-class woman from Monterrey, with a graduate degree from Smith College in the U.S., seems to be unsympathetic: "If you want to get the best out of a man, you must let him be a man," she says. "Any woman should be able to handle it."

You are not convinced and you suspect a certain "classism" is at work among these attitudes, as well as fear of potential competition: Mexican upper and middle managers are all upper-class members with advanced education and powerful, wealthy families, and the lower-level employees are from poorer backgrounds.

POSSIBLE SOLUTIONS:

Although your instinct might be to implement an anti-sexual harassment policy, the success of the policy is dependent on women reporting harassing behavior. Initial conversations indicate that women do not perceive sexual harassment from their male colleagues. In addition, forcing a policy to solve an unacknowledged problem will most likely create resentment from male employees. You may well be right in your first perceptions and intuitions, but, since you come from a very different cultural background, you should not assume similar evaluations and effects of similar behavior. Possible approaches include

- Invest additional time to get to know your colleagues, the work environment, and the impact of culture on gender dynamics. Ask open ended questions to clarify behaviors while maintaining a non-judgmental attitude. Others may define sexual harassment in ways that are different from yours.
- If you find underground resentment and frustration on the part of some women because of certain male colleagues' behavior, explore the reasons for their silence and inaction to date. Consider how best to provide a voice for their concerns in a safe way by gathering information and presenting it in a confidential format that does not link comments to individuals. Exercise caution so that retaliation against employees in lower status roles does not become an unintended consequence of your efforts.
- If you determine that an anti-sexual harassment policy is an appropriate step (or if an anti-sexual harassment policy is mandated by your company) then take the time to clearly communicate the policy and provide training that is behaviorally focused with specific examples and outcomes explicitly described. Also, take the time to tailor the training program to the work environment in Mexico, ensuring that video clips, cases, and workplace examples are culturally appropriate.
- Employees may need time to learn just what the policy entails and how to use it without damaging their careers. Support ongoing training if needed; continue your own conversations with employees in order to monitor the "pulse" of the organizational environment.

Summary Recommendations

1. The large gap in **socioeconomic status** between the "haves" and "have-nots" is clearly visible in Mexican society and in the workplace. At the same time, courtesy, protocol, and respect are universally important across all socioeconomic levels. Pay attention to the level of formality required for the business occasion and demonstrate proper manners at all times. Often, the ideas and input of employees with less perceived status due to socioeconomic background may be overlooked by their Mexican colleagues. Try to create opportunities for such employees to build their credibility through significant work contributions.

2. Be aware of the sensitivities to discussing **race and ethnicity** in Mexico. As a foreign businessperson, take an appreciative and open approach to discovering more about Mexico's history, the important contributions of the indigenous cultures, and the blending of races that comprise Mexican society today. Pointed questions about race and ethnicity are normally not advisable.

3. Many Mexican women with career aspirations are attracted to multinational companies as an opportunity for increased advancement. Tap into this potential workforce and expand beyond the usual **gender** roles in hiring and promotions when there are qualified women candidates. Focus on creating an open environment and maintaining good communication within the company to ensure that there are no barriers because of gender stereotypes.

4. Take into consideration the **regional** differences in Mexico that create very diverse work environments in Mexico City, in Monterrey, in the south, and along the border with the United States. For example, providing employee housing, meals, and transportation to the job site in a *maquiladora* environment can increase retention of economically disadvantaged workers from other parts of the country. In addition, be prepared for potentially diverse working styles depending on the region—these range from a more formal and conservative style in Mexico City to a more direct, fast-paced style in Monterrey.

CHAPTER 7

Diversity in Russia

Maria Kostromina-Wayne and J. Paul Wayne

Why Russia?

- Russia is the largest country in the world in terms of area, being almost double the size of its nearest rivals. The country's abundance of natural resources make it the leading exporter of nickel and gas, as well as one of the top five exporters of oil in the world.
- Russia has a literacy rate of almost 100 percent, with a strong educational system that takes a multidisciplinary approach and emphasizes fundamental sciences such as physics and math. It produces a talent pool that is highly motivated by challenging research work.
- The country's engineering culture is disciplined and up-to-date. Technical talent tends to come from aerospace and military research and development backgrounds.
- Due to a long history of isolation, Russian approaches to technical and business problems tend to be creative, original, and different from the West. Having to work in the context of very limited resources has produced a tradition of practical, cost-effective innovation.

Introduction

Citing statistics on the Russia Federation often seems like an exercise in hyperbole. The country covers one-seventh of the world's landmass, is twice as large as Europe, and is 1.8 times the size of the United States (see Figure 7-1). One lake alone holds an estimated 18 percent of Earth's fresh

FIGURE 7-1. Russia's Vast Land Mass

water, and one-quarter of the world's natural gas reserves are found under Russian soil. Traveling from the country's western border to the Pacific coast is a journey of over 5,000 miles through eleven time zones.

Despite Russia's size, one need not look far to find diversity. The Russian Federation is by no means a homogenous mass stretching from Europe through Asia. People of more than 120 ethnicities live within the borders of Russia, collectively yielding a population just under 144 million people.[1] Eighty percent of this population lives in western or what is commonly referred to as European Russia, and the two largest urban centers, Moscow and St. Petersburg, account for well over 10 percent of the country's inhabitants. The country is divided into 89 federal subjects with varying degrees of autonomy. For example, 21 of the 89 subnational entities enjoy the status of federal republic, which, among other things, gives them the right to establish their own official language.

Rulers of both Russia and the former Soviet Union have long been preoccupied with controlling this vast and diverse territory. Given the sprawling distances, czars, general secretaries, and presidents alike relied on trusted regional representatives and well-placed proxies to extend the power of the center to the regions and to maintain the link between state institutions and the people. Although physical distance poses fewer challenges now than in centuries past, reliance on a wide-reaching network of personal contacts continues to be the foundation for success in Russia. A weak legal system, endemic corruption, and exposure to economic fluctuations further magnify the importance of relationships. *Who* you know is often much more important than *what* you know.

This reliance on personal relationships is so central to Russian business that it is difficult to overestimate. If a team of Russians receives briefs on an upcoming negotiation, team members would most likely turn immediately to the biographies page to familiarize themselves with *whom* they will be negotiating, while the content of the briefs would be secondary. Given this tendency, the characteristics and behaviors that Russian businesspeople regard as key differentiators between residents of their own country are of primary relevance to conducting successful business in Russia today. What are the criteria that make one person *svoi* (an insider) and another *chuzhoi* (an outsider), and how can foreigners working with Russians come to comprehend and deal with such internal distinctions?

This chapter will explore the following:

- Ethnicity
- Regional Origin
- Socioeconomic Status
- Age

A History of Foreign Influences

Russia is often seen as isolated from the rest of the world by geography and climate. Foreigners, however, have played key roles in the country's history, though not always in a positive context. From as early as the thirteenth century, Russia was at war with the Swedes in the north and the Tatar or Mongol descendants of Genghis Khan who invaded from the east. The Swedes were defeated and retreated; the Tatars occupied Russia for more than two centuries until their rule was finally broken by Ivan III in 1480. Ivan's successors successfully expanded the Muscovite state by consolidating surrounding principalities. Despite extensive territorial gains and the centralization of power, however, the Russia of the next two centuries remained largely medieval in character.

Russia's isolation from Europe ended under the reign of Peter the Great (1682–1725), who actively engaged the nations of Europe. The language of the Russian court and Russian nobility became French, and czars routinely offered foreigners key positions in the government, military, and universities. According to one estimate, more than two-thirds of the gentry at that time were of foreign extraction.[2]

The history of Russia's industrial and technological development also owes a great deal to foreigners. Though the industrial revolution started much later in Russia than elsewhere in Europe, Russia managed to bridge some of the gap by effectively adapting and improving upon foreign technologies. Numerous key industrial developments were founded or initiated by foreigners, and many of the country's businesses owe their early development to people born outside of Russia. One of the country's first factories, the Tula Iron Works, was founded by a Dutch concessionaire in 1632. The Donbass coal mining industry was formed in the nineteenth century by a Welshman, the Baku oilfields were founded in 1890 by an Englishman named James Wishaw, and even the Kremlin was designed by Italian and Scottish architects.

During the Soviet years, foreigners, specifically Westerners, were admired and envied by Russians, who at the time were repressed and deprived of almost all material goods. To the average Russian, the West was wonderfully abundant in unheard-of delicacies, beautiful matching clothes, and unbelievably smart gadgets about which one could only dream. Many have even argued that exposure to Western consumer goods did more to foment change in the Soviet Union than the arms race. Put more colloquially, the West might have won the Cold War thanks to its Marlboros and blue jeans rather than its supply of nuclear missiles.

Westerners were admired and envied to such an extent that the phenomenon became a source of jokes. One such anecdote goes "A teacher asks her first graders to tell what they want to be when they grow up. Some say, 'A cosmonaut,' others say, 'a doctor.' Little Vova thinks really hard, and then declares: 'When I grow up, I want to be a foreigner!'"

Despite extensive contributions by foreigners, modern-day Russia perpetuates an ingrained xenophobia. Over the past two centuries, Russia experienced several devastating confrontations with foreign powers; Napoleon burned Moscow in 1812, the Russian Empire collapsed in the First World War, and Hitler's invasion of the Soviet Union in 1941 was eventually repulsed and defeated at a cost of over 27 million Soviet casualties. Although many welcomed the collapse of the Soviet Union as an end to an oppressive regime, others suffered through the tumultuous transition to a market economy and found the promises of democracy unfulfilling. As the Soviet period recedes further into history, this significant segment of Russian society that has experienced severe economic dislocations is increasingly nostalgic about that era and more prone to view the collapse of the Soviet Union as yet another tragedy thrust upon Russia at the hands of the West. The legacy of historical events remains central to current Russian identity and underpins Russia's view of itself as a unique, independent actor among the world's powers.

Ethnicity

The Soviets tried to develop a new global working proletariat, uniting 15 Republics with their different ethnic groups under a common Soviet ideology and identity. One of Lenin's first proclamations declared the "equality of all citizens regardless of status, sex, race, religion, and nationality." Ethnic Russians were acknowledged as the dominant ethnic group both in terms of population and representation in positions of power;

at the same time, diversity in the Soviet Union was not only tolerated, but also celebrated. Affirmative action policies, written and unwritten, required that membership in official organizations reflect national ethnic composition.

Diversity and Dissent

Although Russians are comfortable with ethnic and cultural diversity from an ideological standpoint, when it comes to the diversity of opinions among different groups about concrete matters of economics and governance, they are sometimes far less flexible. The old slogan: "He who is not with us is against us" still has many adherents in Russia. At the core of its meaning in the West, diversity assumes the admissibility, the advantages, and even the obligation to hear dissenting voices and to encourage plurality and open debate. This concept is reflected in the following expression: "Your opinion is offensive and incorrect as far as I'm concerned, but I'll give my life in defense of your right to express that opinion." Over much of Russia's history, however, dissent has been a recipe for trouble. In Russian society there has commonly been a "right" view, and other dissenting positions have, by definition, been categorically condemned as "wrong." During the Soviet regime, which boasted of its diversity, dissent by ethnic groups or individuals was punishable both officially and unofficially, and millions of people were targeted for persecution and even elimination.

Are you Russian?

While Russia has always been a very diverse society, ethnic Russians still constitute the overwhelming majority. According to a recent census, Russians accounted for 79 percent of the population, followed by Tatars and Ukrainians at 3.8 percent and 2 percent respectively.[3] Many of the Russian Federation's 89 federal subjects are, in fact, republics organized primarily around a distinct ethnic minority. Some better-known examples include the Tatars in Tatarstan, Bashkirs in Bashkortostan, Dagestanis in Dagestan, and Chechens in Chechnya. Although no one ethnic minority makes up a substantial percentage of the national population, the tendency of these groups to cluster in specific regions often means that they comprise a substantial percentage of the population in those areas.

The Soviet government promoted some movement of different ethnic groups between regions, partly based on social ideals, and partly with the aim of consolidating control over a far-flung empire. The central government in Moscow sent highly placed party officials (usually ethnic Russians) to the republics, where they held influential posts and maintained a suitable political environment in keeping with the accepted policies of the Kremlin. The children of the local elite in the republics were, in turn, sent to Moscow for their higher education, thereby ensuring that future leaders of minority ethnicities would be responsive to Moscow's bidding.

Since the dissolution of the Soviet Union, many more people have migrated to Moscow and St. Petersburg from the outlying regions and former Soviet republics, giving these two urban centers a particularly diverse citizenry. But, despite the rich mixture of different ethnic groups, those who are ethnic Russians retain a profound sense of their central place in the country's national identity.

In the Russian language there is a distinction between the word *russky* (referring to Russian ethnicity) and the word *rossiysky* (referring to inhabitants of the Russian Federation as a country). Using the English word *Russian* to describe the latter often creates awkward misunderstandings. Soviet-era passports contained a line identifying the holder's ethnicity, thereby requiring each citizen to declare whether they were part of one of the minority nationalities. This practice proved extremely unpopular among ethnic minorities, who claimed it led to discriminatory treatment. Current Russian passports no longer identify ethnicity, but instead use the term *rossiysky.*

Russia's internal ethnic diversity was augmented during the Soviet period by visitors from other parts of the socialist bloc. These seldom included black Africans, who have never been widely represented. However, Koreans, Chinese, Cubans, and later Vietnamese visitors were more visible. Students from other Soviet republics were encouraged to come to Moscow and study, and perhaps lived in some measure better than their Russian counterparts because of government-sponsored stipends. Ideology actually seemed to take precedence over ethnicity when it came to these stipends. Those who were raised in the Soviet Union and were acquainted with its institutions and practices were accepted as "ours." They may have been "our" Korean, or "our" Cuban, but acceptance was granted.

Persecution of Minority Groups

Today, national origin and ethnicity are still important factors in Russian society. The country is large enough that its various ethnic groups are thought of as citizens who come from a collection of national republics. Opinions among Russians and non-Russians vary on how much stereotyping and discrimination results from differences in *natsional'nost* (nationality), yet members of ethnic minorities are quite vocal about the negative treatment they receive from Russians. Most citizens of Russia would agree that awareness of one's ethnic background is continually present and often discussed. At various times during the Soviet regime, holding a passport with the wrong ethnicity resulted in discrimination and significant hardships.

In the social hierarchy by which Russians measure themselves, Europeans, Americans, and Canadians are generally considered as the "most equal" or closest in status to the Russians, followed closely by the petroleum elite of the Middle East, those from Saudi Arabia, the United Arab Emirates, and Kuwait. Smaller European countries come next, followed by South America, Japan, China, the rest of the Asia, and the impoverished developing countries of Africa and the Middle East.

Russia's relationship with some former Soviet republics and Eastern bloc countries is becoming increasingly contentious, as many Russians feel that these nations are disrespectful of their former ideological and economic "big brother." Tensions are greatest with the former Soviet republics of Estonia, Latvia, and Lithuania; this becomes evident through ongoing border disputes, clashes over the status of Russian minorities, and conflicting interpretations of more recent history, particularly with regard to World War II.

Within Russia, prejudice based on ethnic or racial background and nationality is rife. In particular, two ethnic groups prominent in contemporary Russian society suffer from discrimination: Jews and people of Caucasian nationality. Russia's Jewish population has long been an active and visible force, and the persecution of Russian Jews has a long history as well. Russia's anti-Semitism is a painful theme that resurfaces even today. It is unfortunate, but true, that the infamous word *pogrom,* signifying large-scale persecutions, is one of the Russian terms that has been exported into almost all languages and is associated with Russian culture, along with *sputnik* and *perestroika.*

As recently as the 1970s, many of the so-called Soviet dissidents were Jewish intellectuals who dared to openly disagree with the Soviet regime and maintained forbidden connections with the West. A number of these dissidents ended up in prison; some were allowed to immigrate to the West after years of waiting for exit visas. Today, some émigrés are returning to Russia, dissatisfied with the lack of opportunity abroad and encouraged by Russia's recent economic boom. Because they know both Russian and foreign business practices, they are often able to play a bridging role between Russia and the outside world.

Discrimination against Jews, however, remains a serious problem in Russia. During the Cold War, the Soviet Union supported the Arabs in the Arab-Israeli conflict. Because Israel was viewed as a Western ally, Jews were regarded as the enemy. Today, anti-Zionism and anti-Semitism persists and there is increasing concern that the re-emergence of Russian nationalism will continue to fuel anti-Jewish sentiments. A combination of envy and pragmatic political deal making is common in relation to the country's wealthiest oligarchs, the majority of whom are Jewish, but there is also frequent discrimination in the workplace against Jews of more modest means.

Another ethnic group, or rather group of ethnicities, prominent in the Russian workplace are those referred to collectively in common speech as *chornye* (blacks), though the politically correct term people of Caucasian nationality has come into use more recently. This label is applied to anyone from the ethnically diverse Caucasus region in southern Russia and includes Georgians, Azerbaijanis, Armenians, Abkhazians, Chechens, Ossetians, Cherkessians, and Dagestanis.* Especially in light of the war in Chechnya

*It should be noted that these peoples are referred to as Caucasians. When mentioning the term *Caucasian* in Russia, it implies reference to peoples from the Caucasus Mountains and not to whites, or people with light-colored skin, as it generally does elsewhere. Historically, Caucasians had a reputation as astute traders. There were often significant numbers of this group working in the open-air produce and consumer goods markets. However, because of negative associations between trade and the profit motive during Soviet times, there was more of a tendency to see mark-ups on goods as a sign of criminal activity rather than as a positive example of free enterprise at work.

and related incidents of terrorism in Moscow and Beslan, persons of Caucasian nationality are often subjected to arbitrary document checks by security officials and face both overt and covert prejudice in the workplace. Cases of discrimination against this group are more frequent than against any others in the working population.[4]

Ethnicity: Practical Business Implications

Influenced by the historical aversion demonstrated by Soviet institutions toward dissenting groups and individuals, some Russians in the workplace may be reluctant to take initiative and offer unsolicited suggestions. Rather, they often prefer to be told what to do by superiors, and are reluctant to initiate projects or openly question management's strategy, as Russian work culture considers such behavior insubordinate. In the eyes of many Russians, a good worker is someone who keeps a low profile.

Russian workers tend to take their job descriptions literally, often resulting in an inflexible workforce. For Westerners accustomed to receiving input and critiques from their staff, this work culture can be frustrating and may seem lethargic. Attempts by Western managers to introduce dynamism by actively encouraging staff participation in decision making are often perceived as weak and indecisive leadership.

Upon assuming management of an office in Russia, it is often a good idea to meet with each employee individually to understand the employee's role and gauge his or her level of contribution to the overall mission. Such reviews often reveal that a rigid work culture of adhering strictly to a job description has led to a disproportionate distribution of work. Individuals with a larger workload naturally tend to resent those with less; and those with less spend much of their time pretending to be busy. One approach to resolving this problem is to have each employee review and sign off on a new list of responsibilities and also to agree to a series of performance benchmarks. These basic measures significantly reduce tension in the office. By defining each person's tasks in the context of the overall goals of the company, a manager is able to imbue each staff member with a sense of ownership and responsibility.

While this approach can improve personnel organization and provide direction, it still does not address problems stemming from the tendency in Russian work cultures to discourage initiative and teamwork. To encourage creativity and risk taking, a foreign executive must downplay mistakes that arise naturally from risk taking, and also retrain or remove local managers who punish employees who come forward with new or unorthodox ideas.

A decade ago, Russians were extremely hostile and resentful to former émigrés (in part because the Soviets viewed emigration as a betrayal of the motherland). Furthermore, many Soviet citizens came to resent and envy the wealth and freedom émigrés found in the West. In today's Russia, where there are no restrictions on foreign travel and increasing opportunity and wealth, returning émigrés are not singled out to the same degree and can serve as a great asset to a multinational corporation's workforce. Such people, who know business practices in Russia and in other countries, can help to bridge the gap between employees with different ethnic backgrounds and styles of thinking and their foreign counterparts.

A foreign company in Russia may encounter openly discriminatory behaviors toward minority groups that constitute gross violations of its internal policies. The company's management must choose where and how to make a stand, mindful of the fact that certain old prejudices have unfortunately been fueled by recent terrorist events in Moscow and elsewhere that are still vivid in the public mind. Members of minority groups who find that a foreign employer evaluates them on the basis of their performance rather than their ethnic background are likely to respond positively to fair treatment with hard work and loyalty.

Regional Origin

In addition to ethnicity, one of the most crucial aspects of diversity in Russia is that of regional origin. So great is the divide between Moscow and the provinces that this topic often dominates conversations in the workplace. Foreign multinational managers and Russians alike see regional origin as a key workplace variable.

Where Are You From?

One of the first questions Russians may ask one another is, "Where are you from?" There is a tendency for Russians to judge one another based on where they grew up, with Muscovites tending to look down on individuals from the regions. As a result of this attitude, those born elsewhere share a common bond. There is even a special word in the Russian language, *zemlyak* (from the same land) that strongly implies the need for mutual support. The following is an example of *zemlyak* that comes from a foreigner working in Russia.

> I was visiting a Western firm with a parking lot that had a couple of armed guards. These guards were highly paid to prohibit those without permits to even drive to the entrance of the facility. When my car stopped at the checkpoint, Andrei (my driver from the former republic of Moldova) rolled down the window and spent about three minutes speaking to the guard in Moldovian. After that, the guard lowered the chain and let us park right across from the main entrance. What's more, for the next two weeks that I was visiting that office, the prime parking spot by the entrance was ours—no questions asked, no documents needed. I asked Andrei whether the guard was his good friend. "Never met him before," he answered with a big smile, "*zemlyak.*"[5]

The power of the connection of *zemlyaks* on foreign ground often takes precedence over qualifications, competencies, or rules. In the example above, the level of trust based on only a short interaction elicited a response from the guard that some might deem a flagrant violation of security procedures. This *zemlyak* phenomenon of regional kinship is a double-edged sword. On the one hand, it allows the building of quick ties to circumvent official red tape, but, on the other hand, it may be a source of uneven privileges and exclusion for those who are not part of the right group, which results in workplace factions.

Moscow and Everywhere Else

Moscow has always been the economic, historic, and cultural center of the country. Although St. Petersburg is at times called the northern capital—a reference to the city's 215 years as the court of imperial Russia—Moscow distinguishes itself as the focal point of power and wealth in modern Russia. Russia has no equivalent of China's Shanghai, and there are very few economic success stories outside of the polished European splendor evident in Moscow. Despite the fact that Russia's natural resource wealth is spread throughout the massive country, most of the money, power, and populace remain concentrated in the capital. In Russia, the saying remains true: "All roads lead to Moscow."

Moscow is home to the Kremlin, key government bureaus, headquarters of nearly all major companies, and the country's most prestigious educational institutions. Most companies register and pay tax in Moscow even if their operations are located elsewhere. Moscow enjoys far more foreign direct investment than any other region of the country. Major decisions affecting Pacific fisheries, the Siberian forestry industry, and precious metals found within the Arctic Circle are all made in Moscow. The lion's share of commercial and private real estate development also remains in Moscow, and nowhere else can one find a similar quantity of elegant residences, fashion boutiques, and class A office space. The capital is a major recipient of immigrants from other parts of Russia and the former Soviet Union, and, on an average day, Moscow's metro system carries more riders than those in London and New York combined.

The higher social status of Muscovites has always been indisputable. By virtue of access, Muscovites have held an advantage over the provinces—the blanket term used to condescendingly refer to the rest of the country. This term has traditionally been associated with bleak economic circumstances and an unsophisticated and poorly educated population. The aspirations of leading families around the country have centered on escaping the provinces through a transfer to Moscow, a potential marriage to a Muscovite, and, more recently, around the purchase of an apartment in Moscow.

Given Moscow's wealth, economic growth, and resources, it is understandable that many Russians from other regions view moving to Moscow as the best opportunity for improving their quality of life. The government of the city of Moscow relies on Soviet-era registration requirements in an attempt to moderate internal migration to the capital. More specifically, each resident must be *propysena* (registered) to a specific residence and is issued a document called a *propyska* that attests to the possession of this registration. A valid *propyska* is critical for establishing residency, securing authorization to work, attending schools and universities, and collecting pensions. Moscow police routinely perform document checks to confirm that an individual is properly registered and thereby authorized to be in Moscow. Without a *propyska,* even citizens of Russia from the provinces must carry proof (in the form of a hotel registration or return ticket) that they do not intend to settle permanently in the city. This battle against internal immigration further highlights Moscow's status as a state within a state, although the flow of people into the capitol continues.

Other Major Cities

Russia, as a whole, is largely urbanized. About three-quarters of the population lives in urban areas and approximately 35 cities in Russia have populations over 500,000. Moscow is the largest city, with 10.3 million inhabitants, then St. Petersburg, the former imperial capital and Russia's traditional window to the West, with five million.[6] In addition to these well-known urban centers, there are a number of cities specializing in hi-tech industries, including Novosibirsk, Vladivostok, Krasnoyarsk, Irkutsk, Khabarovsk, Omsk, and Tomsk. All have universities and other institutes of higher education that consistently produce skilled physicists, mathematicians, and engineers. This base of talent has helped establish Russia as a major source of software engineers, programmers, and other skilled IT experts.

Here is a short description of several major Russian urban centers that are less well known outside of the country.

Novosibirsk is Russia's third largest city, established in the late 1800s. It is located approximately halfway between Moscow and the Pacific coast of Russia, and is the center of Western Siberia. Novosibirsk is famous for its nearby *Akademgorodok* (Academic City), a science town established by the Russian Academy of Sciences with a number of major research institutes.[7] Novosibirsk was developed rapidly during World War II in an attempt to protect Russia's intellectual and scientific elite from the German invaders. More recently, it has become widely known in the semiconductor industry as a significant base of research talent; it has the most highly developed educational infrastructure after Moscow and St. Petersburg.

Nizhny Novgorod is located 250 miles east of Moscow on the Volga River. One of the oldest cities in Russia, it is an industrial city that is known as the "Russian Detroit" because of its large automotive factories. The city is famous for its five universities and 50 colleges as well.

Ekaterinburg, which also goes by the names of Yekaterinburg and Jekaterinburg, is located west of Novosibirsk, but is still on the Asian side of the Urals. Currently the fifth largest city in Russia, it was developed into a heavy industrial city in the 1920s. Ekaterinburg is known for industries such as gem cutting, heavy machinery, steel, chemicals, and petroleum.

Tomsk is located in the southwest of the Siberian federal district. It is an important administrative center with a history that goes back to the 1600s. From the mid-nineteenth century, Tomsk expanded quickly because of the growth of mining, particularly for gold, in Siberia. The city's surroundings are rich in natural resources, including oil, gas, metals, and timber.[8] Tomsk's most important export commodity is oil.[9]

Russia's larger cities have managed the transition to a market economy relatively well, as size has tended to bring industrial diversity. Smaller industrial centers have fared far worse, particularly as one massive factory or a group of related enterprises often formed the basis for the entire local economy of a town or region. This factor, compounded by the absence of unemployment benefits, makes closing bankrupt enterprises a politically difficult decision. Siberia and the far eastern regions of Russia are less industrialized, having traditionally served as a source of raw materials such as oil, gas, timber, metals, and fish.

Oil and Science

A growing counterweight to Moscow's dominance is Russia's booming natural resource sector. Of the top 10 industrial companies in Russia, seven of them produce oil and/or gas.[10] While the major oil companies are headquartered in Moscow, oil extraction and exploration activities are found in a variety of other widely dispersed locations such as the Caucasus region, portions of Siberia, and the Russian far east (see Figure 7-2).

Another legacy of the Soviet Union is the so-called closed cities, where the best and brightest scientists were once sent to work on secret military

FIGURE 7-2. Russia: Key Locations for Oil Resources and Science Industries

projects. City names such as Zelenograd, Arzamas, Obninsk, Chernogolovka, Sarov, and Dubna carry with them the connotation of an extremely strong scientific education and—for the older generation—a history of working for the military industrial complex under extreme pressure and in complete secrecy. Many entrepreneurs have attempted to harness the knowledge and technological expertise found in these cities for the development of commercial goods and services. Given the lack of a natural business culture among the population and the fact that access to these cities remains severely restricted, most of these initiatives have encountered significant obstacles thus far.

Obninsk, formerly a closed city near Moscow and the location of a research nuclear reactor, has recently become the center of new technopark development initiated by the Russian government. Special tax incentives and other concessions encourage Russian and foreign investment in high-tech startups and the development of office complexes. Other advantages include a well-educated local workforce, ample real estate at much more attractive prices than in Moscow, and a more developed infrastructure than in other regional locations. Obninsk also has the benefit of accessibility, as it is within several hours' driving distance of downtown Moscow.

Regional Origin: Practical Business Implications

While having a presence in Moscow is important, substantial business advantages in terms of both costs and personnel are available to foreign firms that can utilize other strategic locations as well. At present, Russia's hi-tech cities offer attractive opportunities. This can be valuable information to keep in mind when establishing a business and hiring employees.

Indeed, fewer Moscow-born citizens appear to be reaching the heights of Russian business in recent years. A survey of leading Russian business leaders found that the vast majority of such leaders were from the provinces—people who had been born at a disadvantage to Muscovites, but had a hunger for success. One Russian executive phrased it this way: "We hire from all over the country, and find drive, skills, talent, and solid education in the candidates we interview from all over the Urals, from Siberia, and from other regions. In our experience, Moscow certainly has no monopoly on talent, especially entry-level, college graduate-type candidates."

Socioeconomic Status

In Soviet times, social classes were considered to be a capitalist phenomenon, but in today's workplace, several classes that can be categorized under the broader heading of socioeconomic status are worth discussing. They are the middle class, New Russians, the politically connected, and the poor.

The Middle Class

All citizens of the former Union of Soviet Socialist Republics (USSR) were considered as members of just one working class. Today, however, a middle class similar to its counterparts in other developed nations is emerging. With the resurgence of Russia's economy, urban centers such as Moscow and St. Petersburg have witnessed the development of nascent markets for consumer finance and mortgages. Members of this class typically vacation abroad once a year, own a car, and have extensively remodeled their apartments, or have purchased a new one. The middle class usually has a higher level of education and even perhaps an MBA acquired abroad or from Russian universities that now offer such a degree.

Analysts estimate that somewhere between 12 to 30 million Russians, some 8 percent to 20 percent of the nation's total population, qualify as middle class.[11] Many are small business owners or managers at big Russian or multinational corporations. Other common occupations include computer programming, accounting, banking, and small business ownership, with monthly incomes ranging from $800 to $7,000. Russia's middle class now produces some 30 percent of the country's gross domestic product.

Most middle-class Russians live in apartments they received for free during Soviet times and have since privatized for a nominal sum. Saving habits vary, though there is a tendency to spend rather than save or invest. Memories of losing life savings in ruble conversions of the early 1990s and the financial crisis of 1998 remain fresh in many people's minds, contributing to a lack of trust in the banking sector. Even today, many people keep their savings in cash at home or reinvest in their businesses.

Shopping malls and multitheater cinema complexes are sprouting up all over the urban centers of Russian cities. Large cash-and-carry supermarket chains, home improvement stores, and furniture giants like Ikea have opened multiple outlets in Moscow and St. Petersburg. Prices are in line with other global markets, but import duties tend to be high as Russia's government takes a protectionist approach to uncompetitive domestic industries such as automobiles, commercial aircraft, and furniture.

Transportation costs are still somewhat low in Russia, though they are increasing quickly along with traditionally cheap commodities such as gas, electricity, and water. A very unpopular law passed in early 2005 drastically changed the mechanism for distributing the Soviet-era benefits received by a large portion of the population, particularly pensioners. In short, the law terminates such benefits as free public transport and healthcare and instead compensates beneficiaries by increasing cash payouts for pensions and stipends. Pensioners vehemently objected to the law, arguing that increased pensions would fail to cover real transport and medical costs. In addition, pensioners feared that any real increase in pensions would soon be erased by inflation.

Despite an income that is modest by Western standards, members of the Russian middle class can afford a lifestyle that most of their compatriots only dream about. In a country where only 10 years ago owning an old Soviet-made vehicle in the family was a sign of affluence, today's middle class drives foreign-made cars to their new *dachas* (summer homes).[12] Children of the middle class often attend private schools and the family shuns public hospitals for new, Western-style health clinics. Although Russia's middle class will continue to expand along with positive economic growth, most experts believe the government needs to reform the banking sector and encourage small business development if this class is ever to expand outside of Moscow and St. Petersburg.

New Russians

Notorious and envied for their affluence, an economically successful upper class of New Russians emerged in the mid 1990s during the chaos of privatization. This class makes up roughly 2 percent of the population, and comprises in large part former high-ranking party officials and other well-connected individuals who rode the wave of economic and social reforms to build their own wealth, mostly during the era of privatization. New Russians are spread all across the country, though the greatest concentration resides in Moscow. Incomes of New Russians are vastly greater than the population at large, and members of this group are notoriously conspicuous in displaying their wealth.

Not surprisingly, New Russians are looked upon with a great deal of suspicion and resentment by the rest of the population. Because of rampant corruption, those who are rich are widely considered to have earned their fortunes through questionable means. Many Russians believe that there is little chance of making big money while obeying all the laws of the land, and several of the country's richest oligarchs got their start by acquiring state assets through shady privatization auctions. Numerous other former Soviet officials profited from special access to resources and political connections.

New Russians are often associated with the crude and gaudy criminal underworld. When small businesses were legalized during *perestroika,* even some people who had previously been semi-outcasts flourished as businessmen, often retaining their dubious ethics and, at times, criminal connections. In the early 1990s, extortion became widespread, and a new term appeared—*krysha,* or roof, in reference to the criminal group that a businessperson must pay in exchange for protection. Over the past few years of economic growth, such groups have become less prominent, as many have used funds acquired through criminal activities to finance ventures into more legitimate businesses.

When a New Russian appears in a collective work setting, fellow employees immediately wonder "Why? If one has money, why do they need a job? Will they pull their own weight?" Though many New Russians work diligently, there is also the risk that the individual landed in the workplace thanks to a special connection. In these instances, quite often the employee displays little motivation and a poor work ethic. Children of the political elite fall into this category and enjoy a protected status that is likely to remain unaffected by poor performance. In such cases, coworkers tend to view these colleagues as taking advantage of the system at the expense of others. Companies may tolerate such behavior because they can also benefit greatly from having the sons and daughters of ministers and other influential individuals on their boards. Because personal relationships and connections are so essential to successful business, employers may believe that it is worth hiring a well-connected New Russian merely for the access he or she can offer to key officials.

Networked

People with political connections are not limited to New Russians. There are others who have such connections as well, and they cater to the need for businesses to have close ties with people in politically influential positions who can be called on when needed to expedite the removal of bureaucratic logjams. All established businesses have networks and on occasion firms hire based on the merit of an individual's network.

Such individuals are valuable problem solvers; however, until such time as their contacts are needed, they tend not to consider themselves employed so much as on retainer. Their work group realizes that these individuals are a valuable resource for resolving issues with a political dimension, although the well-connected individual will be a limited contributor to the day-to-day workload.

Intelligentsia

A popular term in Russia, *intelligentsia,* defines yet another group that is prominent in some workplaces. The meaning of this word has evolved over the years from "artistic or social elite" (mostly exterminated during Stalin's purges in the 1930s) to the modern, more inclusive "people who make a living by thinking." Many Russians would agree that the opposite of intelligentsia is a stereotypical untidy, drunken laborer. Yet the so-called *intelligent* is much more than just a white-collar worker. He or she is usually a second- or third-generation member of the Soviet scientific, artistic, or humanitarian vanguard, and nearly always from an urban family.

The word intelligentsia has come into the modern global vocabulary from Russia. In the nineteenth century, it meant a type of publicly active Russian intellectual. These people might have been born into various levels of social hierarchy, including the nobility, clergy, or the merchant class.

Intelligentsia typically shunned state service careers and refused to pursue rank for the sake of power and prestige.

During the Stalinist regime, many members of the intelligentsia were heavily repressed and spent years in gulags for crimes of thought. Scientists perished in Stalin's prisons for discoveries that were deemed bourgeois, while artists and poets were executed for disobeying the rough guidelines of social realism. Thought leaders were declared mentally insane and locked in asylums.

To survive, artists, writers, linguists, geologists, playwrights, economists, and biologists mastered the art of expressing themselves through small circles of fellow specialists who shared arcane research papers, famous quotes, plays on words, and subtle satire. Living in infamous communal apartments where the walls had ears, the intelligentsia read forbidden books, shared a passion for poetry, and learned foreign languages. Only in the 1980s did the intelligentsia begin to challenge the state openly.

Perestroika, while permitting more political freedom, brought about a precipitous loss of jobs at universities, research institutes, and in the arts. For many, the standard of living fell toward true poverty. Intelligentsia, who had always tried to place less emphasis on material things, now had to scramble for money. Because of their knowledge of foreign languages, many joined foreign firms as interpreters or managers. Being well-read, educated, and sensitive to others' feelings are undoubtedly positive qualities, but many Western employers have discovered that such intellectuals are often less effective in management positions, as they are more subtle when expressing opinions and often reluctant to stand their ground, finding it difficult to balance their internal sense of tact and fairness with the cruel realities of budgets, deadlines, and return on investment.

A special subset of the intelligentsia is the so-called *tekhnari,* or techies. During Soviet times, people would tease one other by saying, "May your daughter marry an engineer," as engineers received the lowest wages and lived on the verge of poverty. Computer scientists, physicists, mathematicians, and engineers who graduated from the country's high-pressure technical schools and went on to universities and defense-ministry research institutes nonetheless lived on the verge of poverty even by the intelligentsia's standards.

Unlike people involved in intellectual pursuits in the humanities, *tekhnari* were generally left alone by the ideology overseers. Because more than 80 percent of the *tekhnari* were employed by the defense industry, many of them spent their lives in closed towns populated entirely by their colleagues. This segregation spawned strong communities of intellectuals who formed the leading edge for cultural developments in Russia. For example, in the repressive 1970s, when much of the intelligentsia sought refuge in nonpolitical activities, the *tekhnari* turned two hobbies into full-fledged fads: mountain climbing and folk singing. The first Moscow concert of Vladimir Vysotsky, the folk-singing popular hero of the 1970s, was held in the Culture Hall at the Kurchatov Institute of Theoretical Physics, the birthplace of the Russian A-bomb. In 1981, the same hall hosted Moscow's first rock concert.

Today, *tekhnari* tend to have more success in a private business context than other elements of the intelligentsia. A few of the country's richest men are computer scientists and physicists, and small- and medium-sized businesses have absorbed many of the *tekhnari* who formerly remained cloistered in research institutions.

The Poor

Many Russians have been left behind by economic reform and are still struggling to recover from the loss of employment, housing, and status they enjoyed under the Soviet system. Retirees living on government pensions have been particularly hard hit, and the closing of formerly state-owned uneconomical enterprises has impacted whole regions. A large portion of the population feels disillusioned, with some longing for the old days when at least a modest livelihood was assured and economic profiteering by the well-connected was less conspicuous. It is estimated that somewhere between one-quarter to one-half of the country's population now lives below the poverty line. Suicides have jumped 40 percent in the past two years.[13] Russia has experienced periodic protests from those whose lot has worsened since the collapse of the Soviet regime, but so far the country has avoided mass unrest.

Education and Status

Education provides the most direct route to middle-class status. The role of education in Russia has been strong over the last half century, and it is critical in the workplace. The entire population receives mandatory education through high school, and the country's literacy rate of 99.6 percent is among the highest in the world. Competition is intense for places in the better schools. In fact, there are more people applying for university-level education than are graduating from high school on an annual basis, a new phenomenon that speaks to the growing understanding of the need for continuing adult education. It also speaks to the corruption that is rampant within the higher education system. Admission to university is contingent on passing entrance examinations, though graft and bribery is rampant as parents and professionals seek to guarantee admittance. Theoretically, anyone can go to university as long as they have sufficient funds. Young men of conscription age have an increased incentive to seek a higher degree in order to qualify for an exemption from the two-year obligatory service in the Russian army.

Russian universities turn out approximately the same number of graduates each year as India and China and more than twice as many as the United States, with 55 percent of Russians possessing a university degree. In short, education is highly valued (as are avoiding the army and moving to Moscow). Russians recite the names of their alma mater with reverence, as this is very much like reciting one's own pedigree.

Prestigious universities confer a great deal of status on their graduates. The overwhelming majority of first-rate schools are located in Moscow and St. Petersburg, which reinforces the desirability of these locations. Moscow alone, for example, can lay claim to such leading schools as Moscow State University, Moscow State Technical University, Mendeleev University of Chemical Technology, Moscow State Pedagogical University, and Moscow State Aviation Technological University. Students from the provinces can attend such schools but the fees are high, as is the cost of housing, leaving students from out of town at a distinct disadvantage.

Free admission to university based on achievement has dropped to symbolic levels as the costs involved in providing higher education have skyrocketed. Official and unofficial fees for entry, tuition, and mandatory tutoring have outpaced the purchasing power of the population at large. And since universities no longer receive generous funding from the government, the faculty and administration of universities are increasingly susceptible to bribes and other forms of graft.

In 2005, the Russian non-governmental organization Information Science for Democracy (INDEM) published the results of an extensive survey on corruption in Russia. According to estimates extrapolated from interviews with people from more than 1,000 business and 3,000 households, the organization estimates that Russians paid the equivalent of over half a billion U.S. dollars in bribes to enter university in 2005 alone. Increasingly, the only people who can afford to send their children to school are the elite with connections, New Russians, and the already stretched middle class. Access to top-notch education is becoming a thing of the past for the majority of Russian families.

Socioeconomic Status: Practical Business Implications

For most foreign employers, the middle class provides the ideal labor pool in Moscow and St. Petersburg, as members of this group are attuned to the requirements of a global economy and are often ambitious and flexible workers. Russia's middle class, although limited in size, offers capable and well-educated workers. Members of the intelligentsia as well, especially the *tekhnari*, can perform useful roles but sometimes lack the instincts or training to function effectively in a business context. Caution should be exercised in considering job candidates who appear to have the characteristics of so-called New Russians, as they may have expectations for the kinds of duties they would perform (or not perform) that are at odds with corporate performance standards. Although foreign companies will need to build the same kind of social networks for themselves that Russian firms have, they will probably want to ensure that their political connections are created in a sufficiently broad and transparent way that they are not exposed to legal jeopardy back home or political peril in Moscow when power shifts.

Given the dynamic Moscow job market, graduates of prestigious universities have become increasingly choosy and fickle based on the status conferred by their education. Many organizations have come to realize that a potential hire with an MBA or other prestigious degree will not necessarily be a good manager, although such candidates are likely to expect high salaries, generous benefits, and lucrative perks. Progressive companies now recruit from leading universities all across the country. Novosibirsk, Ekaterinburg, Omsk, and Samara all have universities that are well-respected even by the Moscow elite. Tapping universities outside of Moscow or St. Petersburg for employees provides access to capable but less economically privileged young people from the provinces who could not afford to enter or attend the most famous schools. Such candidates are likely to be more accommodating when it comes to salary negotiations.

Age: The Russian Generation Gap

Given the tumultuous events of Russia's recent past, there are markedly different social perspectives in the country today depending upon when a person was born.

The Soviet Generation

The majority of the population in the Russian Federation today is over the age of 30, and therefore grew up under the Soviet system. This older generation was accustomed to being taken care of and, consequently, feelings of entitlement are pervasive to this day. There was also a great deal of structure and homogeneity of thought and action; people were expected to fit in and keep quiet.

The older generation tends to be dissatisfied with the political and economic reforms that have taken place in the years since the dissolution of the former Soviet Union in 1991. They have seen some grow rich without having to work long and hard, and they have seen others who worked long and hard end up with nothing. Bank defaults, monetary reforms, and inflation of the early 1990s literally took away the life savings of a generation. Some are content to leave things as they are, while others would like to see privatization reversed and a redistribution of state property.

Younger Workers

Young workers who never experienced the Soviet system constitute another significant part of the workforce. Companies employing both younger and older workers will have a generation gap within their staff that can be complex and multifaceted. The younger generation normally wants to see more objectivity and more rewards for achievement. They want their education and their individual contributions to be recognized, which represents a huge shift from the relationship-based careers of previous eras.

Many of the younger generation take the New Russians, oligarchs, government elite, and associated corruption as a given. They may want to see a more universal application of the law and reductions in graft and waste, but this newer generation does not want to undo the past so much as to have the opportunity to make a life and a better future for themselves and for their children. Their achievement-based, optimistic value system has become a crosscurrent running in a very different direction from the entitlement and resentment still felt by many older workers.

During the 1990s, young Russians frequently sought better opportunities through education or emigration abroad. As many as one million young Russians may have gone abroad to study in the last decade and have not returned, according to some estimates.[14] But as the economy stabilizes and grows, young Russians are returning to their home country, seeing it as a place that now offers more opportunities.

Age: Practical Business Implications

Some characteristics of the older generation have proven quite positive for Western firms that employ relatively senior Russian scientists; these are often highly accomplished people, with education and accomplishments evidenced by publications in prestigious international journals. This class of employee is normally willing to work for a fraction of the salary that their Western counterparts would demand. Furthermore, they exhibit a high degree of loyalty to the company and are reluctant to change employers once settled. They have a strong work ethic and discipline is almost never an issue.

When managing workers from the older generation, however, it is critical to understand that most Russian scientists tend to be theoretical, more interested in the freedom and elegance of research than developing immediate commercial applications from their work. Moreover, they are extremely proud people who will not tolerate a lack of respect for their accomplishments. They are also often skeptical of Western approaches and ready to cite numerous examples of the superiority of Russian science. As a result, Western employers face the challenge of balancing respect for their Russian scientists' knowledge with the need to extract practical results from their work. Close technical management is absolutely critical. The scope of work must be defined narrowly and clearly, and frequent (weekly) progress reviews are necessary.

With younger professionals, stability is a concern shared by almost all foreign employers. Demand is high for quality candidates, and many young workers switch jobs often in search of a better pay package and brighter opportunities. Foreign employers can cope with this in part by hiring employees from the provinces and maintaining facilities in cities other than Moscow (such as Novosibirsk) that have a deep reservoir of human resources and talent in vital industries.

Generational clashes between pre- and post-Soviet era employees are not unusual. Some firms seek to minimize the impact of age differences by avoiding mid-career hires as much as possible, building their workforce primarily with fresh college graduates. Other companies maintain a young, aggressive sales force and a stable back office of older workers. With careful management of generational diversity, the mix of younger and older professionals can make for a powerful synergy, with mentoring and growth opportunities throughout the workplace.

If not properly managed, however, work teams that consist of mixed aged groups may experience friction and stress, thereby limiting the potential of the team. Older workers sometimes resent the compensation packages, values, and work habits of younger employees, while more recent hires look with disdain on the cautious outlook of their seniors as a holdover from Soviet years. When the dynamics between older and younger workers are not carefully managed, the potential result is a workplace that is replete with resentment and dysfunctional strife. Foreign employers that can avoid or alleviate such conflict and replace it with a healthy integration of generational perspectives have the best chance of coming out ahead.

Applying Global Diversity: *Determining a Growth Strategy*

Regional Origin, Age

SITUATION:

A large software development company has a Russian subsidiary in Moscow, where a team of 20 has been operating for a year. The subsidiary has achieved encouraging but not stellar results over its first year and is poised to grow further. As the regional director for the company's field operations, you are in charge of redefining strategy for the Russia office to enable it to grow aggressively in the next year. You have flown into Moscow to hold a strategic planning meeting with your Russian management team.

One of the questions on the table is the primary location for future development activities. During the meeting, it becomes clear that the management team has different perspectives on the future strategy for the Russian subsidiary. The team seems to be divided into two camps with opposing views:

- Option #1

  Center of excellence strategy: The Moscow office should focus on science and innovation, leveraging the talent pool of senior scientists from Moscow State University and other first-tier academic institutions in Moscow. The team will accelerate the development of innovative mathematical methods for the company's software products.

  Chief Advocate: Andrei Kozhevnikov, a senior scientist and recognized mathematician with numerous publications who worked for a military research center during the Soviet era. He has strong ties to Moscow State University and an R&D team with several talented graduates of the school.

- Option #2

  Low-cost software development strategy: Focus on cost-efficient software development, hiring a team of recent college graduates in Novosibirsk, where the costs are lower than in Moscow. Continue to operate both locations for now, but within a year transition out of Moscow, transferring key personnel to Novosibirsk.

Chief Advocate: Igor Sergeev, who recently became the company's youngest manager at the age of 29, and was born and educated in Novosibirsk. Although he is young, his technical mastery has earned him respect even among programmers at corporate headquarters.

POSSIBLE SOLUTIONS:

The challenge here is to create a strategy based upon what is best for the business while leveraging the advantages offered by each location. A weakness of Andrei is that he sometimes seems to have difficulty understanding the business side of a high technology enterprise; there is a legitimate concern that he and his team could get bogged down in overly academic approaches. Yet if the whole operation were moved to Novosibirsk, it is unlikely that the company will be able to retain these Moscow-based team members because of their preference for life in the capital and their personal loyalty to Andrei. Meanwhile, Igor, although he is a brilliant programmer who would have ready access to a strong talent pool in Novosibirsk, could use the support and mentorship of Andrei to grow into a leadership role.

Rather than select from an either/or set of options that exclusively favor one location or another, it might be better to appeal to the strong pride in Russian science expressed by both Andrei and Igor, and to encourage them to create an integrated solution. The organization could position a relatively small but talented research team in Moscow to generate creative ideas and to maintain a presence in the country's capital, while a lower cost operation in Novosibirsk produces fast, measurable results with a larger number of employees. This solution could combine the best of both academic and practical perspectives while keeping the subsidiary's cost structure low. Regular rotation of personnel between Moscow and Novosibirsk on short-term assignments as well as metrics that both reward collective results and reinforce mutual assistance would help to build cooperation and shared learning between the two locations.

Summary Recommendations

Companies should keep in mind a few summary recommendations that will help them to successfully manage workplace diversity in Russia.

1. Russia's history, while ostensibly embracing diversity, has favored **ethnic** Russians. Other groups bear the brunt of discrimination even though they have valuable contributions to make. Certain groups of people who have lived abroad and returned can serve as a bridge between Russia and the outside world.

2. **Regional differences** within Russia have long favored the capital city of Moscow and Russia's traditional window on the West, St. Petersburg. Western employers are advised to look to other locations for eager, hardworking talent and more cost-effective operations.

3. **Socioeconomic diversity** is a growing dynamic in the workplace. Non-Russian firms may want to focus on aspiring members of the middle class. Russia's intelligentsia, as well as individuals with special networks, can sometimes offer useful contributions.

4. **Age** affects the outlook and values of the Russian workforce. Younger and older workers have had drastically different life experiences that stem from whether they were raised during or after the Soviet era. When workers from different age groups are combined in the same location, special care is warranted to leverage the unique contributions of both younger and older workers while avoiding serious friction.

CHAPTER 8

Diversity in the United Kingdom

Nigel Richards

Why the United Kingdom?

- The United Kingdom currently has the fourth largest economy in the world.
- The U.K. is Europe's leader in software and computer services, it has nearly half of all the publicly traded biotech companies in Europe, and its banking sector is the third largest in the world (after only the United States and Japan).
- The United Kingdom has an excellent infrastructure with the enormous hub that is Heathrow airport centrally driving world travel.
- Five of the top ten business schools in Europe are based in the United Kingdom according to the latest *Financial Times* ranking of European business schools.
- Census data shows that in the past 10-year period, the minority population in Great Britain has increased by 53 percent.

Introduction

Upon arrival at London Heathrow, the world's busiest international airport, the overall impression is one of incredible human diversity and cultural differences. This diversity seems to be at least as true of the employees who work there as it does of the travelers passing through. The employee population at Heathrow provides a revealing window on a modern Britain that is characterized by a wide variety of cultural influences: Asian, African, Caribbean, and Middle Eastern in addition to Northern European. Not too long ago such workplace diversity would have seemed unthinkable.

What are the key factors that define diversity in this new society, and how is it possible to work with and manage that diversity successfully? This chapter will examine these questions, and suggest some strategies for business professionals to understand and effectively utilize this diversity in everyday situations. Areas covered here will include:

- Ethnicity and Race
- Regional Origin
- Socioeconomic Status
- Educational Background
- Language and Communication

Postwar Britain has undergone profound changes, and the result is a modernization and a makeover of traditions, culture, values, behavior, and beliefs. Globalization is affecting the look and feel of the cities and towns of this once insular country, exposing the island mentality to global village influences. Such traditions as the regular changing of the Queen's guard and customary ceremonial pageantry aside, the reality is that the United Kingdom is simply not the same place it used to be or what the rest of the world sometimes thinks it is.

Historical Context

Less than a century ago, the United Kingdom was enjoying the fruits of the Industrial Revolution and, through its colonies, still held sway over a captive world market that was successfully exploited for resources and trading. Run by an elite and prosperous ruling class, Great Britain was a country clearly divided by an extremely hierarchical social order. This was an era of great privilege and wealth for the few and far less favorable circumstances or even extreme poverty for the rest of a rapidly increasing population. It was a time of imperialism, domination of foreign territories, and a formidable ruling class, with an industrialized economy fueled by a large, poor working class. Britain's pre-eminence as an economic power was accompanied by a sense of stability as well as ideological conservatism and a strong and widely shared feeling of patriotism nourished during the long reign of Queen Victoria.

FIGURE 8-1. Map of United Kingdom

At that time, an understanding of social diversity (not that such a concept existed then) would have been based on social class and regional differences; the Britain of that time was a highly stratified, conservative, and extremely traditional society. There was limited social mobility; status was assigned by birth rather than acquired through individual achievement. The status quo was something to respect and to challenge only at great peril. Historical precedent and the conservative national character exercised, and still do to a lesser extent, a powerful check on institutional and even individual change. The educational system of the time reinforced these social patterns, which were innately resistant to social differences and diversity.

The boundaries between the British Isles as a whole and the outside world were a stable and resistant physical reality; they could not be, as in continental Europe, easily redrawn. Boundaries within the islands could be and have been frequently redefined, as evidenced by the often tense relationships between England, the dominant power on the islands, and Scotland, Wales, and Ireland over the course of their history; the same situation pertains specifically to the United Kingdom.

The fabric of society in the United Kingdom tended to be rigid, the government monoracial (allowing for significant ethnic and cultural differences between groups of Celts, Angles, Saxons, Danes, Normans, and others, who settled at various times before the twelfth century), there was one standard language, at least since the fourteenth century, and the prevailing national character was held in check by a stoic "stiff upper lip"* approach to life and hardship. As the leading maritime power from the eighteenth century until World War I, Britannia did truly rule the waves. Unity and social homogeneity were assumed, although these ideas were in part created and imposed by the Victorians in order to justify certain political and economic practices.

However, many factors in the twentieth century provided an impetus for social, political, and economic changes in every sector of society, changes that in turn led to a significant increase in diversity in the country.

*The "stiff upper lip" functions as a mask, hiding pain, discomfort, and concealing feelings. It serves as a metaphor for English public character at its most severe and unemotional, and was promoted through education in the nineteenth and early twentieth centuries. The idea was that suffering should be endured, persecution accepted stoically, and all emotion contained. Detached, cool, dispassionate, this is the traditional face of many public heroes and figures as depicted in history. Even if this behavior may be less common these days, a healthy appreciation for discomfort remains: for some Britains still "pain means gain."

How did a uniquely traditional country with one of the most historically exclusive cultures transform itself into a burgeoning multicultural workplace in less than half a century?

Ethnicity and Race

Britain's history has oscillated between periods of emigration and immigration. These waves have ebbed and flowed along with the political and military fortunes of the British Isles.

Emigration and Immigration

Over the last several centuries, from the 1600s through the early 1900s, emigration to other parts of the Empire was the predominant trend. Emigration offered economic and social opportunities as Great Britain grew by acquiring a global network of colonies. Former colonies such as Australia, Canada, New Zealand, and the United States to this day still have populations with a large proportion of British ancestry. Migration abroad afforded a way to escape the country's highly stratified society and to find wealth and economic opportunity regardless of one's class and social standing.

During the centuries of Britain's growing stature as a global power, immigration into the country occurred only on a small scale, and foreigners were essentially unwelcome outsiders and considered untrustworthy. Militarily and economically powerful countries in close proximity to Britain such as, at various times, France, the Netherlands, or Spain were often seen as rivals for global preeminence in the shifting patterns of European political alliances and power plays, and therefore their citizens were suspect as well. Meanwhile, immigrants of African or Asian descent were commonly treated as slaves or servants. British ships were deeply involved in the slave trade between Africa and the West Indies as well as the American South, and some 15,000 slaves also came to reside in Britain. In 1833 slavery was abolished in Britain, but this did not alter the fact that members of certain ethnic and racial groups were regarded as second-class persons.

The picture of relative British ethnic and racial homogeneity and the mainly outgoing tide of people that took place at the peak of the Empire is a relatively recent one, however. Prior historical periods saw numerous tides of human immigration surge into the British Isles. Celts, Romans, Angles and Saxons, Nordic Vikings, Normans, French, and Flemish, to name a few groups, have found their way to the islands, many of them staying and adding their genetic inheritances and traditions—thus belying any serious claims to British ethnic purity.

In the post-WWII period, the flow swung away from the emigration that characterized the British Empire at its height, and back again toward immigration on a scale similar to that of earlier eras. Enormous changes took place in the twentieth century, driven by the impact of the two World Wars and the gradual disintegration of the Empire. World War II, though technically a victory for the United Kingdom and its allies, resulted in a severe shrinkage of the United Kingdom's resources and international influence, a devastated economy, and an acute lack of manpower. Mass immigration to the United Kingdom from her dwindling Empire and former colonies was encouraged to boost the workforce.

Postwar governments focused on redistributing wealth, nationalizing industries, expanding the country's electorate, and creating greater equality through social and educational reform. A comprehensive welfare state came into being, the gap between rich and poor narrowed, and the middle class expanded quickly in a way that has come to include many different ethnic and racial groups.

Postwar Immigration Patterns

Since 1945 the number of immigrants has risen steadily from a negligible figure to a significant proportion of the population. In 1951, for example, the Caribbean and South Asian population was a mere 80,000, while by the 1990s the figure had grown rapidly to over 3 million. South Asians in particular—Indians, Pakistanis, and Bangladeshis—have become a visible part of society in many areas of the United Kingdom.

Keeping in mind a total population in the United Kingdom of around 60 million, the results for demographic categories used in the most recent census consist of

- White, with subcategories of British, Irish, or other: 91 percent
- Asian or Asian British with subcategories of Bangladeshi, Indian, Pakistani, and any other Asian background: Indian 1.8 percent, Pakistani 1.3 percent, Bangladeshi 0.5 percent, other 0.4 percent
- Mixed, with subcategories of white and Caribbean, white and African, white and Asian, and any other mixed background ("Mixed" is a new category that was introduced in 2001 to reflect growing ethnic integration): 1.2 percent
- Black or black British with any other black background: black Caribbean 1 percent, black African 0.8 percent, black other 0.2 percent
- Chinese or other ethnic group: Chinese 0.4 percent, other 0.4 percent[1]

In summary, the census results show that the Asian and black population in the United Kingdom has gone from a very small number to almost 8 percent. Even though this may not seem like a significant minority in comparison with myriad ethnic and racial populations found in more historically diverse countries such as Brazil, it represents a major reversal of the previous pattern of out-migration from a country with a relatively homogeneous population.

A key fact that emerges from the census is that in the most recent ten-year period the minority population in Great Britain increased by 53 percent. This is dynamic growth by any standards. Indians are at present the largest minority group, representing 22.7 percent of the ethnic minority population.

Social Consequences

The process of integration has not been an easy one, as immigrants have tended to concentrate in certain parts of England and are not distributed evenly across the United Kingdom as a whole. Over 70 percent of the ethnic minority concentration has been in the Southeast England and the West Midlands. The number of immigrants grew to be so large that at times during the second half of the twentieth century there were serious racial tensions and conflict. The more conservative members of the public became alarmed, and for some there was even a fear of "reverse colonization."

Multiculturalism and ethnicity became associated with social problems and were at times seen as a direct threat to the sense of national identity. Most famously, Enoch Powell, a right-wing and influential Member of Parliament (MP) for almost 40 years starting in 1950, was responsible for creating a public backlash in the late 1960s that brought about a temporary halt to mass immigration into the United Kingdom.

This conservative backlash against the arrival of ethnic minorities proved to be a transitory reaction, and it can be said that the integration of minority groups into mainstream society has been more successful and achieved in a shorter time in the United Kingdom than in other countries having a similar demographic development. Despite its history of colonialism abroad, there was not an extensive heritage of slavery within Britain. The integration of new arrivals has occurred through mainly peaceful, if occasionally tense, periods of social adjustment. This is impressive, considering how the numbers of immigrants have risen so quickly.

Immigrants have also introduced their own religious faiths to the United Kingdom. The images displayed on television of mosques and U.K.-based mullahs represent just one manifestation of a widening array of religious options. A new question about religious identity was introduced in the last census, with the following main categories: Christian, Buddhist, Hindu, Jewish, Muslim, and Sikh. Islam and Hinduism have emerged as the faiths with the largest numbers of adherents after Christianity. The figures also show that Asians, black Africans, and Irish are more likely to have religious affiliations—the trend appears to be toward a steady increase in religious diversity and a decline in affiliation with and participation in England's official religion, the Church of England.

In Search of a New Identity

Against this backdrop of immense, yet mainly peaceful, social and political change the country has achieved significant social mobility, increased equality, and opened the doors to ethnic and racial diversity—a diversity that, even if it has affected mainly urban areas, and even if at times there are still racial conflicts and issues of discrimination, has enriched and permanently transformed the face of English and British culture.

Over the same postwar time period the country divested its empire, and in 1973 it became a member of the European Community. From the start, this membership was viewed skeptically by many, and it is still a divisive issue among contemporary citizens of the U.K. The disappearance of the empire, the country's gradual integration into Europe, and waves of globalization over the last few decades have taken their toll on the British psyche. Greatness and world dominion have been replaced with smallness, and the nation feels overshadowed by its own history. Fervent and bellicose patriotism such as that expressed in Winston Churchill's stirring wartime speeches seems strange and distant today, even if at the time the threat was menacingly real and the sentiments widely shared. Given the pace and the scale of the changes described, it is hardly surprising that there has been an ongoing crisis of national identity; what "Great" Britain formerly stood for has simply ceased to be. The national unity at the end of WW II has evaporated, and in less than two generations the spirit and tradition expressed by such rituals as standing at attention when the National Anthem is performed have been discarded, and the anthem itself is rarely played. Yet there is now for some Britons a sense of nationalism that is being driven partly by a lack of a secure sense of national identity.[2]

Race and Ethnicity: Workplace Implications

The obvious implication of the growth of relatively new minority populations in the United Kingdom is that these same trends have had an impact on the workplace in a big way, particularly in major urban centers. Workers are learning to cope with a multicultural environment that did not exist for previous generations, and companies have undertaken an array of diversity initiatives to try to foster equal opportunity for minority employees. Foreign firms must take these changes into account when assessing potential employees as well as growth markets within the country. It is best to encourage managers and employees from other countries to rid themselves of old stereotypes about Brits that may no longer apply.

Because the age profile in the minority communities is much younger than in the country as a whole, the Asian and black population will grow further in the next decade, introducing yet more diversity into the workplace.

The Department of Education and Skills predicts that the number of Asian and black pupils in English schools will grow to 20 percent by 2010 (it was 12.5 percent in 2003). At the same time, the number of people with mixed backgrounds is likely to increase, especially in London.

Regional Origin

Great Britain, England, Britain, Northern Ireland, Scotland, Wales, the United Kingdom, and the British Isles are terms that can and do confuse geographically and politically, but it is important to appreciate the strict differences between them.

A Scot Is Not an Englishman

First and foremost, the United Kingdom of Great Britain and Ireland came into being in 1800 as a political act, and today this means that Great Britain, or GB, includes England, Scotland, and Wales but excludes Northern Ireland. The latter can be explained geographically as Britain is a noncontiguous island. The United Kingdom, which is the favored contemporary expression, includes England, Scotland, Wales, and Northern Ireland.

As a political creation, the term "Britain" or "British" permits diversity, whereas more nationalistic and geographical terms like English or Welsh do not. In 1922, Ireland gained independence as the Republic of Ireland, or Eire, and the United Kingdom retained the six counties that are now Northern Ireland, with its unsettled political situation and a complex history of bitter religious and political divides.

In 2003, 84 percent of the United Kingdom's population lived in England, 8 percent in Scotland, 5 percent in Wales, and 3 percent in Northern Ireland.[3] Interestingly, the question of national identity was introduced for the first time in the 2003 General Household Survey, and 48 percent of people living in England described themselves as British, whereas in Scotland and Wales only 27 percent and 35 percent respectively saw themselves as British.

National identity, and indeed European identity, is a sensitive and topical subject, whereas regional identity is relatively straightforward geography.

Historically, England has always been the dominant partner and Scotland, Wales, and Northern Ireland have felt oppression and loss of identity as subordinated neighbors.

Despite being a small country—the United Kingdom is smaller than the U.S. state of Oregon—the regional differences are significant, and a few miles can mean a different subculture, dialect or accent, social class, and even values. Given that this is a densely populated geographical area with a population of around 60 million, it is essential to know and appreciate the regions and their differences. You can drive all over the country quickly, there is an extensive railway network, and domestic flights are largely unnecessary.

When British people meet face-to-face and actually talk to each other, their geographic origin, along with their socioeconomic background, is telegraphed almost immediately through a variety of cues. The internal code that is transmitted when British people speak to each other is traditionally based on speech patterns and accent—how you speak signals your regional and class origins. Each region has both an identifiable speech location and a distinct accent or dialect. This question of accent and what it means will be discussed later.

For the visitor, it is useful to be aware of the regional differences, starting with a clear appreciation that a Scot can be called British but never English, or that someone from Yorkshire would be identified as such in Surrey, or that Cockneys come from the East End of London. The visitor will simply be seen as a foreigner or outsider. The question "Where are you from?" can yield a lot of information about the background and therefore attitudes of the person you are meeting, assuming you cannot identify this from their speech, which people from the United Kingdom can usually do even without asking. These issues are often exploited (and much enjoyed) as a basis for humor in the nation's television programs.

In many ways people are less concerned with political correctness in the United Kingdom than in other places, and a visitor should not be surprised by the jingoistic comments and humor at the expense of other nationalities. Neighboring European countries toward which history and close proximity have resulted in a love/hate relationship are frequently the objects of such humor. Jokes about working with continental business partners are affectionately critical, and national and regional stereotypes abound.

Historically, it is easy to geographically distinguish England from Scotland, Northern Ireland, and Wales. Each has its own distinct culture and in some cases language, dialect, or unique accent. Devolution at the end of the twentieth century resulted in the creation of the new Scottish Parliament, the Northern Ireland Assembly for a time, and the Welsh Assembly (1999). These different countries had been forcibly united by a dominant England, and understandably there can still be an underlying adversity toward the English that comes from this history.

There are also both obvious and subtle differences between the north, the midlands, and the south of England. Traditionally, there has been a distinct economic relationship between the south and the north. It is in this regional contrast that the idea of old and new money originated. The north and the midland regions of England, with their industrial cities like Manchester, Liverpool, Birmingham, Nottingham, Leeds, and Sheffield generated the "new" money during the Industrial Revolution, while the south has traditionally had a reputation more for its financial markets and services. The older, more institutional money of the "home counties" was typically identified with the regions nearer London.

Governmental power, whether it was by a monarch or now by the democratically elected Houses of Parliament, has always been centralized in London, the crowded and densely populated capital in the southeast. There is definitely a culture of snobbism on all sides that divides these two broad regions, and everyone knows where everyone is from.

London: City of the World

London occupies a unique position both in British society and among the great cities of the globe. It has a pulse of its own, which often seems to have more connection with Hong Kong or New York than with regional England. Despite the elegant and classic architecture and the institutionalized sense of tradition, the populace is mobile, cosmopolitan, and future-oriented, while the workplace is fiercely and unforgivingly competitive. A dazzling, fast-paced, expanding, and hectic metropolis, it is one of the world's most multicultural cities and is a center for every kind of diversity.

The immigration of the postwar years has made by far the greatest impact on London. According to the last census, more than seven million people live in the city, a figure that is boosted daily by vast numbers of commuters, and seasonally by large numbers of tourists. Fully 30 percent of the city's population is Asian or black, over 300 languages are spoken, and second- and third-generation immigrants visibly contribute their traditions, business skills, and popular cuisines to this vibrant community. Impressively, one out of every five small businesses is owned by people from an ethnic minority group.

London, the self-proclaimed gastronomical capital of the world, has more varieties of cuisine, served in thousands of restaurants, than any city in Europe. There is food from over 70 different countries. More tellingly, the ingredients for all these cuisines are readily available in major supermarkets and shops, which indicates how much Londoners in general, and not just minorities, enjoy cooking ethnic food at home. There is an openness and fascination for cultural difference that would have been impossible a few decades earlier.

Ethnic minorities are popular, and there is definitely a relaxed and welcoming attitude to most ethnic diversity, with the many crowded cross-cultural events reflecting this. Unfortunately, this climate of openness has recently been dampened somewhat, particularly in relation to immigrants from the Middle East, by the very real threat of further terrorist incidents.

London itself is often termed a collection of villages, and it is true that each borough has a unique character. The boroughs of north, south, east and west have clear divides and different cultures. This is a place where money is made, spent, and sometimes wasted in staggering amounts. It is here that the 1997 Labour Party's winning electoral slogan of "Cool Britannia"[4] really did apply.

A noticeable change has come from the growth of employment in service industries and the decline of manufacturing, with London being the service industry center. This has resulted in a shift from standard to flexible or nonstandard working hours, as today products and services are needed on a 24/7 basis. Correspondingly, the workforce has become much more diverse, with an increasing number of working women and students, and more foreign workers coming from abroad. Flexibility and new skills are needed to survive in this demanding workplace.

Although London is a huge hub for international business and a major crossroads for tourism, entertainment, and creativity, it can be challenging to do business in this noisy and sleepless city with its out-of-date infrastructure and ancient buildings. For residents of the United Kingdom, it seems that London is either a place to love and visit or to hate and avoid at all cost. In this sense it is not possible to be indifferent to this great city—an interesting point, as indifference often seems part of the national character.

The linguistic diversity of London can be especially challenging for international tourists; in many busy and popular parts of the city native English-speakers can be difficult to find! Working in the city can feel like surviving in a partially ancient and partially futuristic alien metropolis, with only the architecture remaining historically and regally British.

City, Town, and Country: Workplace Implications

The human resource challenges of London's hyperdiversity are considerable, and the skill and training required to manage its workforce is a recurring theme for the Chartered Institute of Personnel and Development (CIPD), the main Human Resources organization in the United Kingdom. Equal opportunity and diversity management are topical themes. Issues of motivation, employee turnover, and long working hours confront the head offices of the many global and national companies that are based there.

In terms of workplace attitudes, it would be fair to comment that the pace of London can lead to burnout, and the magnet and motivators to work there are of course money, opportunity, diversity, and a mobile urban lifestyle. Everything moves quickly; salaries and cost of living are the highest in the United Kingdom and people expect to move upward quickly within an organization as well. Working hours are longer than in most of the rest of the country and in Europe. Bristol, a major city two hours west of London, is a thriving workplace, yet the people there seem more permanent and it is more traditional, less aggressive, and slower-paced. A Lon-

FIGURE 8-2. Major Economic Hubs of the United Kingdom

doner might feel restless in Bristol, while for others London can seem overwhelming.

London is essentially a world city of its own, self-consciously cosmopolitan, whereas other towns and cities in the United Kingdom tend to be more traditionally "British." The London workplace, complete with exhausting commuting conditions, is rough, tough, fun, and recreation is unlimited. Money and a sense of humor help in surviving here. Cities such as Manchester, Birmingham, Edinburgh, and Glasgow are also dynamic, but not to the same degree. Figure 8-2 highlights important economic hubs outside of London.

Multinationals tend to recruit from the London area, as the hungrier talent is more likely to be found there, and the number of recruitment companies based in the area bears this out. In addition, the workplace is full of people with different ethnic backgrounds, definitely a beneficial resource for multinationals. People here generally have a more global perspective and a less insular attitude. It would be more natural for a British businessperson to move to New York for a project from cosmopolitan London than from, say, Ipswich or Bath.

In some national or regional companies there can be a cultural disconnect even between the people of the London head office and the people who work in regional branches. Issues of town and country and the gap between urban and rural are intensified in this sprawling city, which is self-styled "up" and a countryside that is considered "down."

Some regions of the United Kingdom offer more ethnic diversity than others, creating a more distinct cultural workplace, and London is itself a unique environment. The difference in work practices really lies between city, town, and country, or how deep in the country is the town (this means how far it is from London). In the country business will generally take a little longer to develop, who you know and relationship building will be more important, and credibility will take longer to establish. In this respect, it may be clearer to navigate in the greater Britain, as customs and traditions are more transparent, while in London anything goes these days. The sheer diversity and pace of the big city makes for more unpredictability and a different, more global, set of skills is required to succeed.

The heavier industrial regions of the country have experienced the most hardship over the last 50 years; manufacturing is now less than 20 percent of national output. These areas have a more entrenched conservatism, and, not surprisingly, there is a tendency for people and therefore business to be more risk-averse in these regions, whereas London is definitely risk-embracing, as the hub for the service sector. Like in the United States, but much smaller, there are the hi-tech centers of Silicon Glen in Scotland, and Silicon Alley and Silicon Fen in England.

Despite growing diversity in the United Kingdom, regardless of where you travel or work, it is worth keeping in mind that these are islands, and that sometimes means an insular mentality. Depending on the assignment, for example, sales work, it can help to match appropriate regional background with region; a Surrey (wealthy county south of London) salesperson would have a harder time in Glasgow than a fellow Scot. The message here is that any visitor should work, at first, with a regional or local representative to maximize business possibilities, to develop "inside" knowledge and fit, and to become aware of the both the distances and proximities between London and the rest of the country.

Socioeconomic Status

To appreciate today's business environment in the United Kingdom, it is necessary to keep in mind the impact of the past and to know something of how society is organized. While many attitudes and behaviors have changed since the middle of the twentieth century, leveling the playing field significantly, some of the deeper assumptions remain unchanged. If you scratch the surface, tradition and history still play a subtle part in business. Certainly income is distributed much more evenly than 50 years ago, but considerable wealth remains concentrated in the hands of a few.

Exclusivity and Class

In the United Kingdom there has always been a strong sense of belonging to a group, a feeling of exclusivity, and historically the class system itself was heavily restricted. Membership of a class, a club, a team, or a committee—and the list of possible groupings in the U.K. is exhaustive—all have one thing in common: they are exclusive and clannish. In understanding these groups and kinships, the socioeconomic background of the individual plays an important part.

The divisive debate in the United Kingdom on the topic of membership of the EU raises the question of a possible loss of exclusivity. Some people fear that the intricate and sometimes intimate social and economic networks that bind the British could be threatened by loss of sovereignty and cultural absorption into the EU. It is less about the relative economics of buying French apples in England (or English apples in France, for that matter), than it is about this fear of inclusion and annexation. French, or indeed other European managers working in the U.K., can experience difficulties that stem from the culture of exclusion.

The concept of "mate," a word used to describe close friends with shared interests, is significant. Originally a working-class word, it is widely used to explain close social networks with friends who typically have known each other for many years. In a small country these networks remain intact through life, meetings occur frequently, and it would be unusual to have a high turnover of mates. However, the word mate is also used in greetings and exchanges with strangers.

It can be difficult as a newcomer or visitor to break into such intimate groups, and there is an element of exclusivity to these long-term friendships. Predictably, these groups would not normally cut across class or socioeconomic background, and the legendary Old Boy network of the private schools certainly does not. Once you are in, you remain in, and the group serves to enjoy and protect its interests, whether these be economic, social, sporting, fishing, musical, or simply going to the same pub on a regular basis to drink and socialize. This is true of the present. "Cheers, mate!" means many things, but if it is said to a visitor from abroad it may be a good sign in relationship building.

Historically, British society was dominated by the class system. Though the industrial revolution and reforms of the last century have gone a long way toward creating a much more egalitarian society, some remnants of the class system still exist. Like her neighbor, France, Britain has had her revolutions, but these have been quieter and relatively bloodless. Aristocrats remain even if they are now poorer, and the welfare state of the last century was constructed peacefully. For the visitor it can be difficult to detect venerable social codes and networks at first.

Social status, traditionally more important in the United Kingdom than economic status, was acquired by birth rather than through achievement, and it was difficult to break through barriers and improve one's lot. People were judged more by who they were and where they were from rather than by what they did, and certainly they were judged in an instant more by the sound of their speech rather than by its content. Of course some people married "up" or "down," but this was the exception and not the rule. The lines of social demarcation were clear.

Only recently has hereditary peerage in the House of Lords, the upper chamber of Parliament, been abolished. Now members, or "peers," to this upper house of Parliament are appointed for life on the basis of achievement. Breeding used to be more important than merit, and privilege was comprehensively protected.

Socioeconomic Status: Workplace Implications

The stereotypes that have typically been used to characterize the British have their origins in traditional times and do not resemble present reality. Streets full of restrained city workers in pinstripe suits and bowler hats have long since disappeared, though the work attire is, generally speaking, still relatively formal. Despite casualness in some of the newer sectors, this relative formality holds true across all levels of society and ethnic diversity, the norm in the workplace being "business smart." Most people like to dress up and to look professional, and this is one aspect of traditional formality that has not disappeared.

Titles continue to be used, and these days they are given by the Queen and government as rewards for unique achievements. A look at the composition of many boards of directors in large corporations will show the presence of titled directors, often in nonexecutive roles, included to gain access to specific networks as well as prestige and credibility for attracting investors. This practice depends on the type of business more than where that business is located, and some titled businesspeople participate on a variety of boards.

An interesting and revealing question is to look at traditional attitudes toward money, still something that is generally less directly addressed than in the United States. Money was historically not enough to earn higher social status, and in some subtle ways it still isn't. Historically, wealth was the prerogative of an exclusive few. Britain's stratified society had both "haves" and "have-nots," and those who were upwardly mobile in an economic sense would nevertheless be met with social exclusion. New membership to the club was hard to come by. The class conflict of old and new money and the concept of a "self-made" man (or woman), which had a negative feel to it, hardly encouraged individual achievement. The nouveau riche were what they were—called disparagingly "new" money by people with old money. An individual who was successful and then moved to a more prosperous area to live would not be socially accepted for some time.

An upper-class individual can be impoverished, and because of tax changes many are, but even today everyone knows they are upper class. It has never been something you could buy. Snobbery played a powerful and unpleasant role in keeping people in their places, and those whose background was different were never as welcome as people with the same background. This was not a society keen to embrace diversity and inclusiveness or pluralism at any level, and snobbery worked in both directions and was not exclusive to the well-bred. Again, subtly, this can still be the case, and the adversarial social makeup has been thoroughly stratified throughout history. Only in parts of London and in a few urbanized areas is there any real erosion of this.

Surnames and given names, addresses, schools and universities, newspapers, hobbies, sporting interests, and political persuasion have always reflected class in some way in the United Kingdom. Traditionally some names are classless and therefore inclusive—for example, John—but others are more exclusive. For instance, Bill is usually a working-class nickname and Will, or William, would be the more upper-class version. The names Kevin or Sharon have always been associated with the working class. The tendency is that the working-class names are more often abbreviated, Kevin becoming Kev, and are used in this way to be more intimate and friendly. Upper-class names are less often abbreviated. The beauty of being a visitor is that none of these social rules apply, so there is a freedom in being outside the system. However, it is valuable to have an insight into these social-class issues, and learning about them can be both useful in business, and a humorous, if bewildering, process.

The old class structures are breaking down gradually, but they are still pervasive. Foreigners who are aware of their lingering influence will be better able to decode workplace interactions between local employees. They will also become sensitive to the ways that accent, deportment, table manners, and language convey messages regarding social status or the lack thereof. The visitor will observe much more social mobility these days, and membership in a club (any kind of elite group), while helpful, is not enough anymore. However, if a visitor is living in the United Kingdom for an extended period, joining a club to socialize provides an effective way to create networking opportunities.

Educational Background

Educational background was historically linked to the class system. Indeed, Britain's system of expensive private and state-run public schools effectively perpetuated class divisions. The educational reforms of the last century have challenged this privileged world by providing free or affordable education for everyone from elementary school up to the university level.

The sudden social impact of the equal education of the postwar welfare state meant that in one generation children had access to an education that their parents did not, and opportunities in the workplace have become far more equal. The hugely positive significance of this should not be underestimated, as prior to these egalitarian changes the majority of talent, creativity, and skill remained trapped in a class-bound society, where only the moneyed or the elite enjoyed the privilege of a "character-forming" education.

Of course, the ultimate goal has always been to build a career, but in times past more emphasis was put on building character rather than achieving a grade, and in the privileged private schools the objective was clearly grooming young men for colonial life in the British Empire. Somewhat stereotypically, yet true, all manner of compulsory endurance sports, games, and physical competition were considered to be equally as important as academic achievement—those celebrated qualities of fairness and integrity were deliberately cultivated. Certainly this was the place where the stiff-upper-lip attitude to controlling emotion was inculcated.

The private boarding schools, confusingly called "public schools," still guarantee status and privilege in certain professions. Everyone has heard of Winchester, Harrow, and Eton, to name but a few, and they are patronized by children of wealthy families. It can be said that class segregation and distinction are perpetuated by this. Traditionally such schools were for boys or girls only, though many are coed now. Like it or not, there is in some professions an Old Boy network that persists today, and where you went to school, rather than what you studied or how well you did, still has an influence. Arguably this is true for some branches of the legal profession, for example.

University Background: Ancient, Red Brick, and Glass-Plate

Oxford and Cambridge have long dominated the university hierarchy and are also globally famous. Probably because they have existed for centuries, the schools attract distinguished faculty members and clearly give prestige to students who attend. In these famous schools and universities, their name, longevity, and reputation can give as much, sometimes more, status to the students who attend than students' individual academic achievement.

There are, however, hundreds of excellent, less-famous universities and state schools, and these operate on the basis of academic achievement. Like in many countries, a degree from a top-ranked university will give much better access to top jobs or professions in the United Kingdom's extremely competitive labor market, but it is not as important as, say, in Japan. Often the right degree with a reasonable grade is enough. Once in the workplace and in most jobs, the question of where you graduated from is usually of limited networking interest. During the hiring process with big-name companies it of course adds somewhat to your competitiveness as a job seeker.

The main categories of universities in the United Kingdom are "Ancient," founded before the nineteenth century, "Red Brick," founded in the nineteenth and early twentieth centuries, and "New," or "Glass-Plate," founded in the 1960s. Cambridge, Manchester, and York, respectively, fall

TABLE 8-1. UNIVERSITY RANKING- GUARDIAN UNLIMITED

Rank	School Name	Category	Specialty Areas	Main Location
1	Cambridge	Ancient	arts and sciences	Cambridge
2	Oxford	Ancient	humanities, social sciences, science, medicine	Oxford
3	Imperial College	Red Brick	science, technology, medicine	London
4	School of Oriental and African Studies	New	arts, humanities, languages, law, social sciences in the regions of Africa, Asia, Near East, and Middle East	London
5	London School of Economics	Red Brick	economics, finance, law, politics, international relations	London
6	University College London	Red Brick	history, law, anthropology, languages, geography, fine arts	London
7	King's College London	Red Brick	humanities, modern language center, law, history, dentistry, medicine	London
8	York	New	psychology, modern languages, computer science, educational studies, music, archaeology	York
9	Warwick	New	American studies, sociology, educational studies, economics, politics, film and theater, science	Coventry
10	Nottingham	Red Brick	psychology, manufacturing, engineering, agriculture, art and design	Nottingham

Source: Copyright Guardian Newspapers Limited, 2006. Reprinted with permission.

into these three categories. There is no official university ranking in the U.K., but the main newspapers, such as the *Times,* publish their versions. These versions look very similar.

Although there are some slight changes in these rankings, the same universities appear more or less consistently year after year. They offer comprehensive programs, and their location is suggested by their names. They rank quite closely and many enjoy good international reputations. Indeed, the foreign students who attend British universities each year provide crucial income to the schools and colleges.

One side issue to mention here is that, unlike in the United States or other countries, the concept of private universities is basically unknown. Some argue that this lack of private universities has educationally disadvantaged Britain, resulting in a lesser reputation for research work and an increasing lack of resources. Faculty salaries are lower than in some competitive locations. In the rivalry within the expanding English-speaking world for foreign students, this gives other places an advantage, and can make Britain a less attractive choice for study and research. The London School of Economics is an outstanding exception here.

Apart from formal education, the United Kingdom is a country of readers where information is devoured, complimented by a rich heritage in theater and the arts. It boasts a diverse and high-quality print media, which may often reflect the diversity and political orientation of readers. You can often identify someone's outlook by the paper he or she reads: if it is the *Daily Telegraph,* you would probably be looking at a conservative; *The Guardian* would indicate a liberal.

The BBC, the British Broadcasting Corporation, operates free of commercial activity and advertising, and consistently attempts to broadcast educational and informed commentary through its programs. A visitor can learn much about the United Kingdom, and about everywhere else for that matter, from this valuable resource.

Education: Business Implications

At the end of the day, the issue confronting an employer will be that hiring, managing, and retaining a high achiever with a first-class honors degree from Cambridge may be challenging. Depending on the industry sector, a compromise solution of hiring from less elite second-ranked universities (not ancient, anyway) may result in less turnover, as in some sectors companies and search firms aggressively headhunt or recruit former top university graduates.

One must also keep in mind the impact of a given mix of educational backgrounds on workplace dynamics. Factionalism based on university and other social networks can wreak havoc with workplace relationships; likewise, when graduation from a prestigious university is regarded as a fast pass to higher rank, those with less privileged backgrounds can lose faith in the organization's judgment of their capabilities. When recruiting, employers should look further than qualifications and school, and it may be worth including travel, work, or study experience outside the U.K. as a requirement. It is quite common for young people to invest time, work, and money in extended international travel, and this could add value to workplace participation in global teams. Britain has a long tradition of work-related expatriate assignments as well, and such people with prior "expat" experience are a resource a global employer can definitely tap in the workplace for global strategic purposes.

Language and Communication

When people speak of linguistic diversity, they usually refer to a pluralistic society with a multicultural population speaking a variety of different non-standard languages, and with varying degrees of bilingualism. In the United Kingdom, there is much non-English linguistic diversity, and over 300 languages are spoken in London alone, with corresponding issues of English as a Second Language (ESL) in schools. Even though the standard language of the country is English, it is the diversity within this English that will be discussed here.

Dialects, Accents, and Vernaculars

Tacitly, the English language is the standard language of the country. Because of linguistic globalization and the reality of English as a world language for international communication, Britain lost control of the English language a long time ago. There are many varieties of English spoken around the world by native and non-native speakers, and a huge number of nonstandard dialects, a tribute to the language's functional utility.

Adversely, in many places British English is still associated with colonialism and the imperialistic hegemony of the English language. Many businesspeople in the United Kingdom don't realize this, and, as in the United States, most native English speakers speak second languages poorly or not at all.

The visitor to the United Kingdom will hear much new vocabulary, indirect language, and a huge range of accents. Although the standard language is English, the speech of the regions and the classes can be difficult for a visitor to understand. Across the country there is substantial diversity in dialects, accents, and vernaculars. There is significant variety in the English spoken by the different ethnic minorities. Whether it be the speech patterns and phonetics of London Jamaican or Indian English, or indeed the Geordie dialect (Newcastle), or Scouse dialect (Liverpool), the visitor will need to learn how to tune into these varieties at first.

Scotland, Wales, and Northern Ireland have unique and immediately identifiable speech dialects of their own. At the same time, three Celtic languages have survived as mother tongues in small populations in the United Kingdom: Welsh, Irish Gaelic, and Scottish Gaelic are spoken in Wales, Northern Ireland, and the Highlands of Scotland, respectively.

Counties such as Yorkshire have a very distinctive form of speech. In the north and south, in cities and towns like Manchester, Liverpool, Birmingham, London, and Newcastle-upon-Tyne, to name a few, all have unique and distinct accents or dialects, and, for the non-native of those cities or towns, comprehension can be difficult. Any visitor, and indeed British people from different regions, will be outsiders and immediately identifiable as such. Of course, once one is familiar with the local form of English, difficulties should diminish.

Different social classes can be identified by their speech. Not only is there the contrast in accent, but there are differences in vocabulary. Of course these are generalizations, but such variations do exist. Even when the expressions are linguistic relics of the old class system, they are still used. Here are some persistent examples to be taken humorously.

Middle–Upper Class	*Working Class*
At home	Indoors
Drawing room	Lounge
Loo or lavatory	Toilet
Sorry	Pardon
Sofa	Settee
Lunch	Dinner
Dinner	Tea
Napkin	Serviette

RP, Cockney, and Estuary English

Historically, the Received Pronunciation (RP) of "Standard" English was the most prestigious form, and other regional or urban dialects and accents varied in prestige according to how closely they follow it. As the standard, and therefore status, form of the language, it was endorsed at the educational, social, and institutional level. In the past the BBC maintained that standard through its broadcasting activities worldwide, and the resulting "accent bar" was a well-documented (and often negative) feature of British English. It is against this historical background that the social status of Cockney should be discussed.

Long a divided society with adversarial relationships between classes and institutions, London itself has been split by at least two varieties of English. Cockney dialect speakers inhabit the East End, and those who use the standard variety inhabit the West End. There are further speech varieties in north and south London. As the speech of a lower-class community, Cockney could be viewed as inferior, yet the cheery and creative dialect speakers of this community have been linguistically obscure and defiant for hundreds of years. One example, "To take a butcher's" would confuse a visitor, as it essentially means "butcher's hook," which rhymes with "to look," and therefore means to take a look. So, historically, speakers of Cockney could hide in their language and exclude those outside their speech community.

Estuary English provides a very interesting evolution of dialectical forms in recent years. This is a form of English spoken in the southeast of England, along the River Thames and its estuary. It has been built on Cockney, challenging RP and Standard English. Estuary English has some syntactical features of Cockney, a characteristic vocabulary including more American terminology, different intonation and phonetic sounds from RP, a much higher incidence of question forms, and a potentially confusing stressing of prepositions.

Estuary English appears to be a democratization of speech affording neutral ground where both the privileged and less privileged can communicate equally. Certainly in the general community in the southeast where this mode of speech is gaining usage, it is thought to neutralize the accent bar and, therefore, social class issues, especially in the workplace.

Here are some examples of standard and Estuary English's phonological differences.

Standard English	*Estuary English*
Planted	Planid
Plenty	Pleny
Twenty	Tweny
Something	Somethin or somethink
Nothing	Nothin or nothink
Bath	Baf
Father	Faver
Mother	Muva
Wanted	Wanid

This leveling of differences in education and class, especially when applied to the business community, comes at a time of intense sociocultural change within a society that has historically been extremely stratified linguistically. The BBC has, for a long time, appeared to promote diversity by employing a much wider variety of speakers for its broadcasting. Those caricature upper-class voices of the last century are long gone.

Linguistic Diversity: Workplace Implications

Across the United Kingdom and its social classes, there are subtle messages conveyed by speech that mean that even in a simple telephone conversation it is possible for each party to almost immediately identify the other speaker's geographical and often socioeconomic background. Naturally, education can have a leveling effect, but the accent of a given speaker communicates the most information. This is not necessarily a positive, as typically there is sort of mutual and rapid judgment about each other's social standing. Historically, this was a barrier to socioeconomic mobility and was fabulously dramatized in George Bernard Shaw's satirical play, "Pygmalion" (popularized in the musical "My Fair Lady") where the central character improved her accent to gain access to higher society and privilege. In more recent times, Margaret Thatcher impressively and successfully trained her voice to gain wider appeal. The voice is still an immediate socioeconomic indicator.

In a kind of "Pygmalion" reversal, Estuary English, used with increasing frequency in business and sometimes in government, advertising, and the media, has become a more consumer-friendly speech form. It is middle-of-the-road and therefore the speaker who adopts it is less subject to social judgment. With an increasingly diverse population in the workplace, it would now seem to be a disadvantage to sound too educationally privileged, whereas in the past, increased credibility and authority came from this very same thing.

If this form of English does facilitate business relations between people by relaxing class differences it may be a good thing. If, on the other hand, it lacks the intelligibility of Standard English because of its Cockney content and syntax, it will be far less accessible to non-English native speakers. In short, it could be bad for international business. It may come across as the United Kingdom's dry and ironic sense of humor, as who, except the British, get the joke?

Because of the international position of English, a society such as the United Kingdom, or any part of that society, especially the business community, may not be well served by adopting a less intelligible form of the language at a time when globalization proceeds apace. Cross-culturally, and specifically with reference to functional communication, it can be argued that the more traditional and standard form of English is easier for the non-native speaker of English to understand.

A visitor in the British workplace will encounter such linguistic diversity, a hugely interesting but challenging reality in terms of communicating effectively in business. At the same time, he or she will be immediately identifiable as someone not from the United Kingdom, which can be a good and a bad thing—good in that none of the rules and snap judgments apply, and bad in that comprehension of the different communication styles, dialects, and accents take time to develop. The indirect communication style, combined with understatement and the generally ironic sense of humor, often leave visitors baffled until they invest the effort to get to know their local counterparts and their preferred speech patterns.

Even though some of the linguistic developments may prove transitory, changes in the language and how it is used have occurred over the last 50 years and are emblematic of wider social trends. They are therefore worthy of consideration by foreign companies as they seek to expand their range of customers and employees.

Applying Global Diversity: *Managing a Multicultural Team*

Race and Ethnicity

SITUATION:

You have come to London to manage the office of an advertising agency specializing in IT hardware and electronics, including PDAs, MP3 players, and all-function cell phones, as well as desktop and laptop computers. Your top-level staff is made up of two ethnically English members with elite university backgrounds, several Indians and Pakistanis who grew up mostly in the U.K., an Australian, a Burmese, a Nigerian, and a Scot. The support staff is made up mostly of Jamaicans; your secretary is ethnically English as well, an experienced and forthright woman in her mid-40s. Most of the staff have worked in the branch for two years or more, the English woman having been there since it opened almost five years ago.

There appear to be a number of tensions among management team members, with exclusionary modes of communication being used by some. In your capacity as the team leader, you are also not being given the automatic respect you have experienced elsewhere, and the consultative method of decision making that you have tried to use doesn't seem to help; there seems to be some free-floating resentment being directed toward you. You are wondering what the best first steps would be to better understand the team dynamics and establish your own credibility as the team leader.

POSSIBLE SOLUTION:

It might be tempting to start with a "teambuilding" intervention or to have a meeting where everyone is asked to air their differences frankly and get on with problem solving. However, this approach assumes that team members from all ethnic backgrounds are comfortable with direct communication methods and that major differences between them can be constructively addressed. If the divisions between team members are severe, this strategy could backfire and actually worsen the tension in the office, adding fuel to the fire as the teambuilding and attempts to practice direct forms of communication are ridiculed or resisted.

It would be best to get the lay of the land first, and you can initiate this through regular one-on-one meetings with each person to better understand their backgrounds and perspectives in a more private setting. As you begin to know them better, you can help to position the strengths of each individual with others on the team. In addition, the secretary is in a neutral position and has the longest "institutional" memory in the office. It might be useful to ask for a history of the office staff as she understands it, and for her suggestions. She is likely to have insights into the office dynamics that could take you a long time to acquire, as well as insights regarding what actions or policies would have the best effect on the team. You can also set an example of inclusive behavior and respect for others through your own conduct in team meetings and daily interactions; this may be the quickest way to gain the respect of the team.

Summary Recommendations

The United Kingdom is undergoing a significant transformation that is resulting in more diversity of every kind in the workplace. This is especially the case in the major urban areas. If you are a visitor to the country, the gap between preconceived expectations and the reality in meeting rooms may be considerable, and the country is clearly a different place compared to even a decade or two ago.

Equal opportunity has directly influenced the trend toward a more diverse workplace. In a strange way, the flux and transition have also led to a desire for increased unity in the midst of diversity. There are contradictions everywhere. The unifying effect of World War II has passed with the generations, and the institutions echoing the past jostle with rapid urban change to redefine the national identity. The tug between history and the present is palpable. The insular, stratified, class-bound society has moved forward to allow significant socioeconomic change and greater diversity across the board. There is certainly more workplace opportunity than ever before. London has re-emerged as a unique world city and a strategic location for local, regional, and global business.

Much has changed in recent years, yet much remains the same. The challenge for the visitor lies in appreciating and balancing both the old and the new. Here are five summary recommendations to help individuals and companies to both adapt and succeed in Britain's new and dynamic workplace.

1. Find opportunities from the recent and rapid growth of **ethnic** minorities, as these expanding sections of the population will have a significant role in the future of the United Kingdom. This newest section of society is driving many changes and is making important contributions to the workplace. You may find valuable employees who are undervalued and overlooked, and who don't currently have access to the full range of opportunities available to others.

2. Know the **regions** of the United Kingdom. Appreciate regional differences and expect to encounter pride in both regional and national accomplishments. Remember to acknowledge the particular identity of each part of the United Kingdom when dealing with its inhabitants. Consider leveraging the economic and human resources of key locations outside of the capital. This is a small country with a history as an important actor on the world stage, and it continues to have consider-

able world influence. Nationalism still shapes the attitudes of many residents. Your British colleagues will assume that you regard London as a world-class center for global business.

3. Be aware of what creates **socioeconomic** status and understand the contradictions that come from the present colliding with the past. Avoid being locked into either elite associations that are unsuccessfully standing in the way of social change or contacts at one social level that are likely to exclude you from business opportunities at other levels. Find ways to build on present trends in which equal opportunity, mobility, and diversity are all on the increase.

4. Remember that many of the traditional networks, the exclusive and insular club mentality, and the perpetuation of the class system, come from British **education**. The hierarchy is not so formal these days, but in the eyes of some people *where* others are educated can be more significant than *what* they studied, and clubs and shared interest groups are formed young and last long. Consider tapping the capabilities of strong Red Brick or Glass-Plate universities and their graduates.

5. Be ready for the **language** challenge. Linguistic diversity in the U.K. comes from the huge number of languages that are used, and especially from how English itself is spoken. Accents among even native English speakers give away regional and class origins almost instantly. An all-British team in the modern workplace knows much about itself from how its members speak. Try to learn how to decipher such different forms of English so you will have an idea of the many signals that local team members are reading into each other's verbal expressions.

CHAPTER 9

Diversity in the United States

Pamela Leri and Anita Zanchettin

Why the United States?

- The United States has the world's largest economy; its GDP comprises nearly one-third of the total global economy.
- On measurements of global competitiveness and innovation, the United States ranks highest in the world.[1]
- The population of the United States includes all races and people from every country in the world among its 295 million inhabitants, with more than 35 million foreign-born immigrants.
- According to the U.S. Census Bureau, Latinos comprise about 14 percent of the U.S. population currently and will increase to nearly 25 percent of the population by 2050.
- Purchasing power for Latinos, Asian Americans, African Americans, and Native Americans is increasing rapidly.

Introduction

The place of diversity in daily, educational, and workplace life in the United States is well established. Coverage of diversity-related issues is inescapable in the national media. There are regular stories in weekly magazines on the challenges women face in balancing childrearing and work, news reports about how a person might be stopped by police based on racial background, or accounts of the triumph of a person with a disability who manages to overcome an obstacle.

Americans are deluged with demographic data that compares how people with different racial, ethnic, age, or gender profiles are watching television programs, attending movies, and tuning in to radio stations. For example, it is not unusual to hear a movie labeled according to its anticipated audience: African Americans, women, couples on a date, or children. The mention of various groups, such as NASCAR racing fans, soccer moms, born-again Christians, or residents of the city of San Francisco, conjures up a variety of stereotypical images. These include what people look like in terms of race and ethnicity, how tolerant or lacking in tolerance they might be, what kind of jobs they have, the amount of money they make, and the political party they belong to.

Labeling, categorizing, and measuring on the basis of the ways in which people differ is a constant in daily U.S. discourse. Oftentimes, the stereotypes and assumptions behind these categories are inaccurate and incomplete, lacking in complexity and individual differentiation. Yet real differences do exist and have an impact on the ways that people interact in U.S. workplaces and governmental institutions. The level of complexity and the profusion of data that exists make the task of painting a succinct picture of diversity in the United States a difficult endeavor.

While the corporate field of diversity can trace its origins to a number of countries, certainly much of the history of diversity in the business world has been impacted by changing approaches to diversity in the United States over the past 50 years. With its history of slavery, waves of immigration, and advocacy movements, the United States has struggled in myriad ways to address diversity issues, both socially and legislatively. Rights for blacks, women, union members, military veterans, farmworkers, people with disabilities, and homosexuals have all been the subject of intense disputes and shifting policies over time.

In attempting to determine which diversity variables impact workplace interactions for the broadest number of people in the United States, it might be tempting to focus on the six primary dimensions of diversity—race, ethnicity and national origin, sexual orientation, age, gender, and physical ability—represented on the Diversity Wheel in Figure 9-1. In fact, from the perspective of diversity professionals and of individuals who see their lives as being profoundly affected by the fact that they are disabled, a person of color, older or younger, gay or lesbian, or a woman; it may seem heresy not to do this. However, taking a fresh look at the subject of U.S. di-

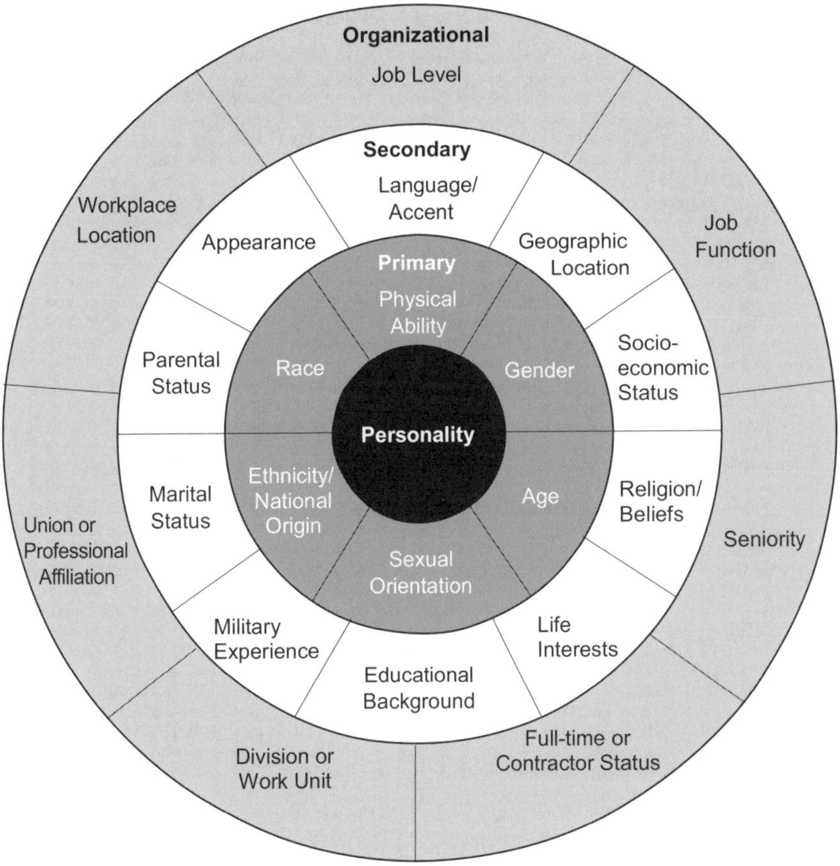

FIGURE 9-1. The Diversity Wheel

Note: Similar models of concentric circles representing the various dimensions of diversity are widely used by U.S. diversity practitioners and reflect the U.S. experience of diversity. Traditionally U.S. companies have focused on the primary dimensions, the innermost circle, based on legal requirements (EEO and Affirmative Action legislation, the Americans with Disabilities Act, federal, state and local anti-discrimination statutes, etc.). In certain corporations, as diversity efforts expanded and focused on inclusion of all employees, addressing the concerns related to the outer circles drew more attention in terms of corporate policies, programs, and recognition. This diagram is adapted with permission from John Wiley & Sons.[2]

versity and reflecting on workplace realities, there are other variables, such as geographical or regional differences, which deserve attention as well. It should also be acknowledged that a dimension such as gender clearly overlaps with other factors including age, family issues, life stage, and marital status. Race and ethnicity, the historical basis for the diversity movement in the U.S., continue to be important, but in new ways as the profile of the country's population continues to change.

The diversity variables covered in this chapter include:

- Regional Origin and Immigration
- Race and Ethnicity
- Gender
- Religion and Values

Regional Origin and Immigration

Regional differences are a longstanding feature of U.S. life. These have been strongly influenced by historical patterns of immigration and internal migration. The mobility of the U.S. population and the proliferation of fast food and shopping malls across the country may lead some to expect that variations in regional character are becoming less pronounced, with only minor differences in spoken English separating north, south, east, and west. However, not only accents, but also basic values, as well as communication and work styles, still tend to vary widely across regions according to the ethnic makeup of the population.

There is also considerable variation from one region to another in the extent of ethnic and linguistic diversity. The experience of driving through the ethnic neighborhoods of the greater Los Angeles area is markedly different from the cityscapes and signage one would encounter in Topeka, Kansas or Birmingham, Alabama. The residents of Manhattan, Silicon Valley, and Miami expect their days to be a swirl of languages and cultures. A bilingual English and Spanish speaker from Miami, of Cuban descent, would find it surprising to be told upon relocating to Boston that the conversation he has with his wife in Spanish may make others uncomfortable—in Miami, speaking his mother tongue had never been an issue.

A History of Immigration, Slavery, and Internal Migration

While the first arrivals to the land that would become the United States were groups later labeled as Indians or Native Americans, the new waves of immigrants who began to arrive in the seventeenth and eighteenth centuries were mostly Northern Europeans. English, Scotch-Irish,* Germans, Dutch, and Swedes were among the early European settlers who came in search of economic opportunities as well as religious and political freedom. These immigrants settled the eastern seaboard and gradually moved inland as Native American lands were purchased or seized outright.

The early years of settlement and nationhood also saw the arrival of Africans who were forcibly abducted and brought to the United States as slaves. It is important to differentiate the experience of early European immigrants from the experience of the African slaves, who were clearly not immigrants. As Malcolm X said, "We are a people who formerly were Africans who were kidnapped and brought to America. Our forefathers weren't the Pilgrims. We didn't land on Plymouth Rock; the rock was landed on us."[3]

In the 1800s, new waves of immigration, influenced by events in Europe such as the Irish Famine from 1845 to 1849, or the failure in Germany of a revolution in 1848 that sought to unify the country with a constitutional government, brought fresh groups to a burgeoning nation. These groups tended to displace earlier occupants of urban centers such as New York, while more established residents moved on to other areas. New immigrants, Germans and Scandinavians in particular, also found their way to the rich farming country of the Midwest. The influx of settlers from the east and from Europe into California after the discovery of gold there was accompanied by importation of Chinese laborers to work on farms, mines, and in the construction of the transcontinental railroad.

The late 1800s and early 1900s saw another enormous influx of people from southern Europe, particularly Italy, and Eastern Europe, including

*Scotch-Irish were people of Scottish descent who lived for some time in the northern part of Ireland (particularly Ulster) before immigrating to the American colonies prior to the Revolutionary War. They are commonly distinguished from Irish Catholics, who immigrated in large numbers beginning in the mid-1800s.

many Jewish immigrants from Russia, Poland, and elsewhere. The all-time peak of immigrants as a percentage of the total U.S. population was the nearly 15 percent level reached between about 1870 and 1910.[4]

TABLE 9-1. WAVES OF IMMIGRATION TO THE UNITED STATES[5]

Time Period	Largest Groups by Size
Pre-1790 immigration; original thirteen colonies	English, Scotch-Irish, German, Scottish
1790–1880	German, Irish, British, Austro-Hungarian, Canadian
1880–1930	Italian, Austro-Hungarian, Russian, German, British
1930–1965	German, Canadian, Mexican, British, Italian
1965–2000	Mexican, Filipino, Korean, Dominican, Indian (from India)

As for African Americans, when the Emancipation Proclamation was issued on January 1, 1863, less than 8 percent of the black population lived in the Northeast or Midwest. Yet the end of the Civil War and the years of Reconstruction did not see a mass exodus of former slaves from the southern states. Although in the late 1800s tens of thousands of African Americans moved into Kansas and others settled in the Oklahoma Indian Territories in search of social and economic freedom, even in 1900 approximately 90 percent of all African Americans continued to live in the south.

In the early decades of the twentieth century, the movement of blacks to the northern and midwestern cities gained tremendous momentum. Thousands of African Americans boarded buses and trains, nicknamed the Chicken-Bone Express, bearing brown paper bags with food packed by female relatives to sustain them on trips from Mississippi to Chicago or from Alabama to Detroit. There were many reasons for this great migration. Leaving behind the southern states to escape sharecropping, worsening economic conditions, and the lynch mob, they sought higher wages in manufacturing jobs, better homes, and political rights, although they did encounter discrimination in the North as well as the South. Between 1940 and 1970 continued migration transformed the country's African American population from a predominately southern, rural group to one with a strong presence in northern industrial cities such as New York, Detroit, and Chicago.

Recent Shifts in Immigration Trends

There has been a marked shift in immigration patterns over the last several decades, with Latinos and Asians dominating the mix. A huge tide of Latino immigrants has entered the border states of the Southwest and West, as well as urban centers such as Chicago and New York. About half of these Latinos are from Mexico, with the Dominican Republic, Cuba, and Puerto Rico as other prominent countries of origin.

Asians of multiple nationalities—Chinese, Filipinos, Vietnamese, Koreans, Japanese, and Indians, to name the largest groups—have favored California as an initial destination; South Asians, such as Indians and Pakistanis, have immigrated in large numbers to the East Coast. Figure 9-2 illustrates the transformation in the blend of immigrants toward a preponderance of Latinos and Asians: at present, more than half of the foreign-born residents of the United States are from Latin America, while a quarter are from Asia.

Latino immigration, both legal and illegal, has had such an enormous impact in recent years that Spanish is now the second, or even the first, language of many communities in the Southwest and in California. In some respects, the increased Mexican presence in the border region represents a return to the past, as much of the Southwest and California was Mexican territory before the Mexican-American war of 1846–1848, and it has seen many different eras of civilization from the Native Americans to the Spanish conquistadors and missionaries, Mexican ranchers and farmers, and, more recently, European settlers.

Immigrants from Latin America have been concentrated in just five or six states: California, Texas, New York, Illinois, and Florida. California in particular has been affected disproportionately in relation to the rest of the country by immigration, as one-quarter of the state's population is now foreign born. More than one-third of people in the United States with Latino ancestry live in this one state.[7] However, over the past decade, growing

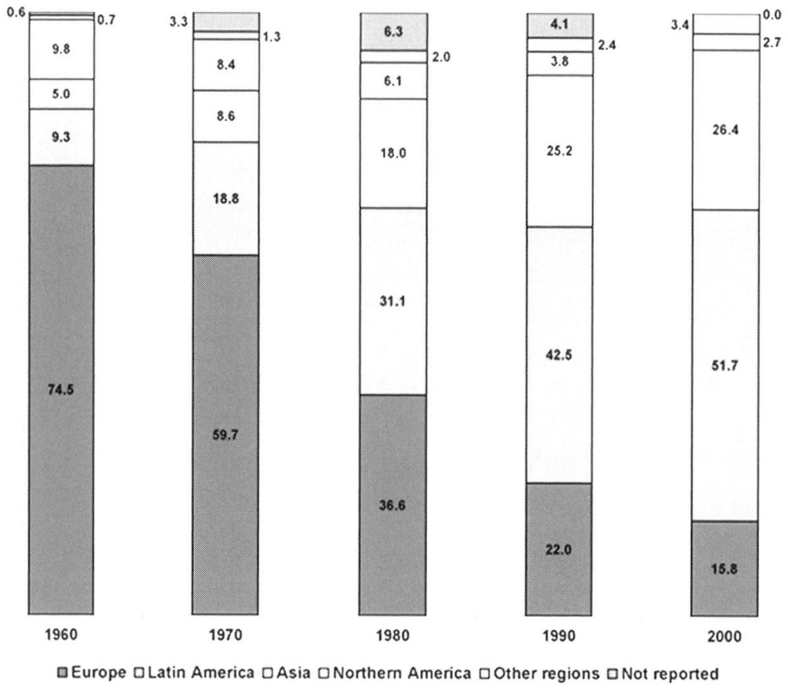

FIGURE 9-2. Foreign-born Population by Region of Birth as a Percentage of the Total Foreign-born Population for the United States: 1960 to 2000

Source: Used with permission. Originally published by the Migration Information Source, (www.migrationinformation.org), a Project of the Migration Policy Institute.[6]

numbers of people, most recently immigrants from Mexico, have been moving north and east to other states in search of work in industries such as agriculture or construction.

Regional Identities

The net result of these changing historical patterns of immigration into the United States and migration within the country is a mosaic of different cultures that have intermingled and taken on particular regional identities. Figure 9-3, for example, shows the U.S. distribution of Native Americans, the original inhabitants of the continent, along with people of black, Asian, Pacific Island, and Latino ancestry. It is readily evident that Native Ameri-

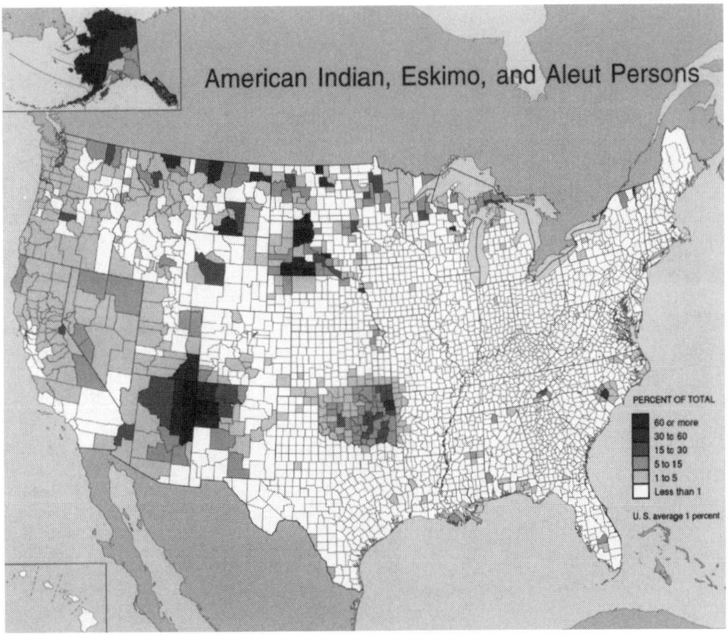

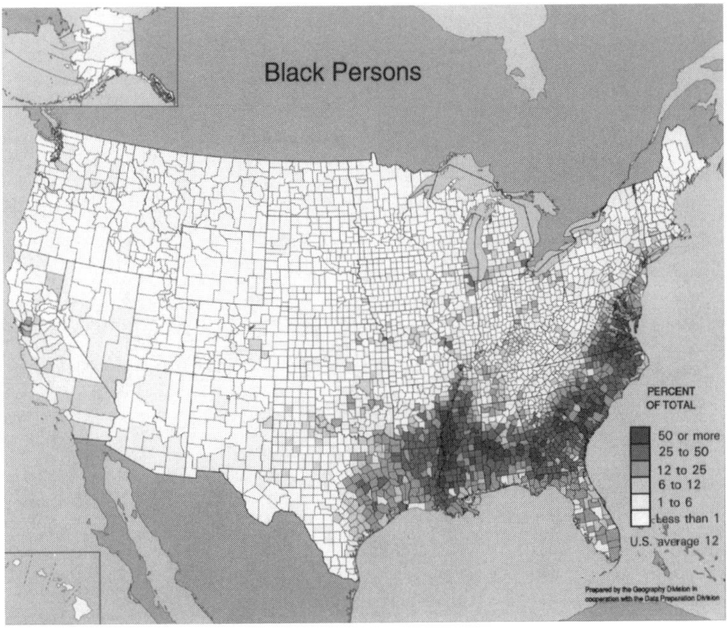

FIGURE 9-3. Population Density of Native Americans, Blacks, Asians and Pacific Islanders, and Latinos in the U.S.[8]

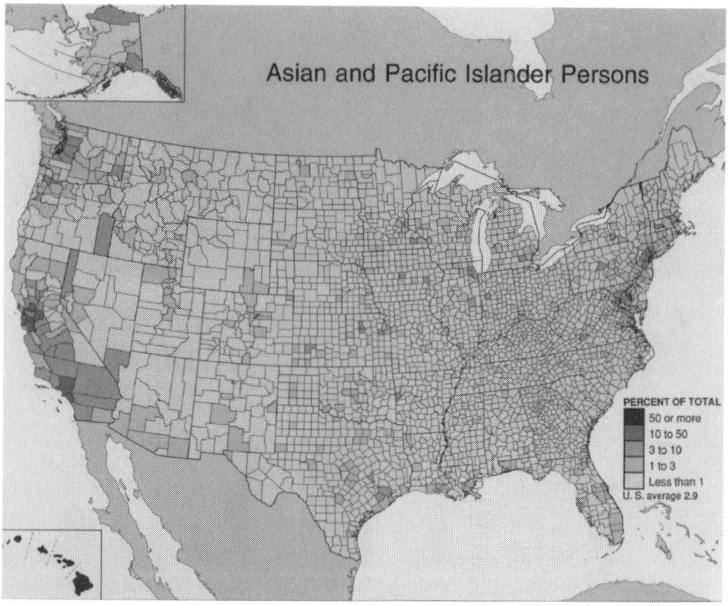

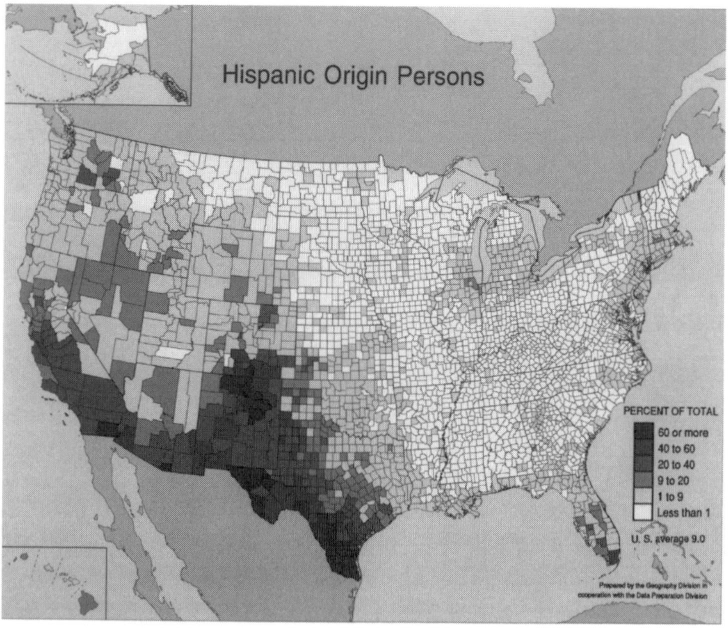

FIGURE 9-3. *Continued.*

cans are most heavily clustered in the Southwest, the northern plains states, and Alaska. Blacks are still concentrated in the South as well as in major urban areas in the upper Midwest and Northeast. Asians and Pacific Islanders favor urban areas on the West Coast and the Northeast, while Latinos have initially gravitated toward locations within several hundred miles of the border with Mexico.

The distribution of these groups, plus the movements of European and other immigrants, has affected regional character in various ways. Some examples from different locations, including popular images that represent a generalized description of the region based on the racial and ethnic makeup of the locations, are listed in Table 9-2.

The Midwestern state of Minnesota provides an interesting illustration of America's layering of immigrant waves. During the 1800s, this state was the destination of many Scandinavians and Germans, and also became home to a number of large Native American reservations. Minnesota has traditionally been a major farming state with a strong educational system and a liberal political tradition. Much of the state's commerce came to be focused on the metropolitan center of Minneapolis and St. Paul known as the Twin Cities.

In the wake of the Vietnam War and other global conflicts, Minnesota experienced an influx of refugees, most notably Hmong tribespeople from Laos. Minnesota's immigrant population has continued to grow, more than doubling in the decade of the 1990s. It now comprises 5 percent of the state's population and has become far more visible, especially in urban areas such as the Twin Cities. The top three nationalities of foreign-born residents of Minnesota today are Mexican, Laotian, and Vietnamese.[9] As a result, work and community dynamics have changed. Over the last several decades, many Minnesotans have learned to live and work for the first time with non-native speakers of English (once-familiar jokes about Norwegian farmers are especially bewildering to immigrants from Mexico or Southeast Asia). Workplaces that were previously staffed almost exclusively by Caucasians now include people with a completely different historical experience of village life, tribal loyalties, and labor patterns.

More broadly speaking, in states and cities where the non-white

TABLE 9–2. IMMIGRATION AND REGIONAL CHARACTER

City or State	*Prominent Groups*	*Popular Images*
New York City	Irish, Italian, African-American, Eastern European/Jewish, Puerto Rican, Dominican	global financial center; so-called Capital of the World; corporate headquarters; highly competitive work environment; ethnic neighborhoods; first destination for immigrants
Boston	English, Irish, Italian, African-American	early colonial center; long history; European influence; elite universities; liberal politics; socioeconomic, ethnic and racial divisions
Chicago	German, Polish, Mexican, African-American	Midwestern business center; steel and other manufacturing; former stockyards; music and nightlife; segregated neighborhoods
Miami	Cuban, Haitian, Dominican, Puerto Rican	Spanish-speaking; U.S. center for business with Latin America; conservative Cuban immigrants
Los Angeles	Mexican, European, Iranian, Korean	movie and aerospace industries; sun and surf; large Spanish-speaking population; smog and congestion; social extremes
Texas	Mexican, English, German, African-American	oil and cattle industries; brash manners and risk-taking attitude; fondness for "bigness"; religiously and politically conservative; proximity to the border
Iowa	German, Scandinavian	hard-working farming communities; modest and plainspoken; high educational standards; fiscally conservative, socially progressive; predominantly white and middle class

population is rapidly becoming the majority, there are varying patterns of segregation and integration that affect local culture as well. Chicago and Atlanta can both be considered African American cities in terms of population percentages, yet they are highly segregated cities where much of the mixing between whites and blacks, for example, may occur primarily in the workplace. Diversity professionals comment that one of the major impediments to ongoing progress on the issues of diversity in the United States is that while interactions may occur between different ethnic and cultural groups in the workplace, people return home to neighborhoods or to other venues dominated by people like themselves in terms of race, ethnicity, and economic status. A case in point is religious institutions. There is an often-repeated comment that in Chicago the city is at its most segregated on Sunday mornings and in the early afternoon. It can be difficult for foreigners who are unfamiliar with a particular region or locality to understand the nuances of how diverse populations interact with each other.

Regional Background and Corporate Culture

Corporate cultures of major corporations may reflect the headquarters location. For example, a company whose corporate headquarters is located in a rust belt and relatively homogeneous city such as Pittsburgh could find that there are complications involved in dealing with colleagues located in northeastern urban centers such as Boston and New York, or other cities such as Miami or Los Angeles. There can be differing expectations regarding such basics as work hours and flexibility, punctuality, level of directness, socialization outside working hours, and respect for authority.

A company headquartered in Houston or Atlanta is likely to have a very different image than one in Seattle or Denver. This could affect public perception of the industry it represents, the kinds of employees it is able to attract, the political persuasions of top management, and the role of religion in the workplace. A history of lost jobs and severe economic dislocation, as in certain Rust Belt cities, can affect the receptivity of residents to globalization, offshoring, and diversity in general, with the potential for backlash toward foreign workers greater than in other regions where the foreigner may actually be in the majority.

Regional Origin: Workplace Implications

Regional and urban/rural differences may affect workplace interactions in the general level of tolerance expressed toward individuals perceived as being outside the local mainstream, including employees who are from outside the United States, members of minority groups and/or recent immigrants, as well as gay, lesbian, bisexual, and transgendered (GLBT) employees. One corporation, in the process of relocating employees from Silicon Valley to one of the western mountain states, encountered issues related to differing levels of receptivity to differences. It recognized a business imperative in dealing with issues of regionalism because it was spending a great deal in relocation costs, only to see highly skilled employees quit the company because of their unhappiness in a new location. This company set up a series of community awareness days and diversity-related efforts advocating acceptance of Latino, African, and Asian American, as well as GLBT employees.

Another example of how such differences play out regionally can be illustrated by the experience of a diversity consultant conducting training sessions for thousands of employees of a large U.S.-based multinational in the South and Northeast. One exercise asked participants to choose from among four individuals which person they would most like to be and which person they would least like to be. The choices were an African American woman with a high school equivalency diploma, a recovering drug-addicted father living in a car with his children, a Southeast Asian merchant with limited language skills and uncertain citizenship status, and a gay, white unemployed executive male. The exercise raised issues related to values, assumptions, and the impact at work.

At the southern locations of the corporation, the gay executive was never selected as a person they would like to be and was the overwhelming choice for the one they would least like to be. When asked why, participants spoke of their Christian faith and strong family values. The so-called lifestyle of the gay executive was labeled as sinful. Even closeted gay and lesbian employees who revealed their sexual orientation to the consultant avoided the executive option. When asked who they would like to be, the choice in the South was often the father in the car, based on reasoning related to the importance of family and the notion that a path to recovery includes a spiritual or born-again Christian awakening.

In the northern locations, the choices were the reverse, with participants selecting the gay employee as the person they would like to be because of a perceived ease in regaining employment and the assumption that he had a nice apartment and a comfortable life of affluence. While some expressed concern about the perceived loneliness of the gay employee in the workplace, there was considerably less discomfort with the character than in the South, even in predominantly Catholic but liberal Boston. The father in the car was the least likely to be chosen, with little mention of the possibility of redemption or faith.

Deeper inquiry revealed that many of the tensions on work teams comprised of people from different regions came from the perception that individuals were judging one another based on assumptions related to perceived differences in life interests, values, sophistication, and mental agility. Some in the North confessed to being put off by the accents of their southern colleagues. There was a presumed mindset—conservative, prejudiced, anti-intellectual, slow—that the accent represented in their minds. Southerners commented on the fast-talking directness, lack of relationship-orientation, and brusque manners of their northern colleagues, and were highly sensitive to stereotypes held about them.

Foreign employers are advised to consider regional differences when shaping their entry strategy into the United States. What sort of corporate image do you seek to establish? How attractive is your location to a diverse employee base? What is the potential level of receptivity to employees from around the world based on regional diversity in your location? Once operations are up and running, it is wise for such employers to also focus on shared goals and performance criteria that are applied fairly across regions, and to be alert for tensions between regional offices or problems that come into play when moving people from one place to another. When such issues do exist, it can be useful to stress the values of the corporation worldwide and how those are applied in each location. It is best to encourage employees to embrace, in a positive way, being part of a global enterprise rather than to allow regional differences to become an object of excessive focus or to permit differences in work styles to escalate into conflicts.

Foreign managers will have different day-to-day working and living experiences in different parts of the United States, based on the regional diversity described in this chapter. It is important to take a proactive approach to ensure that employees from around the world are valued and provided the opportunity to contribute to their full potential in all locations in the

United States. Location-specific information is vital to increase understanding of regional nuances and to accelerate the adjustment process. In addition, it is important to provide training programs and systemic support focused on increasing awareness of the impact of cultural diversity on teamwork and the development of effective working relationships.

Race and Ethnicity

Clearly, one of the most intractable issues in the United States continues to be race and ethnicity. It was the starting point for diversity awareness in U.S. institutions, and its relevancy has only increased over time. The most blatant historical contradiction to the U.S. ideal of equality was almost a century of institutionalized slavery. The tragedy of slavery and its legacy continues to haunt the United States. Thomas Jefferson, in his "Notes on the State of Virginia," warned of a catastrophic calamity as America's potential fate: "Deep-rooted prejudices entertained by the whites; ten thousand recollections by the blacks of the injuries they have sustained . . . will divide us into parties, and produce convulsions which will probably never end but in the extermination of the one or the other race."[10] Although the dire consequences of Jefferson's prediction have thankfully never been realized, there continues to be a sense of the U.S. as a nation divided along racial lines. A few years ago, *The New York Times* won the Pulitzer Prize for its series "How Race Is Lived in America," which explored the differences in the daily life experiences of blacks and whites in the United States and acknowledged that while progress has been made, many barriers and obstacles remain to equality for African Americans.[11] Because this is still true in many corporate settings as well, the subject of workplace diversity holds ongoing challenges. Thought and practice related to establishing equal rights for blacks have been linked with other social advocacy movements over time under a broader diversity umbrella.

Discrimination: Overt to Subtle

For the most part, U.S. corporations have put an end to blatant discriminatory behaviors based on race and ethnic origin. Racial slurs, racially and ethnically based jokes and humor, sharing pictures and cartoons depicting negative stereotypes, and so on, have mostly gone underground to the extent that such conduct remains. Much of this is the result of prominent lawsuits and the imposition of zero-tolerance policies by many corporations. While pockets of such behavior exist and the pain they inflict is still very real, diversity professionals, many of whom are African American, agree that discrimination based on race and ethnicity is almost more difficult to deal with in the current U.S. work environment because it has become more subtle, nuanced, and sophisticated. Today, it is the questions an African American business traveler might face when waiting in the first-class check-in line at the airport; it is the people who are greeted with their names pronounced properly in the workplace and those who are not; it is leadership meetings involving the top 10 percent of company leadership where special programs have to be implemented to involve more than a handful of people of color; it is who gets feedback to improve their performance—some managers hesitate to offer feedback to people of color for fear of being sued or accused of discrimination if the feedback is misinterpreted. References to lingering forms of privilege and favoritism or to "microinequities" point to those subtle messages, sometimes subconscious, that devalue, discourage, and ultimately impair performance in the workplace, particularly on the part of people of color.[12]

America's Changing Racial Profile

The recent waves of immigration to the United States make the current scene even more complex. The number of Latinos in the U.S. population as a whole has recently surpassed the number of blacks, making Latinos America's largest minority group. The birth rate among Latino residents of the U.S. is far higher than the birth rate for other groups (2.8 births per woman for Latinos versus 2.0 for blacks and 1.9 for whites, which has significant implications for the future).[13] The U.S. Asian American population, while still accounting for less than 5 percent of the total, grew by about 50 percent between 1990 and 2000.

Each group of immigrants, based on their ethnicity, skin color, level of education, socioeconomic class, and English language ability, experience the

United States differently, and the quality of welcome they receive may vary considerably. For example, a light-skinned Cuban or persons from northern India may be viewed as white, while a dark-skinned Afro-Cuban or a person from southern India may be labeled and treated as a racial minority.

The current and projected growth in minority populations reinforces the business case for the continued need to fight discrimination as well as to leverage growing market opportunities and sources for talent in the workplace. In places such as Miami or Los Angeles, the minorities have become, or are becoming, the majority. The numbers of minority workers and simple observation in the workplace signal a different balance of people than one would find on the street. African Americans and Latinos continue to be underrepresented at the higher levels of corporate, educational, and governmental institutions. Latinos and African Americans have lower incomes and levels of education on average than whites.

Asian Americans present a different set of issues. While they still represent only about 5 percent of the population in the United States, they have made significant strides in terms of economic prosperity and visibility in corporate America, even though their representation at the CEO and senior management level is low. Asian Americans have the highest median household income and are the highest percentage of college graduates among all groups, including whites.[14] They tend to cluster in medical and high-tech fields and represent a large number of small- and medium-sized business owners. In general, Asian Americans are no longer considered a disadvantaged group in admissions to universities and colleges because of their high levels of representation and academic success. In Silicon Valley companies, where Asian Americans are more readily visible at upper levels of management and professional positions, there is a concern about the lack of attention and support for diversity-related issues for Asian Americans. A number of surveys indicate that Asian Americans in corporations believe that diversity efforts do not apply to them.

The relative affluence of Asian Americans does not extend to all groups, with recent immigrants from Vietnam, Cambodia, and Laos experiencing greater rates of poverty and un- or underemployment. This is often because of the contrasting circumstances in which those people have entered the United States. Regardless of their country of origin, those who arrive as political refugees are less well positioned than those who come with strong educational credentials, professional goals, prearranged contacts, and plans to seek economic opportunities.

People of Color

Given this complex mixture of racial and ethnic groups, discrimination and prejudicial stereotypes are not simply an issue between whites and blacks or whites and Latinos but between African Americans and Asian Americans, African Americans and Latinos, and different Asian groups with one another. *People of color,* a term often used to refer to minority, non-white populations, assumes a shared experience between these various groups. However, Asian Americans and certain groups of Latinos, such as light-skinned Cubans, may not see common cause with other people of color. In fact, the labeling and naming of racial, ethnic, and cultural groups in the United States continues to be a source for much debate—including heated discussion about the need to even provide a racial or ethnic category, which has been labeled as unpatriotic by some in the media. A representative comment based on this viewpoint is "Why do people have to say they are African American or Mexican American. Aren't we all just Americans?"

The assumption of similarity within each group may or may not be applicable. In addition to varying levels of economic achievement, Asians have a diverse set of cultural backgrounds ranging from India to Southeast Asia to Japan and may have very little shared sense of community between them. Latinos could have originally come from any Spanish-speaking country in the Americas, and common cause between them may or may not be felt based on economic status, job type, religion, and the path that brought them to the United States. African Americans come from all different socioeconomic strata and professional or vocational backgrounds, yet many do see themselves as part of one community that shares an experience of oppression. On the other hand, how that community is defined and who qualifies as a legitimate spokesperson for it—whether liberals such as Jesse Jackson or Al Sharpton, the conservative J.C. Watts, or a newcomer like Barack Obama—are causes for continual debate.

What Am I?

The issue of self-identification is also complicated, as people assign different labels to themselves. Based on generation or experience, an individual may prefer to be referred to as black and feel no affinity with the term African American, having no sense of connection or allegiance to Africa. Others simply want to be referred to as Americans. Terms such as Latino or Hispanic may each have advocates based on cultural, community, or individual experience. The term "Latino" is used here because many people object to the association of "Hispanic"—the term often used in citing census data—with Spain and Spanish colonialism, and also to the potential exclusion of Brazilians, whose heritage is Portuguese rather than Spanish.

In addition to the question of preferred labels, there are growing numbers of individuals with mixed racial and cultural backgrounds. Tiger Woods, one of the most famous individuals with a mixed-race background, refers to himself as a "Cablinasian," pointing to his white (Caucasian), black, Native American, and Thai heritage. Many U.S. nationals have a difficult time selecting racial and ethnic categories for the census, finding the category "Other" to be too general, not taking into account their unique diversity dimensions.

Race and Ethnicity: Implications in the Work Environment

Beyond the very visible issue of lack of representation at the leadership level of corporations, here are several concerns of racial and ethnic minority employees in U.S. business.

Access to Opportunity: Many cite the lack of viable role models and mentors or sponsors to guide their way through the unwritten rules of corporate America. There is limited opportunity to become part of informal networks that allow one to learn about potential job opportunities or high-profile assignments. People tend to mentor or sponsor individuals like themselves who continue, in many U.S. corporate settings, to be white males. There are patterns in some corporations of minorities reaching a certain grade or job level and then plateauing, with limited opportunity to move up the promotional ladder. A recent article in *Harvard Business Review* presented the results of a study that indicated a disturbing trend: whites tend to fast track early in their careers and move quickly up the hierarchy, while minorities tend to advance only after years in middle management.[15] Racial and ethnic diversity may exist at the lower levels of a corporate organization but become rarer at the higher levels. Differences in work, communication and conflict resolution styles, patterns of socialization and community involvement, appearance, and educational background all may create subtle divides between minority and white employees.

Some minorities feel that their white managers and colleagues are uncomfortable with them and quietly and possibly unconsciously exclude them from certain settings and opportunities. Others feel that their managers don't trust their capabilities and tend to micromanage, creating the sense that the minority employees need to prove themselves on a constant basis. The pressure to prove oneself in every meeting and professional interaction creates a high level of stress and tension that increase alienation.

In order to eradicate the more subtle forms of discrimination and provide truly fair access to opportunity, the next step in many companies involves the day-to-day conduct of individual managers who are working with minority employees or peers. This is particularly true for foreign companies and expatriate managers in the United States, as for them racial and ethnic differences may be compounded by cultural contrasts with the home country, potentially creating an even greater sense of distance and exclusion. They need to consider matters such as

- Invitations to casual lunches where business is discussed
- Assignment of high-profile and risky projects
- Air time in meetings and presentations
- Accessibility for consultation
- Their own level of comfort in interacting with minority colleagues and subordinates

On an organizational level, employers can address the more subtle forms of exclusion and limited access to opportunity by paying attention to systems and processes such as hiring, promotions, succession planning, mentoring, professional development, and leadership competencies that are free of unintended bias.

Positioning for Success: Another consistent theme in the comments made by hiring managers and recruiters is that they can't find qualified minority candidates. Then, when a minority employee is hired or promoted, comments may be made that the only reason for the selection was minority status, not qualifications. Recruiters need to be ready to look beyond the usual sources for minority candidates, utilizing the insights, recommendations, and networks of minority employees to locate qualified candidates. For example, employee affinity networks based on race, ethnicity, and gender are excellent sources of contacts for untapped, diverse hiring networks. Then, instead of the harmful pattern in which a minority candidate is hired, positioned to fail, and then fired or persuaded to leave, resulting in the affirmation of negative expectations, companies must put in place as many ways as possible to support individual success: training and development, access to resources and contacts, capable management and mentorship, and a strong team.

Handling the Increased Complexity: As the workplace becomes increasingly diverse and racial and ethnic categories more complex, employers must keep up with the changing demographics and workplace dynamics. The term people of color can suggest a false sense of unity around issues of diversity and inclusion for minorities. Race and ethnicity are still critically important diversity dimensions in the United States that require even more focused attention, increased understanding, and agile responsiveness. A diversity consultant shares this perspective: "Many people say to me that I'll know we're there when we don't have to talk about diversity anymore. I say I'll know we're there when we do talk about diversity more: we pay close attention to changing demographics, understand the potential issues, value the differences in the workplace, notice the uniqueness, and invite that in." According to this viewpoint, the most effective way for firms to deal with diversity issues will be to highlight them still further and to make them a key ingredient in corporate strategy.

Foreign managers may find themselves in an ambiguous category related to race and ethnicity in the United States. Although they may be from the same cultural background as their diverse counterparts in the U.S., the cultural connection may be close or distant depending on the generation of immigration of their U.S. colleagues. In addition, foreign employees may be unfamiliar with issues of diversity and inclusion related to their racial or ethnic background as experienced in the U.S. business context. Finally, despite the dialogue that has taken place in many diversity training programs, senior leadership and diversity council meetings in U.S. corporations over the years, foreign employees will experience a wide range of reactions to race and ethnicity from their U.S. colleagues: enthusiasts who recognize the business case for diversity and inclusion, skeptics who have observed time and energy spent on diversity with limited impact, and naysayers who claim not to experience any racial or ethnic issues in corporate America today.

Gender

Women in the United States have yet to achieve pay parity with men (according to the Census Bureau, women in general make 73 cents for every dollar received by a man, with great variation between different ethnic groups, the lowest being Latinas at 53 cents to the dollar) and continue to be represented in limited numbers in executive positions. In the past few years, the issue of gender in the workplace has become interwoven with issues related to life stage, age, and family. Although substantial efforts have been exerted to make workplaces more family-friendly, these efforts are often seen as perks or remedial assistance for female employees with children. Women frequently do not take advantage of them for fear of being viewed as lacking in career commitment.

The Juggling Act: Work and Family

Though much has changed, the predominant assumption in the United States continues to be that it is the responsibility of women to provide care for children and other family members. When the composition of senior management teams is evaluated, this trend is confirmed: men at the top tend to have either stay-at-home wives, or spouses with schedules flexible enough to deal with childcare and other home issues. Expectations about face time (the amount of time an employee spends at his or her desk at work and in meetings) often fit into a framework that is more feasible for men who have a spouse to take care of family responsibilities. Women with children are forced to juggle family and home responsibilities with work, limiting their ability to advance to top-level positions. Even today, flex-time and virtual work options are limited, especially as one goes higher up in the organization. In recent years, men with children have also expressed frustration with rigidly defined workplace expectations and have pressed for a more flexible working environment.

In addition to work environment pressures, the assumptions and expectations of coworkers can get in the way of the advancement of women at work. As opportunities arise for high-profile, high-pressure projects requiring extensive travel or overseas assignments, women with children may be excluded based on the good intentions of their colleagues, who assume they have no interest in taking on such assignments. Conflicting expectations about the role of working mothers can also create challenges. Women frequently report that the pressure to be a supermom is intense, and leads to stress that affects their ability to be effective at work. Negative assumptions about working mothers and about women who stay at home full-time create what has been called the "mommy wars"—a no-win situation for women with children. Much has been written about affluent, well-educated women taking themselves out of the workplace in order to focus on childrearing. Of course, the opportunity to opt out of work altogether is not available or desirable to many women. This either/or scenario—either you are a working professional or a committed parent—creates unnecessary stress for women and limits the potential contribution of a key segment of the U.S. workforce.

Singles and the Family-Friendly Workplace

Another group with increasingly vocal concerns in the workplace is comprised of singles without children, including single women. Work/life balance and family-friendly initiatives often appear to exclude the needs of this group. The complaint they often express is that others think they have no personal life, and so they are tasked with excessive travel and overtime responsibilities with little or no support from their companies. Singles tell stories of being asked to travel on holidays with the explanation that their colleagues need to spend time with their families (children and spouses). An organization may receive an award from *Working Mother* magazine for its efforts to accommodate the needs of mothers, yet single women in the same company are left shaking their heads because they don't see benefits or support being extended toward them. It often comes as a shock to employers when their single workers start asking for flexibility in order to care for aging parents.

Employees in their 20s and 30s (so-called Yers and Gen Xers) have other concerns about their access to flexible scheduling and work/life balance offerings. They may feel that the quality of their work/life is declining because of perceived needs to cover for older employees or for those with children or aging parents. Tensions in work teams may have much to do with generational, gender, and life stage issues. Accounting and consulting firms often have high turnover among entry-level employees and women in general. Some have initiated structured approaches to addressing the work/life issues of team members who work in fast-paced, travel-heavy, and high-pressure environments in order to address concerns related to fairness.

Lack of Diverse Leadership Models

Authors and speakers like Deborah Tannen and Pat Heim have documented ways that women and men approach communication, leadership, and teamwork differently, and have stressed the fact that there are often different rules governing the expectations of behavior for women in the workplace.[16] One consulting firm that hired an equal number of men and women in entry-level positions, but had only 12 percent women in partner positions, found that women's performance appraisals differed substantially from those for men. The comments "does not speak up in meetings" and "does not stand up for her ideas" appeared frequently in women's evaluations, reflecting differing behaviors related to participation in meetings;

women tended to practice more turn-taking than men and shared the airtime. What is labeled as assertive behavior in a man may be seen as overly aggressive and unacceptable behavior when demonstrated by a woman. Another difference can be as simple as word choice. In studies related to women's acceptance into MBA programs and whether women entrepreneurs received investments from venture capitalists, women tended to use phrases in their application essays or sale pitches like "I will try," or "I hope to," whereas men used more confident-sounding phrases like "I will."[17]

Gender: Implications in the Work Environment

Women continue to lack adequate role models for success at the highest levels of corporations even though their numbers are growing. Often, women are not part of networks that would lead them to work assignments with Profit and Loss (P&L) responsibility which, in turn, lead to executive positions. Even in areas such as human resources, where females tend to dominate in terms of numbers, leadership positions are often held by men. In engineering and scientific fields dominated by men, women often struggle for credibility or experience the anxieties and loneliness that can come from being in the minority.

Although progress has been made for U.S. women in the workplace, there is much work left to do. Some foreign employers may be surprised by aspects of the U.S. social climate and corporate norms that are less generous than they would expect in terms of maternity leave or childcare; on the other hand, they might find a heightened sensitivity toward issues such as workplace discrimination and sexual harassment that can result in major legal damages for companies that take them too lightly. A work environment that is open to flexible work schedules and virtual work options and also accepting of a wider range of leadership, communication, and teamwork styles will enable U.S. women to achieve more responsible positions and contribute more fully to the success of the organization as a whole. Companies need to exert conscious attention to ensure that corporate networks, performance evaluations, meeting styles, and written or unwritten expectations for everyday behavior take gender differences into account and reinforce fairness on the job rather than the opposite.

Religion and Values

The United States as a whole is a relatively religious nation when compared with other major countries in Europe or Asia, for example. This proclivity toward religion undoubtedly reflects in part the fact that many of the founders of the original colonies, as well as immigrant groups who have entered the country over time, came to America to escape religious persecution in their homelands and to find a place where they could express their own religious faiths freely.

Religious affiliation in the United States, to some extent, mirrors the patterns of immigration that were discussed at the beginning of this chapter. Among all U.S. residents, about half identify themselves as Protestants, and a quarter as Catholics. Protestants live throughout the country, but adherents of the socially conservative Baptist denomination comprise from 35 percent to 55 percent of the population in southern Bible Belt states such as Mississippi, the Carolinas, Georgia, Alabama, and Tennessee. Catholicism is particularly strong in the Northeast and in the border states next to Mexico, reflecting the presence of families with southern European or Latin American ancestry—more than 40 percent of people in New York, New Jersey, and New Mexico, for instance, identify themselves as Catholics. And the percentage of those who claim they have "no religion" is highest in the far western states where people have historically been less enthusiastic about organized religion; in California, Nevada, Oregon, Washington, and Wyoming, the number in this category is 20 percent or higher (in several of these states it is the largest category).[18]

Workplace Expressions of Religion

In recent years the U.S. workplace has been caught up in an increasingly vocal debate about spiritual and religious expression. Often there is a conflict between those expressing fundamentalist values and those holding more secular and liberal values. Those espousing a more secular perspective may or may not be very religious in their personal lives, but they see the workplace as a venue where is it more appropriate to separate church and religious activities from business, and keep their spiritual perspectives to themselves. Those with more fundamentalist or evangelical beliefs may want to break down the separation between religion and work, and are advocates of prayer meetings, open discussion of religious beliefs during work hours, and embedding explicit religious principles into corporate structures.

A recent NBC News poll found that 58 percent of respondents said their religious beliefs played a role in the decisions they made at work, and 65 percent said those beliefs influenced how they interacted with coworkers. So whether religious beliefs are held privately or expressed openly, their influence is indeed pervasive in the workplace. Many workers credit religion and spirituality as one of the top factors in making them the people they are today. Since the events of September 11, 2001, many in the United States have experienced a reawakening regarding the importance of faith. When this is combined with the fact that some take their faith to work with them, it is easier to understand why the faith-at-work movement has become more visible in recent years.

Legal Framework

While protections in the workplace exist that allow for reasonable accommodation for religious expression under Title VII of the Civil Rights Act of 1964, those accommodations are typically presumed to apply to people who pray at designated times during the workday, such as Muslim employees, those who need time off for religious holidays, such as Jewish employees, and those whose religious beliefs require dietary and clothing restrictions, including headscarves for Muslim women. Provision of these accommodations is not consistent within the workplace. The number of formal allegations of religious discrimination received by the Equal Employment Opportunity Commission has almost doubled over the past decade. Even when formal complaints are not filed, human resources and diversity professionals hear complaints by evangelical or fundamentalist Christians that these accommodations do not extend to providing them the opportunity to openly express their own religious faith, which includes proselytizing about their religion and its associated values and beliefs. Several years ago, the *Harvard Business Review* included a case study on the issue of employee affinity groups based on religion.[19] In fact, many companies that establish affinity networks for different ethnic and cultural groups, employees with disabilities, and women make it a point that such networks exist for business reasons and should not be venues for proselytizing or recruiting members for a specific church or religious organization.

Religion: Implications in the Workplace

Employers in the United States must carefully consider issues of religion in the workplace and stay abreast of changing social circumstances that could impact their workers.

Faith-at-Work and Tolerance: Many of the concerns expressed in response to the growing faith-at-work movement are related to a perceived lack of tolerance toward various groups: those belonging to non-Christian religions, individuals who do not conform to traditional Christian models, those holding secular or atheistic beliefs, and GLBT (gay, lesbian, bisexual, and transgender) employees. Different regions or locales may have a different level of receptivity to other groups based on their own sincerely held religious beliefs or values. Some fundamentalist employees concede that they attempt to limit their interactions with people they assume to be gay or lesbians because of their evil lifestyle. The fear of being negatively judged in the workplace for one's life situation, politics, and values is a fundamental issue related to diversity of religious beliefs and individual freedoms.

A schism even exists in the U.S. diversity field, where diversity facilitators or trainers with strong religious beliefs may find it hard to discuss sexual orientation from a non-judgmental perspective or to condemn discrimination against GLBT employees. In fact, it is not Christians alone who may have strong issues with sexual orientation but many cultures and religious traditions, including Islam. Those with a sexual orientation other than heterosexual continue to find themselves the object of jokes and judgments that would be unacceptable in the workplace if directed to a specific ethnic or racial group, women, or people with disabilities. This may lead to a climate where GLBT employees feel unsafe being open about their sexuality and relationships with significant others. The ongoing debate about gay marriage has brought heightened attention to the differences between religious fundamentalists and others regarding this issue.

Potential for Religious Coercion: Concerns about religion in the workplace also relate to the overt, or even subtle, pressure that leaders and managers can place on their employees related to religion. If an employee is fired for not attending a prayer meeting or religious event, there is a case for discrimination on the basis of religion. However, if an employee attends a prayer meeting or religious event because he or she is fearful about the loss of future developmental and professional opportunities, there is no easy remedy for this more subtle form of coercion. Religion and associated values can become a means to include or exclude people on teams and workgroups and provide unearned advantages to certain individuals over others.

Attitudes toward Muslim Colleagues: 9/11, the war on terror, and the war in Iraq have created strains between Muslims and others in the workplace. The unwarranted linking of Muslims in general with terror and terrorists leads to unfortunate patterns of stereotyping and misunderstandings. There is an appalling dearth of knowledge in the United States regarding the history and values of Islam and the role that fundamentalism plays. Cultural and ethnic diversity among Muslims in the U.S., encompassing all races, causes confusion among some mainstream U.S. Americans who have a narrow view that Muslim equals Arab. Some Muslims feel uncomfortable asking for reasonable accommodation for prayer time, making ablutions, and changing their attire because they do not want to call attention to themselves or for fear they will not fit in with their colleagues. In some companies, Muslims find signs in the restrooms saying sinks are for hands, not feet, preventing them from performing purification rituals that are required for prayer.

Muslim women report that the wearing of veils or headscarves often makes other employees hesitant to interact with them and prevents them from being considered for managerial positions. Twenty-something Muslim women in the workplace comment that their colleagues act surprised upon hearing that they enjoy music, shopping, and partying—albeit without alcohol—like other young people. "It is amazing how a piece of clothing can make people act so unnaturally with me, as though my headscarf makes me somehow less than human," said one Muslim woman after hearing colleagues speculating about her after-work activities. "The other response is that I am like a Catholic monk or nun, someone totally removed from society or having a 'normal' daily life. People can't seem to believe that my life is enjoyable." Muslims in general, like other minority groups, are concerned about lack of opportunity in majority, Christian-dominated institutions.

In each of these situations—whether the question is tolerance of different lifestyles, the potential for religious conversion, or attitudes toward Muslim colleagues—foreign companies are advised to follow a two-part strategy. First, they must ensure that they are in legal compliance with provisions against overt religious activity or proselytization in the workplace as well as provisions for accommodation of reasonable forms of religious expression such as prayer, special holidays, or particular forms of dress. Beyond such basic compliance, however, they also need to look for ways to create a company culture that welcomes various perspectives while requiring that employees remain primarily focused on achieving their own job objectives as well as the goals of the organization as a whole.

Applying Global Diversity: *Religious Expression at Work*

Religion

SITUATION:

An Asian company with its U.S. headquarters based in North Carolina is experiencing difficulties with its branch operation in Minneapolis. The Human Resources Department recently informed corporate headquarters that employees in Minnesota have complained about "intimidating" behavior on the part of the branch manager based on the activities of his "faith-at-work" group.

Further investigation of the branch manager's conduct has revealed that his behavior is no different from that of company managers in several other locations. A devout Baptist from North Carolina, he has brought a number of religious objects to his office, including a Bible that he often reads at lunch, before which he always says grace. He holds regular prayer breakfasts, open to all employees, and tends to use religious homilies at office staff meetings.

When asked about whether these activities would be perceived as exclusionary, the manager asserts that these are free expressions of faith that are similar to the allowances made for Jewish staff who are not expected to work on Saturdays, or for Muslim women who wear headscarves to work. Indeed, he notes that the faith-at-work group is a significant comfort and source of motivation to other employees who have moved to Minneapolis from corporate headquarters in the South and miss contact with the community churches that they grew up with. The manager notes ironically that he feels it is his group that is being made to feel unwelcome through criticisms of their behaviors in this so-called diverse workplace.

POSSIBLE SOLUTIONS:

Human Resources' recommendation, based on advice from legal counsel, is for the manager to refrain from any expressions of religious faith in the workplace in order to limit the company's legal exposure to claims of intimidation. The current situation could be interpreted as making adherence to a particular religion an implicit requirement for advancement. However, it would probably be difficult for the manager and his fellow religious believers to accept a ban on any forms of religious expression in connection with work.

A compromise that might be more acceptable to the manager would be to cancel the prayer breakfasts on work time and to hold them on weekends at his home or outside the office, while also refraining from religious references in his public communications at the office. This would signal to employees that he believes religious observances are to be respected but are also private, and that no one in the office should either impose or feel imposed on by a particular religious belief. The manager can keep his Bible in his office, though it might be a good idea to close his office door when consulting it. He can set the tone for a mutually respectful office atmosphere through his own example, and will not have to feel that he is hiding his faith or that coworkers resent the imposition of his faith on them.

Summary Recommendations

1. Be prepared for the impact of **regional origin** on the nature of diversity at work as well as attitudes toward it. Relocating employees to different parts of the United States, for example, can have a profound effect on the overall work experience. Work locations with considerable diversity of languages, ethnicities, races, and geographic backgrounds may require new skills for working effectively across style differences; locations that are more homogenous may require awareness of subtle and often unconscious exclusion that can happen when people who are different enter the workforce.

2. It is important to not only attract and retain diverse talent, but also to effectively leverage diversity for competitive business advantage. Employees from diverse **racial and ethnic groups** provide insights about how to best serve local customers with the same background; they also may interface more effectively with counterparts abroad who are from their country of origin in order to foster rapid and efficient communication.

3. Management training programs in the United States often fit a narrow mold that does not take **gender** differences into account. Ensure that leadership models and development programs incorporate a wide range of management and communication styles. Analyze succession planning for unintended bias and consider the potential benefit of mentoring programs to broaden the exposure of women to senior leadership.

4. Be sensitive to issues related to **religion** and tolerance in the workplace. Based on the distinctive history of the United States and high rates of formal religious affiliation in parts of the country, some employees are likely to have religious beliefs that they feel quite passionate about and would like to bring into the workplace in a way that comes as a surprise to foreign managers. At the same time, there are those who are equally adamant about their own more secular views or forms of spirituality that do not involve organized religion. An example of a current flashpoint is the backlash from groups of employees who feel that their religious convictions are affronted by policies and benefits for gay

employees such as healthcare for partners. Whether employee affinity groups based on religion should be permitted is another bone of contention, especially when this leads to attempts to convert other employees. Companies must stress values and goals that respect each individual's rights to his or her own beliefs while offering equal opportunities to every employee. There is a fine balance between allowing permitted forms of religious expression and letting these become intrusive in the eyes of other workers.

CHAPTER 10

Conclusion: Moving from Knowledge to Action

How can knowledge about the rich diversity that exists within each country be translated into action? The complexity of cultures within cultures around the world may appear daunting, yet there are practical ways to leverage such diversity successfully across a global enterprise.

An Approach to Global Diversity: Six Steps

Here is a set of straightforward steps that can guide approaches to global diversity. This same list could be employed by a company, a global manager, or an individual contributor. A description of each step as well as examples of possible applications are also provided.

1. Engage country partners and establish a common purpose.
2. Identify the core diversity variables that are relevant for a particular country environment.
3. Consider both positive and negative implications of these differences in the workplace.
4. Prioritize the variables that have the greatest impact on the organization and propose alternatives for action.
5. Examine the local social environment for forces that might support change.
6. Implement changes to realize business opportunities and promote greater inclusion.

Step One: Engage Country Partners

The best way to begin a global diversity effort is, of course, to engage counterparts from the country of interest in an ongoing dialogue. This type of effort can be initiated within a diverse management team, among members of a global diversity council, or with an individual colleague who is willing to serve as a cultural guide.

Establishing a common purpose is a good place to start. This usually takes the form of an interrelated set of goals to grow the business and to develop employees to their maximum potential. It is also important to have shared values or principles; these are often part of the organization's basic charter.

The good news for those who seek to promote global diversity efforts is that principles that form the core of some domestic initiatives also tend to be valued by employees around the world. These include, for example

- *Developing the strongest possible business network* of customers and suppliers.
- *Creating an inclusive work environment* that provides access to opportunities such as promotion, mentoring, and feedback.
- *Avoiding bias and stereotyping,* including the impact of subtle and often unconscious behaviors based on limited or faulty information about others.

Step Two: Identify Core Diversity Variables

It is all too easy to pass judgment on another country from the outside looking in. As previous chapters have indicated, the views of people within any given country with respect to diversity may involve a distinctive combination of variables that does not mirror the diversity profile that exists in another location. For someone who has just arrived, it may seem relatively simple to diagnose problems and propose solutions in a host environment based on one's own experience and cultural background, yet this type of approach seldom provides a promising basis for action.

If an organization seems to lack representation of women in management, or people in a certain ethnic group are clustered in lower positions in a corporation, for example, a visitor may be quick to point this out and begin making suggestions. While such observations could be valid, there might be historical and cultural factors involved that are obvious to the country insider but less visible to the outsider. In any global diversity effort, acknowledging the complexity of the diversity issues present and gaining a variety of input, including local views, before introducing changes is a critical part of the process.

The list of 14 possible diversity variables mentioned in Chapter One can serve as a reference point for identifying the particular variables that are most crucial in a given country environment. Previous chapters have illustrated different possible combinations of variables country by country. For example, core variables discussed for China, Egypt, and the United States are contrasted below.

China	*Egypt*	*The United States*
❖ Regional Origin	❖ Family Background	❖ Regional Origin
❖ Socioeconomic Status	❖ Socioeconomic Status	❖ Race and Ethnicity
❖ Language	❖ Religion	❖ Religion
❖ Educational Background	❖ Gender	❖ Gender
❖ Age		

Establishing a set of diversity variables that reflects the perceptions of local employees and business colleagues requires patient inquiry and a willingness to set aside preconceptions based on one's own background and agenda. There may also be distinctive aspects of the local organization that cause one or more diversity variables to take on greater or lesser prominence than would be the case for the country as a whole.

Step Three: Consider Positive and Negative Implications

It is important to explore the positive and negative implications of the diversity variables that have been identified. On the positive side, there are often business *opportunities* that flow from underserved markets or uneven allocation of resources in different parts of a country. Examples cited in previous chapters include

- Linguistic groups that would like to have products or services delivered in their own language (India).
- Regions of a country that are targeted by the national government for future development (China).
- Potential customers among recent immigrant populations who are not reached by a traditional sales force (United States).

Explicit recognition of key diversity variables can help to shape a strategy that seeks to expand market coverage, reach new customers, and enhance the company's image. Qualified new suppliers may also emerge from exploration of neglected regions or population segments.

Less positive impacts of perceived differences between people usually involve forms of *exclusion.* One method for pinpointing harmful forms of exclusion is to examine key diversity variables in relation to the stages of human resources development (see Figure 10-1). Each of the stages noted below can either propel one's career forward or hold it back.

It is worth asking whether people are excluded from fair and reasonable opportunities to be hired, trained, retained, evaluated, compensated,

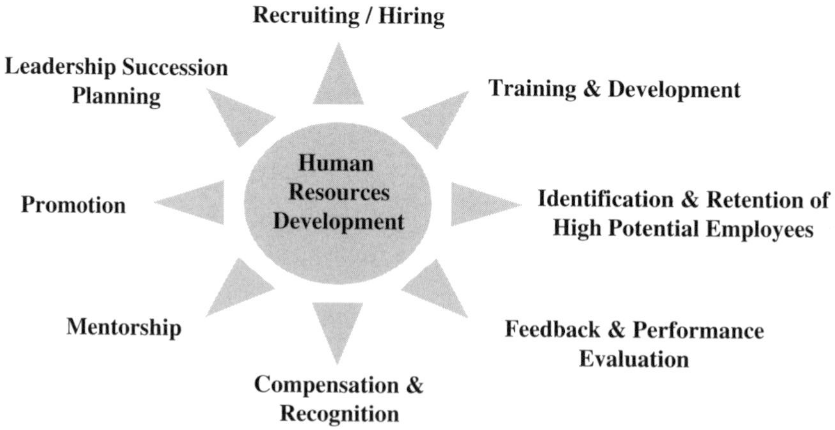

FIGURE 10-1. Human Resources Development Stages

mentored, promoted, and selected for top leadership positions based upon the diversity variables most prominent in their environment. Are some parts of the employee population automatically given preference over others because of factors such as age, regional origin, educational background, gender, or racial differences? Systematic forms of exclusion are likely to lead to competitive disadvantages while they also imply potential sources of fresh advantage. They may represent significant violations of corporate values as well.

Workplace exclusion can appear as a broad social trend such as the persistent reluctance to appoint women to top management positions in many Japanese-owned companies, or hiring discrimination against people of indigenous background who seek elite white-collar jobs in Mexico. This can also take more subtle forms such as the micro-inequities that have become part of the diversity dialogue in the United States: reluctance to offer appropriate feedback because of uncertainty about the recipient's possible reaction, or the failure to invite a person with a disability to a business lunch because of unwarranted concern over the complications involved with transportation, seating, and so on. In any case, there is likely to be a significant cost to the organization when qualified people are excluded from chances for professional advancement.

Step Four: Prioritize Variables and Propose Alternatives for Action

Some diversity variables are bound to be more critical than others for business success in a particular country. There may also be global corporate values that are so important that they add greater emphasis to certain themes. When core diversity variables have been identified and their positive and negative implications explored, it is time to set priorities and examine possible actions.

What opportunities offer the biggest potential benefits to the organization, and what forms of exclusion are holding its employees back? What can we do to realize business opportunities or to promote inclusion over exclusion? It is always best if the proposals come from local country residents rather than from well-intentioned outsiders.

Examples of diversity variables based on previous chapters that could be designated as high priority from a business standpoint, along with possible actions to address the opportunities or issues they represent, are listed in Table 10–1.

TABLE 10–1. HIGH-PRIORITY DIVERSITY VARIABLES: EXAMPLES

Country	Diversity Variables and Related Business Issues	Possible Actions to Better Leverage Local Diversity
China	*Regional Origin:* Salespeople from Shanghai face obstacles selling to customers in Guangzhou.	Salespeople based in Guangzhou prep colleagues from Shanghai prior to customer visits to familiarize them with local requirements and key phrases in Cantonese.
Egypt	*Family Background:* A company is seeking a new executive to head its regional operations and needs to identify candidates who will be most effective in this role.	A multinational enterprise is able to select the most appropriate candidates for top leadership positions based on knowledge of how their personal history, educational qualifications, and prior military service will shape their ability to get things done in the local business environment.
India	*Language:* Customers in many states prefer to buy software products in their own language.	Employee language skills are leveraged to develop new business in selected states or regions that require products in a specific language.
Japan	*Age:* Top management lacks technical skills that are important to shaping strategy in a changing market.	Young employees with technical skills offer reverse mentoring to senior managers to foster a two-way flow of information between different age levels based on expertise rather than seniority.
Mexico	*Socioeconomic Status:* Factory absenteeism and turnover are high because employees are from other parts of the country, live far from the factory site, and do not have reliable forms of transportation.	Employee housing, meals, and transportation to the job site are provided in a *maquiladora* environment in order to increase retention of economically disadvantaged workers from other parts of the country.

Russia	*Regional Origin:* Lack of cooperation between employees located in the capitol and in other sites causes project delays and lack of delegation to a lower-cost location.	Short-term employee exchanges between Moscow and Novosibirsk improve teamwork and help the organization to better realize the advantages of both locations.
United Kingdom	*Race and Ethnicity:* Highly qualified job candidates are increasingly available from minority groups whose members the company has not sought out in the past.	Qualified minority employees are recruited aggressively in order to make the company an employer of choice with a fast-growing segment of the population.
United States	*Race and Ethnicity:* Large potential business opportunities are available with immigrant communities and with the immigrants' countries of origin.	Immigrant employees from various racial and ethnic groups provide insights about how to best serve local customers with the same background; they also interface with counterparts abroad who are from their country of origin in order to foster rapid and effective communication.

Step Five: Examine Forces That Support Social Change

Most cultures are dynamic and changing, and this is also true of cultures within cultures. In each country there are likely to be at least some trends towards social transformation related to the core diversity variables—for example, changes in gender roles, educational practices, attitudes toward older and younger age groups, opportunities for racial and ethnic minorities, or perceptions attached to different regions of the country. A corporate diversity initiative, even if it appears to address an issue with real business impact that has been designated as a priority within the organization, may have only limited chances for success if it is pitted against traditional customs and beliefs that are still strongly valued by the general population. On the other hand, an initiative that intersects with larger social forces supporting change can benefit from a cultural tailwind that enables rapid and efficient implementation.

A company that tries to provide greater opportunities for women, for instance, could meet with accolades, difficult but surmountable obstacles, or broad social condemnation and even banishment from the country depending upon the national setting. The social environment should not necessarily determine a company's approach—initiatives that run contrary to broader social trends may be undertaken anyway because they are based upon fundamental corporate values—but it should be taken into account. Companies that find allies and supporters for change in the wider society will have a better chance of not only succeeding but also being held up as a positive role model for customers and industry peers, and capable job candidates will come knocking. When change appears to be essential (as with restrictions on black workers under the former apartheid regime in South Africa), yet powerful local institutions and citizen groups are opposed, the ultimate response may be to restrict commercial activities or even to withdraw from the country and do business elsewhere.

Over the past several decades, there have been a number of instances of diversity initiatives championed by global companies in local country markets that have coincided with broader social changes and brought significant business benefits. Among them are

Japan: Foreign capital companies have employed and promoted women into management roles over the past two or three decades in much greater numbers than companies headquartered in Japan. This has happened at the same time as women's roles have been changing and has also helped to accelerate that change, resulting in a significant influx of first-rate employee talent.

China: The training and development and technology transfer efforts of Western, Japanese, and Taiwanese firms have transformed the capabilities of millions of Chinese workers who come from economically disadvantaged backgrounds. Such training and development efforts are now making an important contribution to the government's objectives for developing the western part of the country.

United States: Foreign manufacturers have located large, new facilities in poor, rural communities, decreasing the economic imbalance between urban and rural areas and gaining a cost advantage. These manufacturers have provided welcome employment opportunities while becoming significant contributors to the local tax base that funds schools and other infrastructure.

Step Six: Implement Changes

A diversity strategy for a country will have the best chance for implementation if it is shaped according to the steps outlined above. That is, it will include a set of diversity variables that accurately reflect local perspectives, have been analyzed and prioritized according to their business impact, and are translated into practical steps ideally supported by social trends. It may be best to go with a short list rather than a long list of change initiatives, and to build momentum with initial successes.

An example of a comprehensive strategy outline for one country, China, is provided in Table 10-2. The priorities listed could be addressed simultaneously or in succession. Some of them may overlap with global diversity efforts being implemented across multiple world regions; others could be unique to China but faithful to the company's basic diversity principles. This model condenses the steps previously described into a three-point framework that is often useful in working with cross-border differences: *What?* (What are the differences?) *So What?* (Why do they matter?) *Now What?* (What can we do about them?)

Implementation of global diversity initiatives can occur on a grand scale or through the actions of a single individual. On an organizational level, initiatives that require major financial investments, altering the behavior of a sales force, the modification of established management practices, and/or changes in human resources systems may warrant the application of a full-scale change management process. This could include extensive project planning, overt support and modeling by top leaders, alignment of organizational structure and systems, carefully targeted rewards and sanctions, and training for employees who might otherwise resist changes.

TABLE 10–2. COUNTRY STRATEGY EXAMPLE: DIVERSITY IN CHINA

What? (Core Diversity Variables)	So What? (Practical Business Implications)	Now What? (Proposed Actions)
Priority Number 1: Socioeconomic Status	Chinese government emphasizes development of poorer western provinces; significant difference in cost of labor between east coast and western interior	New company branches are opened in major western cities; manufacturing operations with high labor component are relocated to the west to take advantage of the lower wage structure and government incentives to develop economically disadvantaged areas; wages are targeted to be in the top quartile of the regional norm.
Priority Number 2: Regional Origin	Salespeople from Shanghai face obstacles selling to customers in Guangzhou	Salespeople based in Guangzhou prep colleagues from Shanghai prior to customer visits to familiarize them with local requirements and key phrases in Cantonese; training and development of Guangzhou sales personnel is accelerated to enable them to sell a full range of products.
Priority Number 3: Age	Annual turnover of high potential employees under the age of 35 is more than 20 percent per year	Young, high-potential employees are targeted for training and development opportunities abroad, with a minimum commitment to ongoing employment required upon their return.
Priority Number 4: Language	Low brand identification among consumers in provinces with different dialects	Television advertising in local dialects is created to build brand recognition and increase nationwide market penetration.
Priority Number 5: Background	Employees from less prestigious universities face discrimination in compensation and promotion decisions	Human resources policies enforce compensation and promotion based upon workplace performance rather than educational pedigree.

The reason that input from local employees is so crucial at every stage is that the ultimate fate of any diversity initiative depends upon local ownership of new patterns of action. Many people cling to familiar forms of behavior even when these are clearly dysfunctional. Old loyalties and established prejudices die hard, and most of us would, perversely, rather live with our own defects than correct them when they are pointed out by somebody else, especially someone from outside of our own country or cultural context.

Fortunately, with or without a major change initiative, it is possible for each individual contributor in a global enterprise to address diversity issues for a particular country through daily actions. When traveling or living abroad or even working with others through a virtual connection, we can take advantage of fresh business opportunities and support inclusive practices in another country based on ongoing dialogue with our colleagues there. This might mean electing to visit new and different customer sites, seeking out possible new suppliers, scheduling meetings with promising employees whose merits have been neglected, greeting younger workers in the hallway, or taking the time to interview a wide range of job candidates. Assuming that a common understanding has been established around basic diversity principles and that others recognize our interest as being sincere, simply asking the question, "What can I do?" or, better yet, "What can we do?" is a good place to start.

From Strategy to Results

The approach to global diversity that is offered in the six steps described here makes the opportunities clear and provides a framework for action, but does not predetermine the results. It sets the table without fixing the menu, requiring a consistent set of processes and principles while leaving specific actions and their implementation up to the employees in each location within the global organization. The practical form that implementation of a diversity initiative takes within each country can and should reflect its particular business and social circumstances.

Diversity at Home and Abroad

The momentum in the diversity world has been shifting from "Why should we do this?" to "How can we get this done?" Although leveraging diversity on a global scale is a journey rather than a destination, along the way it offers compelling benefits worldwide such as access to new markets and customers and the sourcing of superior talent. It would be a mistake for companies to assume that they are finished with diversity issues in their home country and move on to tackle diversity elsewhere. Yet they should also not be so preoccupied with the challenges and opportunities at home that an even wider set of potential advantages in other countries is neglected.

We can keep creating our own story even as it is interwoven with, but not forced upon, the forms of diversity that exist elsewhere, learning about ourselves as we learn about others. Cultural competence takes on a new and more complex meaning when global diversity and cultures within cultures are considered, but the opportunities are greater as well.

Appendix A
Approaches to Diversity in Canada, South Africa, and Sweden

In addition to its multilingual and multicultural heritage stemming from both French and English immigrants, Canada's foreign born population now amounts to more than 18% of the total, versus 11% for the U.S. and 22% for Australia. These new immigrants have included a large contingent of what the Canadians call "visible minorities," the largest proportion being from Asia, particularly Chinese. Canada also has a significant First Nations population of 2%.

Canadian multicultural policies were promulgated in deliberate counterpoint to the historical tendency in the U.S. to favor assimilation. Canada's brand of multiculturalism encourages its citizens to retain their cultural heritage while sharing the national experience. Some fear that multicultural programs have encouraged immigrants, especially recent immigrants, to avoid associating with other cultural groups.

Cross-cultural issues arise primarily in Canada's large cities, because 90% of Canadians who were born abroad live in the 15 largest cities in the country. The backgrounds of Canadian citizens have changed and will continue to do so in the foreseeable future. Since the population pool is undergoing a transformation, people from different ethnic groups will increasingly replace retirees. That will automatically be reflected in the workplace.

The Royal Commission on Equality in Employment developed a model for achieving equality that is distinctly Canadian, and in 1995 the government passed the Employment Equity Act. The name *Employment Equity* was meant to move beyond the "Equal Opportunity" measures already available in Canada at the time, and to distinguish it from the U.S. model of *Affirmative Action*. The Commission recognized that pervasive discrimination was to blame for most of the disparity in employment. They outlined a systemic response, and coined the term *Employment Equity* to describe it.

The goals of Employment Equity are to

- Eliminate employment barriers for the four designated groups identified in the Employment Equity Act: women, persons with disabilities, Aboriginal people, members of visible minorities;
- Remedy past discrimination in employment opportunities and prevent future barriers;
- Improve access and distribution throughout all occupations and at all levels for members of the four designated groups;
- Foster a climate of equity in each organization.

Employment Equity is an ongoing planning process used by an employer to

- Identify and eliminate barriers in an organization's employment procedures and policies;
- Put into place positive policies and practices to ensure the effects of systemic barriers are eliminated; and
- Ensure appropriate representation of "designated group" members throughout their workforce.[1]

South Africa: The Legacy of Apartheid

South Africa's labor market has undergone a transformation since 1994, with an emphasis being placed on strategies that eliminate the race-based inequalities of the past and improve general working conditions for all South Africans. Although much progress has been made since the demise of the apartheid establishment, issues of inequity still afflict South African society. In the workplace, employees must continue to cope with old mindsets that have not changed, and the courts, in dealing with racist language and harassment, have declared racism in the workplace to be grounds for dismissal. Judges have noted that racism is akin to a cancer in society, and that racial insults in the workplace are counterproductive to good business relations, not to mention degrading to the dignity of the employees who are on the receiving end of such insults.

Discrimination in employment based on an individual's HIV status is also common. According to Clem Sunter, AIDS expert in South Africa, there is a general lack of concern about the impact of HIV infection on employees and the workplace, and there is little or no mention of HIV/AIDS in annual reports. In spite of these issues, efforts are being made to eliminate discrimination.

The South African Employment Equity Act was passed in 1999. The purpose of this Act is to achieve equity in the workplace by

- "Promoting equal opportunity and fair treatment in employment through the elimination of unfair discrimination; and
- Implementing affirmative action measures to redress the disadvantages in employment experienced by designated groups, in order to ensure their equitable representation in all occupational categories and levels in the workforce."[2]

Before the fall of the apartheid regime, the common enemy was easily identified: the Apartheid regime itself. The struggle for equity in the workplace was overt, and the division lines were clear. However, since the establishment of a democratic government the lines have become blurred. There is still conflict in the public and private sectors based on race and ethnicity, but those who were formerly oppressed have now become the ruling party, and they must balance their desire to share resources and promote social justice and equality with the need to keep the country's economy growing. The government and top managers, many of them whites who prospered under apartheid, have to forge a new reality together. Companies that are part of this new South Africa are also part of a legal and moral climate that now strongly encourages more inclusive practices.

Sweden: Gender Equality

The prevalence of a supportive cultural atmosphere conducive to the achievement of gender equality in Sweden is widely known. Swedish culture is in general very egalitarian; workplace examples range from an emphasis on gaining input from employees at all levels to the relatively small income gap between the highest and lowest hierarchical levels. Within this context, regulations on gender equality are generally regarded very positively by both men and women in Sweden.

Since policy associated with gender equality influences all sectors of the populace, every minister in the government is accountable for analyzing, following up, and presenting plans related to equality between women and men in their particular spheres of accountability. The Ministry for Industry, Employment, and Communications addresses gender equality concerns through the Division for Gender Equality. The Office of the Equal Opportunities Ombudsman handles questions concerning legislation and equality between men and women in the workplace, and is under the direction of the Minister for Equality Affairs. The Equal Opportunities Ombudsman was fundamental in eliminating unwarranted wage disparity, and has developed wage statistics and designed a gender-neutral job evaluation system.

Wage disparity still persists—Swedish women earn on average 25 percent less than men—mostly due to segregation of men and women into certain occupations. The Government is attempting to offset the condition of gender segregation in the labor market not only through legislation but also through taking effective measures to transform attitudes and eradicate structures that contribute to gender separation in the allocation of employment. The Equality Affairs Division publicizes information and organizes conferences and seminars to address this issue, and public as well as private organizations contribute to the forming of public opinion on the rights and obligations of men and women and other equality matters. Emphasis has been placed on efforts to eradicate violence against women, and in 1993, the Government appointed a Commission on Violence against Women.

The Government assigned a working group in 1997 to accelerate the development of methods for ensuring gender equality. Specialists on gender equality issues work with each county administrative board. The Government has also allocated funds to the Swedish Association of Local Authorities for a project that will research, develop new methods, and include a gender perspective in the work of local authorities. The Swedish government believes that gender awareness should pervade both political and administrative work in all areas and on all levels. As indicated above, all government ministers are obliged to take into account the objective of equality in their particular area. The Minister for Gender Equality is accountable for the follow-up and further development of the policy and directs the work. The Ministry of Justice is considering proposing a new law to increase the percentage of female board members in publicly listed companies.

In an effort to create greater gender balance, the government also stresses the importance of increasing the household responsibilities of men, and tries to convince fathers to take parental leave. It has augmented the number of men working in schools and childcare and supports men concerned with lowering the incidence of violence against women.

Swedish Gender Equality Policy Objectives

"Women and men shall have the same opportunities, rights, and responsibilities in all significant areas of life:

- Equal division of power and influence between women and men;
- The same opportunities for women and men to achieve economic independence;
- Equal terms and conditions for women and men with respect to owning their own business, work, employment conditions, and career development opportunities;
- Equal access for girls and boys, women and men to education and the development of personal ambitions, interests, and talents;
- Shared responsibility for work in the home and with children;
- Freedom from sexual (gender-related) violence."[3]

Appendix B
Questions for Starting Global Diversity Initiatives

Key questions to consider and honestly answer include:

1. Who is the global diversity effort for? Whose needs is it truly addressing?

   Possible answers may include the following:

   - Advocates of diversity and inclusion are based primarily at corporate headquarters. These advocates may include highly placed executives, the chief diversity officers or leaders, or members of an internal team of diversity professionals, diversity councils, and/or affinity network groups. These individuals and groups may feel that the next logical step for diversity is to extend its scope and take it global or, at the very least, to a larger number of locations.
   - The impetus comes from local employees of a global organization who want to see greater inclusion and respect for their capabilities. Or they may have diversity issues and concerns that they would like to address with the help of corporate resources. For example, they may be experiencing recruiting and/or retention issues, lowered productivity among diverse teams, and challenges in communicating across locations, including with headquarters.
   - A need has been identified that exists among employees in a number of countries. The organization is increasingly using global,

virtual teams to accomplish critical tasks, employees are more frequently working across boundaries, and there is a desire to learn more about the diversity that exists across the entire organization in order to communicate more effectively. The corporation has a commitment to respect and value the contributions of all employees, but to accomplish that task its members must learn more about the priorities and requirements of employees in different locations.

2. What are the key drivers for the initiative?

   Possible answers may include the following:

   - Diversity and inclusion are deemed to be key factors in achieving global competitive advantage.
   - There is a desire to spread the good work related to diversity and inclusion being done at headquarters and other locations to the company as a whole.
   - Parts of the organization are seen as being dysfunctional in terms of dealing effectively with dimensions of diversity that are regarded as crucial (i.e., gender, race, ethnicity, sexual orientation, and/or disability).
   - Diversity and inclusion are viewed as critical components of Corporate Social Responsibility or "triple bottom line" actions being undertaken by the organization.
   - Pressure is being exerted in the form of lawsuits, threatened class action suits, changing legal requirements, and governmental directives.
   - Diversity and inclusion are part of a package of organizational change activities driven by headquarters. Diversity goals in alignment with other globalization goals are being cascaded throughout the corporation.
   - There is a need to fix longstanding problems in the relationship between headquarters and other locations, and diversity and inclusion practices are seen as a method to mend fences.

The answers to these questions should be considered carefully in making decisions about whether or not to proceed, what resources to invest, and how to structure any initiatives to ensure a broad base of support.

Appendix C
Examples of Effective Global Diversity Goals

- *Ensuring the organization is an Employer of Choice by attracting the best talent.*

  Our competitive advantage is our employees. We want our company to be the Employer of Choice in an industry that is currently experiencing a decrease in the available talent pool due to demographic trends.

- *Recruiting employees from diverse backgrounds to better serve and grow in diverse markets.*

  Delivering products and services that meet the needs of our customers is a business imperative for our company. In order to make sure that we understand our diverse customer base in each country where we do business, we have identified recruitment of employees from diverse backgrounds as an important element of our global diversity strategy.

- *Retaining employees.*

  Our current business environment—and projections for the near future—dictates that we must retain and develop our key people. It is critical that we retain employees so that our workforce operates at a high level of productivity, even though in some locations the average industry turnover rate is much higher than ours. In addition, the costs associated with hiring and retraining employees have been put at 1.5 times annual salary per employee based on our internal research. In order to keep these costs down, retention is a business imperative.

- *Creating and maintaining an inclusive environment that allows all employees to contribute fully.*

  We have identified the following business costs associated with a lack of full contribution by employees:

  Lower productivity;
  Ineffective communication and teamwork;
  Increased safety issues;
  Lower morale;
  Increased absenteeism.

  It is imperative that we create and maintain an inclusive environment that allows all employees to contribute fully so that we are productive.

- *Developing, leveraging, and fully utilizing the diverse ideas, perspectives, and contributions of employees.*

  Our recent employee survey indicates that employees are concerned that we have a culture that only values the contributions of employees with a certain industry background and number of years of experience. In order to remain competitive and successful, we can not afford to limit the contributions of employees.

- *Strategically focusing on leadership development and succession planning to ensure there is a pipeline of employees from diverse backgrounds.*

  Our company has changed significantly in the past five years: we are in more global locations, our customer base is more diverse, and our employees are working on multicultural project teams across geographies. We need leaders who can meet these new challenges, and have identified leadership development and succession planning as key business imperatives in our global diversity strategy.

Endnotes

Introduction

1. William James, in his classic work, *The Varieties of Religious Experience*, uses this "blooming, buzzing" phrase.
2. Actually, the facts related to this apparent gaffe, allegedly a mistranslation of "Come Alive With Pepsi," apparently remain unconfirmed; see http://www.snopes.com/business/misxlate/ancestor.asp. A similar claim about Coca-Cola, that its name was first transliterated as "Bite the Wax Tadpole," or the even more vivid "Horse Flattened with Wax" seems to have been an urban legend based on the actions of Chinese shopkeepers rather than the company itself. See, for example, http://www.snopes.com/cokelore/tadpole.asp. Accessed February 22, 2006.
3. Edwards reportedly cited two other errors: one product used chanting of the Koran as soundtrack for a computer game, and resulted in a Saudi Arabian ban and demand for apology; another gave Latin American users a selection between gender choices, with the three alternatives being "not specified," "male," or "bitch" due to an error in translation. Best, Jo, "How eight pixels cost Microsoft millions," c/net News.Com, August 19, 2004. See http://news.com.com/How+eight+pixels+cost+Microsoft+millions/2100-1014_3-5316664.html. Accessed February 21, 2006.
4. See, for example, Yadav, Babulal, "Bill Gates Visit to India—November 11–14, 2002, An Exercise in Corporate Environmental Management," http://www.cemanagement.org/cem_case.htm. Accessed February 22, 2006.These events took place well before the generous gifts from Bill Gates and Warren Buffett that made the Gates Foundation the largest charitable organization in the world.
5. India is rivaled in the number of languages only by a few other nations such as Nigeria or Papua New Guinea.
6. See, for example, http://home.c2i.net/kwhitefoot/LatinDictionary.html-d. Accessed February 22, 2006.
7. Nancy Adler, *International Dimensions of Organizational Behavior,* Fourth Edition. Cincinnati, Ohio: South-Western, 2002), pp. 141–147."Groupthink" refers to the tendency

of group members to perceive and to judge events in the same way based upon the social pressures of an in-group environment.

8. For a summary of Hofstede's research, see *Culture's Consequences: International Differences in Work-Related Values* (Thousand Oaks, California: Sage Publications, 1997). The dimension called Power Distance refers to the degree of differences according to hierarchical status; Uncertainty Avoidance is a label for attitudes toward situations that involve risk.
9. Ibid.
10. See Bibliography for references to each of these authors.
11. See, for example, Ernest Gundling, 2003. *Working GlobeSmart: 12 People Skills for Doing Business Across Borders* (Palo Alto, California: Davies-Black, 2003).
12. Aperian Global is a company with offices in North America, Europe, and Asia that provides Web-based tools, consulting, and training for companies that do business across borders.

Diversity in China

1. See, for example, *Ethnic Minorities in China,* Chinese Cultural Center of San Francisco. Available from http://www.c-c—c.org/chineseculture/minority/minority.html; or, *China's Population Mix,* China Internet Information Center. Available from http://www.china .org.cn/e-groups/shaoshu/mix.htm. Accessed February 22, 2006.
2. Ibid.
3. Tibet is a particularly sensitive subject for China because of the support from outside of the country for Tibetan independence and the aspirations of indigenous Tibetans themselves. Indeed, rather than promoting genuine political and cultural autonomy, China's government appears to have adopted the opposite policy of exerting strong military control and encouraging Han Chinese to emigrate to Tibet in order to build a Han demographic base that will counteract Tibetans' claim for political independence.
4. Here a note of caution is in order: For foreign businesspeople with families, the one serious drawback of many interior cities is the lack of good international schools. If you are considering an expatriate assignment and have children, the availability of good schools should be at the top of your research list.
5. China's regional differences are sometimes replicated in more local rivalries. The lovely city of Suzhou, not far from Shanghai, has a venerable history of more than 2,500 years as one of China's great cultural centers. So famous is Suzhou as a symbol of China's cultural tradition that it, along with its cultural cousin, Hangzhou, are the subject of many traditional Chinese sayings. One of the best known translates as "above there is heaven, here on earth there is Suzhou and Hangzhou." Citizens of Suzhou often find their Shanghainese neighbors insufferable: Shanghainese who come to Suzhou will inevitably compare Shanghai's much greater economic output and status as China's trendsetter and make comments about Suzhou's relative backwardness. It is always a tremendous delight for residents of Suzhou to point out to snobbish Shanghainese that for most of China's history, Suzhou was a vibrant leader of China's cultural development when Shanghai was nothing but a dirty, fly-infested fish camp.
6. Companies that make a genuine commitment to addressing the educational needs of SOE employees or of China's rural poor have a far better chance of winning the support of government officials than competitors who remain focused solely on how China can

benefit them. The Chinese government is acutely aware of the country's history of relations with other nations: during much of the nineteenth and twentieth centuries, Western powers and Japan took advantage of a weak China, much to China's shame and humiliation. Particularly troubling to many Chinese are Britain's deliberate policy of selling opium in China in the mid 1800s to pay for its imports of Chinese tea, and Japan's invasion and occupation of China as part of its imperial ambitions from 1937 to 1945. As a result there remains deep in China's national consciousness a residual suspicion of outsiders' motives: while Chinese welcome outside investment, they want to be sure that any investment benefits them at least as much as it benefits the investor.

Diversity in Egypt

1. See, for example, *Energy Information Administration,* Country Analysis Brief: Egypt. Available from http://www.eia.doe.gov/emeu/cabs/egypt.html; Accessed February 22, 2006.
2. Yasmine El-Rashidi, Jason Singer and David Pringle, "Egyptian Mogul Makes Big Bet on Cellphones," *The Wall Street Journal,* April 18, 2005, p. B1.
3. Robert B Cunningham, and Yasin K. Wasta Sarayrah, *The Hidden Force in Middle Eastern Society.* (Westport: Praeger, 1993).
4. Egypt publishes little information about its military, and its bases and the areas surrounding them are off-limits to Egyptians and foreigners alike. Statistics and details about the military are from external sources and their reliability is unverifiable.

   All males must register for conscription upon reaching the age of sixteen. A local council of military, civil, and medical officers grants exemptions and deferments for those employed in permanent government positions, young men whose brothers died in service, those employed in essential industries, and family breadwinners. It then chooses conscripts by lot from the remaining names, who are on call for induction for three years. If not called after three years, they can no longer be drafted. Alternative forms of national service in which conscripts may be required to participate are the police force, the prison-guard service, or in one of the military economic service units. Conscripts who have completed high school serve two years, and those who have not finished high school serve three years of active duty, after which they remain in the reserves. Those with college degrees serve 18 months.

   Egypt is assumed to supply its military forces with the latest equipment for prestige and as a deterrent. As the strongest military power in Africa and the second largest in the Middle East after Israel, it has contributed to international peacekeeping missions such as those in the Congo, East Timor, Georgia, Kosovo, Liberia, Sierra Leone, and Western Sahara, and it participated in the NATO Implementation Force in Bosnia.
5. Mohamed A Maait, et al., *The Effects of Privatisation and Liberalisation of the Economy on the Actuarial Soundness of the Egyptian Funded and Defined Benefits Social Security Scheme,* International Social Security Association (ISSA) Research Programme, Conference Proceedings, Helsinki, September 25–27, 2000.
6. Leila Reem, "Grow Old, Get Poor," *Al Ahram Weekly Online* no. 691 (May 20–26, 2004); Available from http://weekly.ahram.org.eg/2004/691/fe2.htm. Accessed February 22, 2006.
7. Nagla El-Ehwany and Manal Metwally, "Labor Market Competitiveness and Flexibility in Egypt" (paper presented at the 7th Annual Conference of Economic Research Forum for Arab Countries, Iran & Turkey (ERF), held at Amman, Jordan, October 26–29,

2000). Available from www.erf.org.eg/database/paperresult.asp?d_code=200129. Accessed February 22, 2006. Some of the data cited is from the 1996 census, and circumstances may have changed since that time and should become apparent when the results of the 2006 census become public. Additional sources include the International Labor Organization, and the Labor Force Sample Survey (LFSS) carried out by the Central Agency of Public Mobilization and Statistics (CAPMAS) and analyzed by the Almishkat Center for Research in Egypt.

8. Nasra Shah, "Arab Migration Patterns in the Gulf" (Regional Conference on Arab Migration in a Globalized World, September 2–4, 2003. Cairo, Egypt), pp. 97–109. Available from http://www.egypt.iom.int/eLib/UploadedFolder/Abstracts of Research Papers, Regional Conference.pdf. Accessed February 22, 2006.
9. See, for example, "Arab Migration in a Globalized World" (League of Arab States and the International Organization for Migration, conference, Cairo 2–4 September 2003). Also see Shah, Nasra, "Arab Migration Patterns in the Gulf," pp. 97–109. Available from http://www.egypt.iom.int/eLib/UploadedFolder/Abstracts of Research Papers, Regional Conference.pdf. Accessed February 22, 2006.
10. See, for example, Jackline Wahba, "Does International Migration Matter? A Study of Egyptian Return Migrants" (Regional Conference on Arab Migration in a Globalized World, September 2–4, 2003. Cairo, Egypt). Available from http://wbln0018.worldbank.org/eurvp/web.nsf/Pages/Paper+by+Wahba/$File/WAHBA.PDF. Accessed February 22, 2006.
11. Nathan J. Brown, "Women and Law in the Arab World," unpublished article (1996). Available from http://www.geocities.com/nathanbrown1/WomenLaw.htm., and http://www.geocities.com/nathanbrown1/. Accessed February 22, 2006.
12. See, for example, the research summary, "Measuring the Economic Contribution of Women in Egypt" on the website of the American University in Cairo; http://www.aucegypt.edu/src/wsite1/research/research_economiccontribution.htm#A%20General%20Overview%20focusing%20on%20the%20Different%20Estimations%20for%20the%20Participation%20of%20Females%20in%20the%20Labor%20Force. Accessed February 22, 2006.
13. It is important to note that Christians also comprise 10 percent of the population in Egypt, with the largest number belonging to the Coptic sect. The culture of the Coptic church persists throughout Egypt in the use of what was the ancient Egyptian calendar and is now known as the Coptic calendar. It is divided into 13 months of three seasons of four months each: the season of the flood, the season of cultivation, and the season of the harvest and fruits. Farmers all over Egypt use it to keep track of the agricultural seasons. The feast of Nayrouz marks the first day of the Coptic year, corresponding to the 11th day of September. While Coptics may use their calendar to celebrate religious holidays, it has less impact on the business world than the Muslim calendar.
14. Another source of information for short- and long-term residents in Egypt is *Cairo: The Practical Guide, ed. Claire E. Francy* (Cairo: American University of Cairo, 2004). The book is also read by Egyptians.

Diversity in India

1. Shashi Tharoor, "A Culture of Diversity," *Resurgence Magazine* (August 3, 2005); Available from http://resurgence.gn.apc.org/articles/haroor.htm. Accessed February 22, 2006.

2. The list of Schedule VIII official languages is as follows: Assamese, Bengali, Bodo, Dogri, Gujarati, Hindi, Kannada, Kashmiri, Konkani, Maithili, Malayalam, Manipuri, Marathi, Nepali, Oriya, Punjabi, Sanskrit, Santhali, Sindhi, Tamil, Telugu, and Urdu.
3. The exceptions are three states in the Northeastern region where English is the official state language. English is not included in Schedule VIII of the Indian Constitution, which lists the 22 official languages.
4. The Indian film industry is mainly centered in Mumbai but also located in Chennai, Hyderabad, and Kolkata. Hyderabad has the well-known Film City, where a large number of Indian, as well as foreign, films are shot.
5. *The KryssTal Web Site,* eds. Kryss Katsiavriades and Talaat Qureshi. Available from http://www.krysstal.com/langfams_indoeuro.html. Accessed February 22, 2006.
6. Two classical Indian languages, Sanskrit and Pali, belong to the Indo-Aryan language family. Both of these languages were very influential in shaping Indian philosophy, religion, and culture. Known as the mothers of all Indian languages, they are now gone from daily speech. Sanskrit has been likened to Latin because it is almost exclusively used by holy men in the study of ancient texts and in ceremonial functions. Hindi and Sanskrit terms often share the same root word, so there is academic study of Sanskrit, just as some study Latin as the basis for European languages.
7. Although it is mainly used in religious ceremonies and not a language for communication, Sanskrit is common in both North and South India. The written form is in the local script.
8. Barbara D. Metcalf and Thomas R. Metcalf, *A Concise History of India* (Cambridge: University Press, 2002).
9. The rivalry between India and Pakistan carries over to sports, with a heated rivalry between national cricket teams. For big matches between the two countries some Indian companies in larger Indian cities have been known to project the game in a large conference room, and heated discussion on the topic can be heard in the cafeteria. Outside of the workplace, prayer meetings by every religious group are held all over the country for the victory of the Indian cricket team.
10. In India, some of the largest cities are sometimes referred to as "A" class cities, whereas the second tier, consisting of most state capitals, are labeled as "B" class cities.
11. A good example is Bangalore, where the new business investment seems to have outgrown the infrastructure capacity of the city. As a result, many companies located there are challenging the state government to take appropriate steps or they will move out of the state.
12. It may be worth noting that the words "Hinduism" and "Hindu" are not mentioned in the ancient Indian religious scriptures or literature. The word "Hindu" seems to have been first used by Islamic invaders and rulers who coined the term based on the word "Sindhu" (the river Indus in present-day Pakistan), around which the ancient Indian civilization was born and developed.
13. *Census of India* (database online) 2001, Registrar General and Census Commissioner, India; available from http://www.censusindia. net. Accessed February 23, 2006.
14. India's major religions include the following:

   - Hinduism: The oldest and the most dominant religion in the country was born in the Indus Valley area approximately 4,000 years ago (1500–2000 B.C.). It has evolved considerably over time and today constitutes the largest single religious group in Asia.

- Islam: The second largest religion in India arrived in India with the Muslim traders from the Middle East around A.D. 800, and blossomed during the periods of Islamic rule from thirteenth century onward.
- Christianity: Many foreigners believe that Christianity was brought to India by European colonists after the Portuguese sailor, Vasco Da Gama, discovered the sea route from Europe to India in 1498. But Christianity was probably brought much earlier—either by Saint Thomas or by Syrian missionaries in the fourth century. It grew most rapidly in the country during the colonial periods.
- Sikhism: This group was born in India about 400 years ago and has played an important role in India's cultural history since then. Despite the fact that its followers comprise a relatively small percentage of population (1.9 percent), Sikhs, whose majority resides in Punjab, have had significant influence in the military and with public policies. Currently, fundamentalist Sikhs have some conflicts with the government.
- Buddhism: Buddha is said to have gained enlightenment in Bodh Gaya in Bihar (Northeastern India) during the sixth century B.C., and Buddhism, the religion that grew from his teachings, had a major impact and influence in India over the following thousand years. It then lost influence and has since fallen into a small minority within India.
- Jainism: The birth and growth of the Jain religion took place in sixth-century B.C. Just like Buddhism, its founder, Mahavir, came from a noble family and gave up a good, comfortable life for the betterment of the inner soul. Many of its followers' beliefs are similar to those in Hinduism except that they also believe in complete *ahimsa,* or nonviolence, for every form of life. The faith is practiced by a small minority of Indians.
- Zoroastrianism: This is the religious system based on the teachings of the Persian prophet Zoroaster whose followers are known as Parsis. In the eighth century, Zoroastrians fled to India (mainly to the modern-day province of Gujarat on the west coast around Mumbai) in large numbers for refuge from religious persecution by Muslims in Persia. One of the conditions of their refuge was that they not partake in missionary activities or marry outside of their community. Although not legally bound to these practices, modern Parsis still hold to them and are therefore a dwindling population. The Parsis of India speak a dialect of Gujarati.

15. *Census of India* (database online) 2001, Registrar General and Census Commissioner, India; available from http://www.censusindia.net/religiondata/index.html. Accessed February 23, 2006.
16. *UNDP Human Development Report 2004* (Database online); United Nations Development Programme, 2005; available from http://hdr.undp.org/reports/global/2004/?CFID=91066&CFTOKEN=31302537. Accessed February 23, 2006.
17. Ayodhya is in the northern state of Uttar Pradesh. It is a very sacred place for the Hindus, as it is said to be the birthplace of Lord Ram, whom Hindus worship as an incarnation of God.
18. *Census of India* (database online) 2001, Registrar General and Census Commissioner, India; available from http://www.censusindia.net/religiondata/index.html. Accessed February 23, 2006.
19. *Brief Analysis of Indian Census Religion Data. Census of India* (database online) 2001, Registrar General and Census Commissioner, India; available from http://www.censusindia.net/religiondata/Brief_analysis.pdf. Accessed February 23, 2006.

20. Based on an interview by the author in March 2005 with Mr. Ashutosh Phadke, Director of Human Resources, General Mills, Mumbai, India.
21. Based on an interview by the author in March 2005 with Mr. Ashutosh Phadke, Director of Human Resources, General Mills, Mumbai, India.
22. Based on interviews by the author in March 2005 with Mr. Abhijit Bhattacharjee, Manager of Human Resources, Kyocera Wireless India Private Limited, Bangalore, India.
23. The "Rahu Kala" period lasts for 1½ hours every day, but occurs at different times.
24. Based on interviews by the author in March 2005 with Mr. Ashutosh Phadke, Director (HR), General Mills, Mumbai, India, and with Abhijit Bhattacharjee, Manager of Human Resources, Kyocera Wireless India Private Limited, Bangalore, India.
25. *Shudra* is a broad classification that included untouchables.
26. Gandhi himself was not mainly responsible for winning greater social rights or opportunities for untouchables. The main crusader for their cause was a group of social activists under the leadership of Dr. B.R. Ambedkar.
27. Based on an interview by the author in March 2005 with Professor Hari Krishna Lal, former legislator and former Dean of Law, Ranchi University, Ranchi.
28. Based on an interview by the author in March 2004 with Mr. Abhijit Bhattacharjee, Manager of Human Resources, Kyocera Wireless India Private Limited, Bangalore, India.
29. Nehru was the first Prime Minister of the country and ruled from 1947 to 1964.
30. There is a recent shift in this trend, as the institution of extended families is declining in urban areas and nuclear families are on the increase. However, the wife within the nuclear household is still expected to take full care of visiting relatives.
31. See, for example, http://www.avert.org/indiaaids.htm. Accessed April 30, 2006.
32. Carol S. Coonrod, "Chronic Hunger and the Status of Women," The Hunger Project (website); available from http://www.thp.org/reports/indiawom.htm. Accessed February 23, 2006.
33. Based on an interview by the author in March 2005 with Mr. Abhijit Bhattacharjee, Manager of Human Resources, Kyocera Wireless India Private Limited, Bangalore, India.
34. Ibid.

Diversity in Japan

1. Archeological evidence offers little support for the notion of Japanese homogeneity, racial or social. Various migration patterns of peoples and cultures from both Northern and Southern Asia have been identified that go back for tens of thousands of years. Indeed, scholars suggest that the reluctance of Japan's Imperial Household to permit excavation of Imperial tombs derives from the fear that archeology would establish even firmer links between Japan's historical origins and the Korean peninsula. See, for example, John Nelson, *"Origins of the Japanese," Asian Studies Network Information Center (ASNIC),* available from http://asnic.utexas.edu/asnic/countries/japan/originsofthejapanese.html. Accessed February 23, 2006.)

   Certainly Japanese society was hardly unified for most of its recorded history. Although for centuries nominal authority was vested in the institution of the emperor, and later the shoguns in the name of the emperor, each region within the Japanese archipelago historically regarded itself as its own country (*kuni*). These "countries," often separated by mountainous terrain as well as different accents and customs, fought fiercely with one another through long eras of shifting alliances and sporadic warfare.

The Warring States period of Japanese history, which lasted from approximately the mid-fifteenth through the early seventeenth century, represented the culmination of these brutal internecine struggles. While the Tokugawa Shogunate was finally able to unify Japan under its rule in the early 1600s, rival provinces still regarded one another, and sometimes the Tokugawa government as well, with suspicion and jealousy, and the Shogunate held as hostages family members of feudal lords governing the provinces in order to maintain insurance against sudden defections.

2. *Statistical Handbook of Japan 2004.* Ministry of Internal Affairs and Communications—Statistics Bureau website: http://www.stat.go.jp/english/data/handbook/c02cont.htm. Accessed May 15, 2006. See also http://www.stat.go.jp/data/kokusei/2005/kouhou/useful/u01_z07.htm; http://www.stat.go.jp/data/kokusei/2005/kouhou/useful/u01_z17.htm; http://www.stat.go.jp/data/kokusei/2005/kouhou/useful/u01_z22.htm. Accesssed May 15, 2006.
3. David Matsumoto, *The New Japan* (Boston: Intercultural Press, 2002), pp. 45–47.
4. Ibid., pp. 70–72.
5. Another possible derivation is the combination of the word *free* plus a portion of the word *arubaito.* The latter, which means part-time work in Japanese, is derived from the German word *arbeit,* or work.
6. See, for example, http://www.nri.co.jp/english/news/2004/041101.html. Accessed April 30, 2006. This Nomura Research Institute study also quotes a White Paper on the Labour Economy published by Japan's Ministry of Health, Labour, and Welfare in September 2004, that defines the NEET as "those among the non-labour force population, the number of non-working individuals between the ages of 15 and 34 (unmarried school graduates who neither help with the housework nor attend school)," and estimates their numbers at about half a million.
7. David Matsumoto, *The New Japan* (Boston: Intercultural Press, 2002), p. 76.
8. When badly handled, forced retirements can leave workers depressed or worse—many suicides in Japan are attributed to lost employment. Workers accustomed to giving their all to the company and expecting to be cared for in return may find themselves with no hobbies and no friends or interests outside of an employer that has now rejected them.
9. Sumitomo 3M is an example of a firm in Japan that has carried out its early retirement program in a more voluntary manner.
10. "Statistical Maps of Japan: 2000 Population Census of Japan," Statistics Bureau: Ministry of Public Management, Home Affairs, Posts and Telecommunications.
11. City, age, and gender differences regarding interaction with foreign culture; data provided by David Matsumoto.
12. By comparison, for example, the United States has approximately 32 million foreign-born residents out of a total population of 295 million—this amounts to over 10 percent of the population.
13. Adapted from: http://www.moj.go.jp/PRESS/040611-1/040611-1.html. Accessed February 23, 2006.
14. See, for example, U.S. Department of State (database online); http://www.state.gov/g/drl/rls/hrrpt/2003/27772.htm. Accessed February 23, 2006. "In 2000, a revised law to end the practice of fingerprinting permanent foreign residents went into effect. The Government established a family registry system similar to that used for citizens. Foreign residents still are required to carry alien registration certificates at all times, but the

revised law reduces the penalties imposed on those found without documentation." Another source indicates the exact date of the change in Japanese Alien Registration law as March of 1999. See http://www.isks.org/jhtml/hist/81_00.htm. Accessed April 30, 2006.

15. http://www.moj.go.jp/PRESS/040611-1/040611-1.html. Accessed February 23, 2006.
16. Travel abroad has increased as well. The numbers of Japanese travelers abroad increased dramatically through the 1990s to almost 18 million a year in 2000, more than triple the number of foreigners entering the country. Overseas travel went into a steep decline after the 9/11 tragedy, but has since revived, and although the bulk of these trips are short vacation or shopping stints, their cumulative effect has been to vastly increase the familiarity of the Japanese populace, particularly its urban dwellers, with life abroad.
17. Manufacturing is a different story than corporate headquarters. Japanese companies have long taken advantage of the country's extensive coastline and advanced infrastructure for shipping and transportation to locate manufacturing operations in widely dispersed areas around the country. Foreign firms as well have benefited over the years from utilizing manufacturing operations near one of Japan's smaller cities in places such as Sendai Prefecture in the north or Yamaguchi to the west. Local governments eager to provide stable employment for their citizens are therefore willing to hand out incentives to domestic or foreign firms. Manufacturers in these locations normally have the advantage of a well-educated workforce, a strong work ethic, and a lower cost structure. Japan's continuing strength in manufacturing lies in the ability of a stable workforce to regularly increase its productivity through a factory culture of constant knowledge acquisition and improvement.

    Even such advantages, however, have not been enough in recent years to overcome the cost disadvantage of Japan relative to nearby China. Japanese firms have been increasingly moving their manufacturing operations out of the country unless they require sophisticated worker skills.
18. "Survey on Gender equality in Japan in 2004: Public perception on gender equality"; see http://www8.cao.go.jp/survey/h16/h16-danjo/index.html. Accessed February 23, 2006.
19. Ibid.
20. A recent popular book by Junko Sakai, called *Makeinu no tooboe,* (The Loser's Roar), comments that, "No matter how beautiful or how capable of work she is, a woman who is over thirty, single, and without children is a female loser." See, for example, "Makeinu no Toboe ga Kakareta Riyu." ("The reason why 'The Loser's Roar' was written"); http://media.excite.co.jp/book/news/topics/068/. Accessed February 23, 2006.
21. "Heisei 15 nendo josei koyo kanri kino chosa" kekka gaiyo—kosubetsu koyo kanri seido wa daikigyo o chushin ni minaoshi no ugoki. ("2003 survey on management of female employment," summary of results—movement to revise the management of employment system starting with large companies. July 23, 2004). Retrieved from Kosei Rodosho (Ministry of Health, Labor, and Welfare) website: http://www.mhlw.go.jp/houdou/0105/h0528-1a.html. Accessed February 23, 2006.
22. Ibid.
23. *Statistical Handbook of Japan 2004.* Ministry of Internal Affairs and Communications—Statistics Bureau website: http://www.stat.go.jp/english/data/handbook/c02cont.htm. Accessed May 15, 2006.
24. For an English reference, see, for example, http://www.nigelward.com/top30.html. Accessed February 23, 2006.

25. "Young Persons' Career Assistance Research Committee Report," Ministry of Health, Labour & Welfare, 2003; http://www.mhlw.go.jp/houdou/2003/09/h0919-5g9.html. Accessed May 15, 2006.
26. http://www.livejournal.com/users/imomus/9239.html. Accessed February 23, 2006.
27. http://www.pro-researcher.co.uk/encyclopaedia/english/freetersh. Accessed February 23, 2006.
28. Ibid.; "According to a survey of the Japan Institute of Labor in 2000, the average *freeter* works 4.9 days per week and earns 139,000 yen per month (approximately $1,200 U.S.)."

Diversity in Mexico

1. *Pocket World in Figures, 2006 Edition*, p. 26 (London: *The Economist* Newspaper Ltd., 2005).
2. "Gap between Rich and Poor: World Income Inequality" Development Data Group, The World Bank, Washington DC. 2002. Available from www.infoplease.com/ipa/A0908770.html. Accessed February 23, 2006.
3. "Mexico Makes Progress And Faces Challenges In Poverty Reduction Efforts," News release July 28, 2004; Available from http://worldbank.org/WBSITE/EXTERNAL/COUNTRIES/LACEXT/MEXICOEXTN/0,,contentMDK:20234053~menuPK:338403~pagePK:141137~piPK:141127~theSitePK:338397,00.html. Accessed February 23, 2006.
4. Migration Information Source; see www.migrationinformation.org/feature/display.cfm?ID=163. Accessed February 23, 2006.
5. Rawdon Messenger, "Style Matters," Business Mexico Magazine, July 2004, pp. 32–33.
6. Robert Ryal Miller, *Mexico: A History* (Norman: University of Oklahoma, 1985), pp. 138–141.
7. Ibid.
8. Guillermo Bonfil Batalla, *Mexico Profundo: Reclaiming a Civilization* (Austin: University of Texas Press, 1996), p. 18.
9. National Institute of Statistics, Geography and Informatics (INEGI) www.inegi.gob.mx/inegi/default.asp. Accessed February 23, 2006.
10. "Mexico Makes Progress And Faces Challenges In Poverty Reduction Efforts," News release July 28, 2004; available from http://web.worldbank.org/WBSITE/EXTERNAL/COUNTRIES/LACEXT/MEXICOEXTN/0,,contentMDK:20234053~menuPK:338403~pagePK:141127~theSitePK:338397,00.html. Accessed Februray 23, 2006.
11. Les Christie, "The rush to a Mexican retirement is on," CNN Money.com, (April 12, 2005). Available from http://money.cnn.com/2005/04/11/retirement/mexicanretirement/. Accessed February 23, 2006.
12. http://www.blackwell-synergy.com/doi/abs/10.1111/j.1545-5300.2002.00619.x. Accessed April 30, 2006.
13. For more information on this directive, go to www.gob.mx. Accessed February 23, 2006.
14. The World Bank. http://devdata.worldbank.org/genderstats/genderRpt.asp?rpt=profile&cty=MEX,Mexico&hm=home and http://devdata.worldbank.org/external/dgcomp.asp?rmdk=110&smdk=473885&w=0. Accessed February 23, 2006.
15. Patricia Espinosa Torres, "Seeking for Globalization with Equity," National Women's Institute of Mexico. Inter-American Commission of Women. Available from www.oas.org/cim/English/Mexico-GlobEquity.htm. Accessed February 23, 2006.
16. Ibid.

17. United Nations Development Fund for Women (UNIFEM), Canadian International Development Agency. Available from www.acdi-cida.gc.ca/cida_ind.nsf/0/394f0a61a8a4571485256bf9005d6fbf?OpenDocument#3.3. Accessed February 23, 2006.
18. Census of the National Institute of Statistics, Geography and Informatics (INEGI) 2000 www.inegi.gob.mx/inegi/default.asp. Accessed February 23, 2006.
19. Library of Congress, Country Studies, Mexico, Role of Women. http://memory.loc.gov/cgi-bin/query/r?frd/cstdy:@field(DOCID+mx0050) Accessed February 23, 2006.
20. *World Development Indicators for the World Bank.* (World Bank, March 2004) p. 153.
21. Census of the National Institute of Statistics, Geography and Informatics (INEGI) 2003. www.inegi.gob.mx/inegi/default.asp. Accessed February 23, 2006.
22. Census of the National Institute of Statistics, Geography and Informatics (INEGI) 2000. www.inegi.gob.mx/inegi/default.asp. Accessed February 23, 2006.
23. Susan Ferriss, "Free Trade's Faded Dream: A Panacea Punctured," *Edmonton Journal,* November 23, 2003.
24. BBC, "Migrant Workers Aid Growth at Home," March 28, 2005.
25. United States Hispanic Chamber of Commerce; available from www.ushcc.com/res-statistics.html. Accessed February 23, 2006.

    Mexico is considered among the ten top tourist destinations in the world. Tourism within the services sector represents one of the three pillars (besides agriculture and industry) of the economy. This traditionally strong sector has dropped in its economic contributions to the national coffers in the last few years. Although tourism is spread throughout the country, aside from the central region the most popular destinations are in the coastal states of Yucatán, Jalisco, Guerrero, and Baja California Sur. Economic investment for tourism has created niches of development unfamiliar to most of the rest of the country. In terms of employment opportunities, this sector generally provides low wage alternatives for most of its employees.

Diversity in Russia

1. *All Russian Population Census of 2002.* Data from the census can be accessed on the website of the Russian Federal Service for State Statistics; see http://www.perepis2002.ru/index.html?id=11. Accessed February 23, 2006.
2. In fact, many of the emperors and empresses put their health in the hands of foreigners. Many Russian leaders have also been foreigners. Catherine the Great was born to a German. She moved to Russia at the age of 15 to marry the heir to the Russian throne. She brought in many foreigners to populate the territories and to try to "civilize" Russia's inhabitants. An example from more recent history is Vladimir Lenin, who was half German.
3. *All Russian Population Census of 2002.* Data from the census can be accessed on the website of the Russian Federal Service for State Statistics; available from http://www.perepis2002.ru/index.html?id=39. Accessed February 23, 2006.
4. A recent survey quantifies the attitudes of ethnic Russians toward nine other national and ethnic groups, ranking those groups based on the percentage of Russian respondents who said they would rather not work with them. The Chechens and Roma (gypsies, Moldova) headed the list, with over 50 percent of Russian respondents preferring not to work with them. People from the Caucasus region, Africans, and Chinese came in next, with 30 to 40 percent of Russian respondents stating their reluctance to have

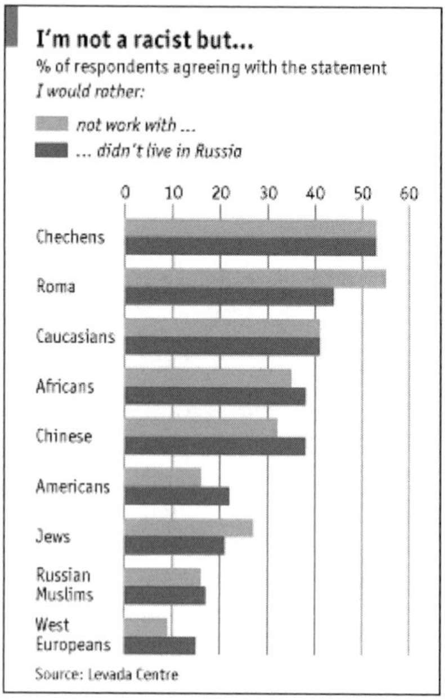

Used with permission of the Levada Center

them as coworkers. Ten to 20 percent of respondents preferred to avoid Americans, Jews, Russian Muslims, and Western Europeans. Chart displayed in "Russian xenophobia: The New Jews," *The Economist*, February 17, 2005; it is reprinted here with permission from the Levada Center. *The Economist* article is also available to subscribers on line at: http://www.economist.com/displaystory.cfm?story id=3672697. Accessed July 31, 2006.

5. This anecdote is based on the author's experience.
6. www.perepis2002.ru/ct/html/ALL_00_01.htm. Accessed Februrary 23, 2006.
7. http://www.f8.com/FP/Russia/Anovo.htmlh. Accessed February 23, 2006.
8. http://www.russiatrek.com/r_tomsk.shtmlh. Accessed February 23, 2006.
9. Ibid.
10. Deborah Palmieri, "The Ultimate Insider's Guide to Doing Dusiness with Russia." The Russian-American Chamber of Commerce (Denver, Colorado 2002), p. 333.
11. *Business Week* online, October 15, 2000.
12. *Business Week* provides the following characterization of Russia's several middle class segments:

Russian Middle Class

	Lower Middle	Average Middle	Upper Middle
Job	*receptionist, security guard*	*computer programmers, junior managers, and accountants*	*senior managers, small-business owners, or investment bankers*
Salary range (Moscow)	$800 and $1,500	$1,500 to $3,500	$3,500 to $7,000
Salary range (provinces)	$300 to $550	$550 to $1,500	$1,500 to $3,500
Car	Late-model Russian-made Lada	new Toyota Corolla	New Opel Cadet or used BMW
Dacha (summer home)	a wooden cottage with no indoor plumbing	contractor-constructed house with indoor plumbing and heating	house with stone and brick walls, terrace, indoor garage
Summer vacation	Soviet-style resorts on Black Sea	Turkish seashore resort of Antalia	Majorca on Spanish Riviera

Source: Adapted from *Business Week;* available from www.businessweek.com/2000/00_42/b3703095 .htm. Accessed February 23, 2006. Data on income per household assumes a family of three (two adults and one child); amounts are given in U.S. dollars.

13. See, for example, http://wired-vig.wired.com/wired/archive/3.05/russians.html. Accessed February 23, 2006.
14. CNN. http://edition.cnn.com/SPECIALS/2001/russia/stories/youth/. Accessed February 23, 2006.

Diversity in United Kingdom

1. National Statistics website: http://www.statistics.gov.uk. Accessed February 23, 2006. Crown copyright material is reproduced with the permission of the Controller of HMSO.
2. Events such as the Golden Jubilee or the behavior of English football (soccer) fans may, in part, be outgrowths of a desire to belong to a securely valuable "something," which the country today seems to be missing when compared with the Britain of half a century ago. The death of Princess Diana seemed to unite the country in an extraordinary display of public emotion and grief, but the effect was short-lived. And there is a divisive nationalism on the question of European integration and being "European." To ask what it means to be a Briton or British, or English, Scottish, Welsh, or Irish, and what the prevailing contemporary culture is, are questions that themselves raise more

questions than answers, especially compared with the responses that would have been given 50 years ago.

3. National Statistics website: http://www.statistics.gov.uk. Accessed February 23, 2006. Crown copyright material is reproduced with the permission of the Controller.
4. "Cool" as in young and hip, not Conservative, a new era for opportunity, change, mobility, and being the "place" to be. This marketing construct succeeded.

Diversity in United States

1. *Pocket World in Figures, 2006 Edition*, pp. 58–60. (London: *The Economist* Newspaper Ltd., 2005)
2. There is a similar version of this model in Gardenswartz, Row, Digh, and Bennett, eds., *The Global Diversity Desk Reference: Managing an International Workforce* (San Francisco: John Wiley & Sons, 2003).
3. See, for example, www2.volstate.edu/socialscience/FinalDocs/1960s/malcomX.htm; this is an excerpt from a speech delivered by Malcom X at Washington Heights, NY, in 1964. Accessed February 23, 2006.
4. Michael Fix and Jeffrey Passel, "U.S. Immigration at the Beginning of the 21st Century," Testimony before the Subcommittee on Immigration and Claims hearing on "The U.S. Population and Immigration" Committee on the Judiciary U.S. House of Representatives; www.urban.org/urlprint.cfm?ID=7321; See Figure 2: Foreign-Born Population: 1850–2000. Accessed February 23, 2006.
5. See, for example, http://www.ellisislandrecords.org/immexp/wseix_5_2.asp? Accessed February 23, 2006.
6. http://www.migrationinformation.org/GlobalData/charts/fb.2.shtml. Accessed April 30, 2006.
7. http://usinfo.state.gov/journals/itsv/0699/ijse/portrait.htm. Accessed February 23, 2006.
8. United States 2000 census results; available from http://www.census.gov/population/www/cen2000/atlas.html. Accessed February 23, 2006.
9. 16 percent were born in Mexico, 10 percent in Laos, and 6 percent in Vietnam. See, http://www.migrationinformation.org/USFocus/statemap.cfm. Accessed February 23, 2006.
10. http://etext.virginia.edu/etcbin/toccer-new2?id=JefVirg.sgm&images=images/modeng&data=/texts/english/modeng/parsed&tag=public&part=all, section 264. Accessed April 30, 2006.
11. http://www.nytimes.com/library/national/race/. Accessed April 30, 2006.
12. See, for example, http://www.insighteducationsystems.com/. Accessed February 23, 2006.
13. See, for example, http://www.prb.org/Template.cfm?Section=PRB&template=/ContentManagement/ContentDisplay.cfm&ContentID=13598. Accessed July 31, 2006.
14. See, for example, http://www.census.gov/Press-Release/www/2003/cb03-ff05.html. Accessed February 23, 2006.
15. David A. Thomas, "The Truth about Mentoring Minorities: Race Matters," *Harvard Business Review* (April 2001), pp. 98–107.
16. See, for example, Deborah Tannen, *Talking from 9 to 5: Women and Men at Work* (New York: Harper Collins, 1994).
17. The difference exists even in the Girl and Boy Scout oaths where girls state "On my honor, I will try . . ." and boys state "On my honor, I will do . . ." These differences in

communication styles may be changing with younger generations and women who came of age after Title IX opened up opportunities to participate in sports in school. However, men and women who coach teams of both sexes still comment that even though boys and girls are both competitive, the styles of interactions vary between boys and girls on same-sex teams. Girls tend to be more collaborative and less hierarchical, take turns and verbally encourage, commiserate with and involve one another. Boys tend to be more hierarchical and assign specific roles and positions, mask emotion, talk over and banter with one another, often employing put-downs and calling each other names.

17. See, for example, Barry A. Kosmin and Egon Mayer, "American Religious Identification Survey, 2001," The Graduate Center of the City University of New York; http://www.gc.cuny.edu/faculty/research_studies/aris.pdf, pp. 40–43. Accessed April 30, 2006.
18. Raymond A. Friedman, "The Case of the Religious Network Group," *Harvard Business Review* (July 1, 1999).

Appendices

1. Public Service Commission of Canada, Employment Equity and Diversity website: http://www.psc-cfp.gc.ca/ee/index_e.htm. Accessed May 17, 2006.
2. South African Department of Labor website: http://www.labour.gov.za/ ; for more detail, see http://www.labour.gov.za/legislation/original_act.jsp?legislationDetail_id=5954. Accessed May 17, 2006.
3. Government Offices of Sweden website at: http://www.sweden.gov.se/sb/d/4096. Accessed May 17, 2006.

Bibliography

Adler, Nancy. *International Dimensions of Organizational Behavior, Fourth Edition.* Cincinnati, Ohio: South-Western, 2002.

Aguilar, Leslie and Linda Stokes. *Multicultural Customer Service: Providing Outstanding Services Across Cultures.* New York: McGraw Hill, 1996.

Batalla Bonfil, Guillermo. *Mexico Profundo: Reclaiming a Civilization.* Austin, Texas: University of Texas Press, 1996.

Blank, Renee, and Sandra Slipp. *Voices of Diversity*. New York: American Management Association, 1994.

Chawla, Sarita and John Renesch., ed. *Learning Organizations: Developing Cultures for Tomorrow's Workplace.* Portland, Oregon: Productivity Press, 1995.

Cox, Taylor Jr. and Ruby L. Beale. *Developing Competency to Manage Diversity: Readings, Cases, and Activities.* San Francisco, California: Berrett-Koehler Publisher, Inc., 1997.

Cox, Taylor Jr. *Creating the Multicultural Organization: A Strategy for Capturing the Power of Diversity.* San Francisco, California: Jossey-Bass, 2001.

Cunningham, Robert, and Yasin K. Wasta Sarayrah. *The Hidden Forces in Middle Eastern Society.* Westport, Connecticut: Praeger, 1993.

Francy, Claire E., ed. *Cairo: The Practical Guide.* Cairo, Egypt: American University, 2004.

Gallos, John V. and V. Jean Ramsey. *Teaching Diversity: Listening to the Soul, Speaking from the Heart.* San Francisco, California: Jossey-Bass, 1997.

Gardenswartz, Lee, and Anita Rowe, et al, eds. *The Global Diversity Desk Reference.* San Francisco, California: Pfeiffer, 2003.

Gardenswartz, Lee, and Anita Rowe. *Diverse Teams at Work: Capitalizing on the Power of Diversity.* Chicago, Illinois: Irwin Professional Publications, 1994.

Gentile, Mary C., ed. *Differences that Work: Organizational Excellence Through Diversity.* Long Grove, Illinois: Waveland Press, Inc., 2000.

Griggs, Lewis and Lente–Louise Louw., ed. *Valuing Diversity: New Tools for a New Reality.* New York: McGraw-Hill Companies, 1994.

Gundling, Ernest. *Working GlobeSmart: 12 People Skills for Doing Business Across Borders.* Palo Alto, California: Davies-Black, 2003.

Henry, Pamela K. *Diversity and the Bottom Line.* Austin, Texas: TurnKey, 2003.

Hofstede, Geert. *Culture's Consequences: International Differences in Work-Related Values.* Thousand Oaks, California: Sage, 1984.

Hubbard, Edward E. *The Diversity Scorecard.* Oxford, England: Elsevier Butterworth-Heinemann, 2004.

James, William. *The Varieties of Religious Experience.* New York: Touchstone, 1997.

Lambert, Jonamay, et al. *Global Competence: 50 Training Activities for Succeeding in International Business.* Amherst, Massachusetts: HRD Press, 2000.

Loden, Marilyn and Judith Rosener. *Workforce America! Managing Employee Diversity as a Vital Resource.* New York: McGraw-Hill, 1990.

Loden, Marilyn. *Implementing Diversity.* New York: McGraw-Hill, 1996.

Matsumoto, David. *The New Japan.* Boston, Massachusetts: Intercultural Press, 2002.

Metcalf, Barbara D. and Thomas R. Metcalf. *A Concise History of India.* Cambridge, England: University Press, 2002.

Miller, Frederick A. and Judith H. Katz. *The Inclusion Breakthrough: Unleashing the Real Power of Diversity.* San Francisco, California: Berrett-Koehler, 2002.

Miller, Robert Ryal. *Mexico: A History.* Norman, Oklahoma: University of Oklahoma, 1985.

Palmieri, Deborah. *The Ultimate Insider's Guide to Doing Business with Russia.* Denver, Colorado: Russian-American Chamber of Commerce, 2002.

Pucik, Vladimir, Noel M. Tichy, and Carole K. Barnett, et al, eds. *Globalizing Management.* New York: John Wiley & Sons, Inc., 1993.

Rasmussen, Tina. *The ASTD Trainer's Sourcebook: Diversity.* New York: McGraw-Hill, 1996.

Rosinski, Philippe. *Coaching Across Cultures: New Tools for Leveraging National, Corporate, and Professional Differences.* Boston, Massachusetts: Nicholas Brealey Publishing, 2003.

Seelye, Ned H., ed. *Experimental Activities for Intercultural Learning.* Boston, Massachusetts: Intercultural Press, 1996.

Simons, George F. *EuroDiversity.* Woburn, Massachusetts: Butterworth-Heinemann, 2002.

Sonnenschein, William. *The Diversity Toolkit: How You Can Build and Benefit from a Diverse Workforce.* Lincolnwood, Illinois: Contemporary Books, 1999.

Storti, Craig. *Cross-Cultural Dialogues: 74 Brief Encounters with Cultural Difference.* Boston, Massachusetts: Intercultural Press, 1994.

Tannen, Deborah. *Talking from 9 to 5.* New York: Quill, 2001.

Thiederman, Sondra. *Making Diversity Work.* Chicago, Illinois: Dearborn Trade, 2003.

Thomas, R. Roosevelt Jr. *Beyond Race and Gender: Unleashing the Power of Your Total Workforce by Managing Diversity.* New York: American Management Association, 1991.

Thomas, R. Roosevelt Jr., et al. *Harvard Business Review on Managing Diversity.* Boston, Massachusetts: Harvard Business School Publishing Corporation, 2001.

Trompenaars, Fons and Charles Hampden-Turner. *Riding the Waves of Culture: Understanding Diversity in Global Business, 2nd Edition.* New York: McGraw-Hill, 1997.

Williams, Mark A. *The 10 Lenses: Your Guide to Living & Working in a Multicultural World.* Herndon, Virginia: Capital Books, 2001.

Zachary, Pascal G. *The Diversity Advantage: Multicultural Identity in the New World Economy.* Boulder, Colorado: Westview Press, 2003.

Index